The Past as Text

PARALLAX   RE-VISIONS OF CULTURE
AND SOCIETY

Stephen G. Nichols, Gerald Prince, and Wendy Steiner
SERIES EDITORS

The Past as Text

The Theory and Practice
of Medieval Historiography

Gabrielle M. Spiegel

The Johns Hopkins University Press
Baltimore and London

© 1997 The Johns Hopkins University Press
All rights reserved. Published 1997
Printed in the United States of America on acid-free paper
06 05 04 03 02 01 00 99 98 97   5 4 3 2 1

The Johns Hopkins University Press
2715 North Charles Street
Baltimore, Maryland 21218-4319
The Johns Hopkins Press Ltd., London

ISBN 0-8018-5555-1

Library of Congress Cataloging-in-Publication Data will
be found at the end of this book.
A catalog record for this book is available from the
British Library.

For My Mother

Contents

Contents

Acknowledgments

A book that draws on research and writing conducted over twenty years cannot hope adequately to thank the host of colleagues and friends who have provided intellectual stimulation and support throughout the length of that period. To attempt to do so would be tantamount to writing an intellectual biography, and so it is with regret that I confine myself here simply to expressing my gratitude to all those with whom I have had the pleasure of often intense and always lively intellectual exchange throughout the course of my scholarly career. In particular, colleagues at the University of Maryland and the Johns Hopkins University have provided that critical daily source of sustenance on which one's intellectual development so greatly depends, for no scholarly life is lived in a vacuum, solely in one's own head.

The range of scholarly work represented here has benefited over the years from a variety of institutions and foundations that contributed to sustaining my work. They are, again, too numerous to name, but I remain profoundly grateful to them for their trust and generosity. The same is true for the many scholarly librairies and manuscript depositories that have facilitated my research and, in a very real sense, made it possible. Finally, my family, in both the narrow and the broad sense, has been for most of my life the central support on which I have relied. I am happy to have this opportunity to dedicate this book to my mother, who long ago insisted that I learn Latin and French and German, not in order to be a scholar, but to become the kind of educated person that, in the Viennese world in which she was raised, represented the highest and most important aspiration. I can only hope that my studies have in some small measure met those expectations, although conducted in a world far different from the one for which they were intended.

Versions of all but two chapters have been previously published. Chapter 1 appeared as "History, Historicism, and the Social Logic of the Text in the Middle Ages," *Speculum* 65 (1990): 59–86; Chapter Three as "Towards a Theory of the Middle Ground: Historical Writing in the Age of Postmodernism," in *Historia A Debate*, 3 vols. (Santiago de Compostela, 1995), 1: 169–76; Chapter Five as "Political Utility in Medieval Historiography: A Sketch," *History and Theory* 14 (1975): 314–25; Chapter Six as "Genealogy: Form and Function in Medieval Historical Narrative," *History and Theory* 22 (1983): 43–53; Chapter Seven as "The Reditus Regni ad Stirpem Karoli Magni: A New Look," *French Historical Studies* 7 (1971): 145–74; Chapter Eight as "The Cult of Saint Denis and Capetian Kingship," *Journal of Medieval History* 1 (1975): 43–69; Chapter Nine as "History as Enlightenment: Suger and the *Mos Anagogicus*," in Paula Gerson, ed., *Abbot Suger and the Abbey Church of Saint-Denis* (copyright 1986 The Metropolitan Museum of Art); Chapter Ten as "Social Change and Literary Language: The Textualization of the Past in Thirteenth-Century French Historiography," *Journal of Medieval and Renaissance Studies* 17 (1987): 129–48; and Chapter Eleven as "Medieval Canon Formation and the Rise of Royal Historiography in Old French Prose," *MLN* 108 (1993): 638–58. I thank the various journals and presses for permission to reprint. All the chapters have been slightly rewritten in order to avoid repetition, but I have not attempted to supply updated bibliographical references, except in a few cases where new work has been too important to leave unnoted.

Introduction

The essays collected in this book span two decades of an intense and challenging scholarly engagement in problems of historical writing, both on the theoretical level of a meditation on the nature and modes of narrating what we call the past and on the practical level of the study of medieval historiography. The essays dedicated to questions of critical theory and historiography are to be found in Part One of this collection, and those dealing specifically with the analysis of medieval historical writing are presented in Part Two. Two new essays have been added to those already published. The first, "Orations of the Dead / Silences of the Living: The Sociology of the Linguistic Turn," explores the early work of Jacques Derrida and his elaboration of deconstruction while at the same time contextualizing his thought in a post-Holocaust environment. The second is devoted to an initial, exploratory account of the traditions of medieval historiography in North America from Revolutionary times to the 1990s, called "In the Mirror's Eye: The Writing of Medieval History in America," a subject that I hope to pursue more fully in a book of that name to follow. The trajectory that my work has followed, one that can be traced in the second section of the book—from an early concern with the "truth" and "fictionality" of medieval representations of history and with the ideological investments that conditioned and constrained the medieval approach to the past, to an increasing awareness of the discursive and constitutive force of representation as such—is a trajectory that characterizes the thinking and writing of a significant segment of the professional academic generation to which I belong.

The earliest essays stem from work begun in the mid-1960s, a time just before the stirrings that were to culminate in postmodernism made their appearance in the academy. Scholarship in medieval historical writing was then largely devoted to the identification of what could be accepted as historically "true" in chronicle accounts of the past and the radical expurgation—most often in the form of scornful neglect—of everything that could not. Now this was not a particularly propitious approach to the historiographical texts of the Middle Ages, even leaving aside the subsequent ways in which the very notions of history and the "real" were to be problematized. It was not, because medieval historiography, like all historical writing, foregrounds the problem of the representation of reality—hence of the relationship between text and referent—by virtue of its deployment of a "realistic" style. But medieval historical writing does this in an especially disturbing way, since, in sharp contrast to modern historiography, where "content"—"facts," data, etc.—is presumptively "real" and style is to some extent optional, medieval chronicles tend to employ a realistic style but to include as morally serious "content" a vast range of material systematically excluded from the precincts of modern historical realism: miracles, resurrections, saints, myths, and visions inter alia.

It was even then apparent to me that if one wanted to understand what was "going on," "being said and represented" in these texts, modern criteria governing the representation of reality, hence of historiographical "realism," simply would not do. Thus, my earliest work, represented in this volume by the articles on the genealogical fiction known as the *reditus regni ad stirpem Karoli Magni* (Chapter Seven), on the cult of Saint Denis (Chapter Eight), and on the "political utility" of the medieval manipulation of the past (Chapter Five), focused on the ways in which that past itself constituted an ideological structure of argument, one that sought legitimacy from the borrowed authority of history understood as a putatively real, though highly permeable and fragile, tradition, hence an artifact of historiography. It was, I sensed, precisely the "truth" of the past that underwrote the utility of historiography to medieval rulers and political actors, whose interests, to be sure, lay not in recuperating an account of "what actually happened," but in the legitimation of their propagandistic and political goals. What made the writing of history important in the Middle Ages, despite its absence from the scholarly curriculum, was exactly its ability to address contemporary political life via a displacement to the past, and to embed both prescription and polemic in an apparently "factual," because realistic, account of the historical legacy that the past had bequeathed.

In this sense, even a cursory acquaintance with medieval chronicles required an investigator to pose the question of the minimum conditions of adequacy for realism in historical writing, not so much from the philosophical perspective of truth and epistemology— though those are by no means insignificant issues—but from that of historical practice, that is, realism not as a metaphysical proposition but as a style of reasoning encoded in a particular form of writing. To ask what were the minimum requirements for realism in medieval historiography was tantamount to asking what was the generative grammar that defined historical writing in the Middle Ages, the linguistic protocols that permitted the transformation of the past into historical narrative? And so, naturally, I turned to literary study for help. My reasons for doing so, let me stress, were pragmatic in the extreme; I needed a guide to fathom these apparently straightforward yet strangely deformed texts.

I will not rehearse the details of my rather undisciplined reading program in criticism, anthropology, and, ultimately, theory. Suffice it to say that, like all historians, I began with that most accessible— and, to me, still useful and insightful—of critics, Northrop Frye, from whom I learned the importance of emplotment as the bearer of the tale's "message," a lesson strongly reinforced by Hayden White's work then appearing on metahistory, itself heavily indebted to Northrop Frye. The notion of emplotment, of a text's structural characteristics and narrative economy, as the submerged vehicle of meaning contributed to the sorts of ideological critiques of medieval texts that appeared in my book entitled *The Chronicle Tradition of Saint-Denis*, an additional specimen of which is represented in this volume by the essay on the historical works of Abbot Suger of Saint-

Denis on behalf of the Capetian monarchs and, in particular, of King Louis VI (Chapter Nine). This essay represented an initial attempt to get below the surface realism of Suger's work to grasp the underlying structure of his historical plot and to show that the historiographical (and ultimately metaphysical) argument of his *Vita Ludovici Grossi* lay in that very structure.

From Frye I wandered into anthropology, since his view of narrative as secularized ritual suggested the potential utility of anthropological models of culture; and as anthropology took a symbolic turn, so, too, did I, acquainting myself with the work of Clifford Geertz, Mary Douglas, Victor Turner, and the like. From there it was but a small step to Bakhtin, whose work on the monologic discourse of "high" genres remains for me one of the most powerful but underutilized critical resources available to medievalists. In particular, Bakhtin's conception of epic as a genre whose "formally constitutive feature is the transferral of a represented world into the past" helps us to understand the epic "toning" of so much historiographical writing in the Middle Ages as a means to create a distant world of beginnings and "fathers" that, by its separation from the present, is preserved from the ravages of the contemporary world and thus provides a source of authority and privilege that is both "absolute," in Bakhtin's sense of a hierarchically valorized category, and immutable, therefore impervious to relativization. Moreover, since the ruling class in patriarchal societies, like that of medieval Europe, does belong, in a certain sense, to the world of "fathers," this absolute past both expresses its distance from other classes in society and argues for its independence. Thus an aristocratic class that wishes to emphasize its social separation from all other classes looks to an "epic" time past, using the *temporal* distance between present and past as a means of expressing the *social* distance that, it believes, rightfully obtains between it and its nearest social competitors, a phenomenon that goes far towards explaining the pervasive rewriting of historical sources in the language of literary epic in the High Middle Ages.

Always, in these intellectual peregrinations, what I was searching for was something that would facilitate my grasp of the texts, some way of reading that could help to negotiate the complexities I sensed beneath the surface barrenness of their discourse, some pathway into the meanings that were being generated almost, I believed, behind my back. The textual object was always my primary concern, and it was my feelings of dissatisfaction with the inadequacies of my readings that drove me to search for new instruments of interpretation, if only as a heuristic.

From a fairly wide-ranging course of readings in symbolic anthropology and literary criticism I learned the importance of being sensitive to the formal properties of the texts I was seeking to analyze, of the need to understand their rhetorical devices and literary techniques as an additional locus where the text's "work" of producing meaning was being carried out, and thus to appreciate the entirety of the textual strategies deployed towards the production of history as a specifically discursive phenomenon. The earliest example of this new approach to reading medieval chronicles represented in the present volume is the essay "Genealogy: Form and Function in Medieval Historiography" (Chapter Six), which sought to investigate the ways in which the patterning of medieval histories on the genealogical model of the agnatic family, of dynastic *lignages*, operated as perceptual grid, conceptual metaphor, and narrative structure. By looking at the ways in which chroniclers deployed genealogical frames to arrange their materials into chronicle form, one could see how this new patterning affected the interpretation of historical events in terms of the model of filiation suggested by genealogy. What resulted was not only a new vision of aristocratic society as a congeries of affiliated *lignages* but also a new conception of time, transformed by genealogical conceptual paradigms into a continuous, secular stream, in which past and present became an interconnected succession, seminally imparted from one generation to the next, and time itself, because human, was historicized. No longer a mere shadow or symbol of supernatural forces, history could now be understood as a fully human process subject to change.

An even more pointed effort to apply a specifically literary analysis to the interpretation of medieval historiography appears in the essay

Introduction

"Social Change and Literary Language: The Textualization of the Past in Thirteenth-Century Old French Historiography" (Chapter Ten). In that essay, I focused on a fact of linguistic change itself—the early-thirteenth-century shift from poetry to prose in the writing of vernacular history, of which the historiographical texts I was then engaged in studying constituted the earliest examples—as a social as well as literary event. Assuming, as modern sociolinguists have taught us, that social groups in the throes of change are highly sensitive to alternative modes of discourse, enabling them to register in revised linguistic patterns the social transformations they are experiencing, I argued that the profound shift in language use from poetry to prose that can be documented among the French aristocracy in the thirteenth century signified its perception of dislocations in the social order, a perception encoded in the use of new discursive forms. Although earlier generations of the French aristocracy had forged poetic forms—and, in particular, the courtly *roman*—to articulate its sense of crisis, I argued that the adoption of prose as the language of vernacular history served, in these texts, to "deproblematize" aristocratic culture, thus seeking to mask the challenge to aristocratic independence and prestige that the rise of a newly powerful French monarchy presented. This changed political and social environment, occurring during the very period that witnessed the birth of vernacular prose history, was the hidden force behind the shift in linguistic practices, and helps to account both for the fact of linguistic change and for vernacular history's evolving narrative structures and forms of discourse.

In my growing insistence on examining the literary modes and narrative economies of medieval chronicles, I was, of course, employing a technique of interpretation that was coming to the fore in literary study itself and that, in its largest sense, has been termed the "linguistic turn." The principal effect of the "linguistic turn," for historians, has been to alert us to the mediating force of language in the representation of the past, and thus to help us to understand that there is no direct access to historical events or persons, so that all historical writing, whether medieval or modern, approaches the past via discourses of one sort or another.

And so, perhaps inevitably, I came to Derrida (especially the early works *Of Grammatology*, *Writing and Difference*, and *Dissemination*). Came to, benefited enormously from, but never wholly espoused. Although I believe that Derrida offers in deconstruction an extraordinary tool of reading, one that has taught me to apprehend the constitutive silences and self-generated divisions and undoings that medieval—indeed, all—texts engage in, I have remained committed to addressing precisely the question of representation with which I began—of the relation of textuality to its referent, however displaced, occluded, or indirect—a question that a total immersion in Derridean deconstruction would preclude investigating, but one that was rapidly becoming the focus of postmodernist concern and contestation. My attempt to come to terms with the power of Derrida's thought and with deconstruction as a mode of reading, while simultaneously holding out the possibility of contextualizing texts, is represented here in the essay "Orations of the Dead / Silences of the Living" (Chapter Two), in which I view Derrida's writing as symptomatic of a much broader problematizing of the categories of Western philosophical thought and literary writing that has been a displaced response, I argue, of postmodernism to the catastrophe of the Holocaust.

Although, finally, I have never adhered to Derrida's radical notion of textuality, I nonetheless, in conjunction with many scholars engaged in articulating the problematics of postmodernism, became increasingly convinced that positivist notions of referentiality and empirical truth which had constituted the governing paradigm of "scientific" historiography since the nineteenth century were untenable, at least in the epistemologically totalizing terms in which they were framed. Because I wished to be both historian and critic—the latter required by my conviction that the medieval chronicle should be considered essentially as a literary artifact—I could accept neither the erasure of the past implicit in poststructuralist accounts of textuality, nor the plenitude of presence posited, as it were, by positivism, that logocentric chimera that deconstruction and its allied critical theories were seeking to dethrone. I found—find—myself, therefore, mired in the middle ground, a bog of theoretical self-contradiction from which one emerges only muddied, if not downright muddled.

It is this bog that spawned my concept of "the social logic of the text," the title of the opening theoretical essay in this volume ("History, Historicism, and the Social Logic of the Text" [Chapter One]). This essay offers a critical review of the various schools of symbolic anthropology and critical theory that, in effecting the "linguistic turn," have raised such troubling problems for the study of history and literature. At the same time, I attempt to resolve those problems from a historian's point of view, in particular in light of the historian's need to preserve some sense of the social world by and through which historiographical discourse itself, both past and present, is generated.

The "social logic of the text" is a term and a concept that seeks to combine in a single but complex framework a protocol for the analysis of a text's social site—its location within an embedded social environment of which it is a product and in which it acts as an agent—and its own discursive character as "logos," that is, as itself a literary artifact composed of language and thus demanding literary (formal) analysis. The play on "logic" as signifying both a structure and mode of linguistic performance and an objective description of a social reality (albeit one mediated in language) was and remains intentional. It signals my conviction that texts incorporate social as well as linguistic realities and that even the purely aesthetic character of a work can be related to the social world from which it emerges. It is because of this dual characteristic that, ultimately, medieval textuality grants us (mediated) access to the past.

An acceptance of the double registers constituting linguistic praxis—the instrumental and the performative—and their mutual involvement in the reconstruction of the past and in the production of history is what I try to theorize in the essay entitled "Towards a Theory of the Middle Ground," which constitutes Chapter Three of this volume. The essay itself grew out my response to a debate conducted in *Past and Present* on the philosophical entailments for historical writing embedded in "History, Historicism, and the Social Logic of the Text." Its fundamental impulse is to combine a recognition of the legitimate and persuasive claims of the "linguistic turn" with an insistence on the still viable notion of empirical research as the foundation of historical scholarship.

Now all this sounds fine in principle. The problem is that it contains an enormous epistemological cheat, one that I seek openly to confront in "Towards a Theory of the Middle Ground." On the constitutive level, the difficulty stems from the fact that there is a profound difference between the materials and aims of historians and literary scholars. Literary texts and historical contexts cannot be approached in precisely the same way, nor do they have the same status with respect to the scholar's ultimate interpretive goals. Broadly speaking, a literary text, one already recognized as such, is an objective given, however open to multiple readings and interpretations. But historical contexts do not exist in themselves; they must be defined, and in that sense constructed, by the historian before the interpretive work of producing meaning, of interpreting the past, can begin. As a consequence, the historian functions as a "writer," in the sense of composing the basic historical narrative out of which significance will flow, while the literary critic stands in relation to the literary object primarily as a "reader," although this contrast is clearly too sharp to withstand close scrutiny. But in a general way it seems fair to say that the task facing the one is largely constructive; the other, largely deconstructive. And behind this pragmatic difficulty lies a fundamental philosophical incompatibility in the ontological status of the "text" *deployed* to constitute context (history) and that of the text *employed* in doing criticism.

This most fundamental contradiction is, then, inescapably, translated into one's strategies of narrative presentation. As an eminent example of the failure to solve this problem, I place in evidence my recent book on Old French vernacular prose historiography, *Romancing the Past*, several themes of which are represented in this volume in the essay "Medieval Canon Formation and the Rise of Royal Historiography in Old French Prose" (Chapter Eleven). *Romancing the Past* examines the rise of vernacular prose historiography in thirteenth-century France as a response on the part of a threatened nobility to newly problematic aspects of aristocratic life in the opening decades of that century. It argues that this response was displaced to the past in such a way that vernacular chronicles came to encode in the disguised form of history the most troubling experiences of contemporary life. In order to demonstrate this, it was necessary to know what those experiences—economic, social, political—were and how they posed a challenge to the political authority and the chivalric ideology of the nobility responsible for patronizing vernacular historiography. But precisely because these nobles sought to disguise their contemporary distress beneath the calm and deproblematized surface of prose narrative, it was impossible to "read" the social and political transformations behind such patronage out of the texts themselves, whose entire rhetorical repertoire was designed to disavow the very changes from which it was born.

In writing *Romancing the Past*, thus, I employed the tools of social historians and literary historians. I turned to the first because I wanted to situate the texts within a social world to which they themselves do not bear witness. I resorted to the second because I wished to investigate the ideological manipulation of the past that occurs in these writings, to which end I submit them to close, essentially deconstructive, readings and attempt to display the ways in which they tacitly inscribe through a variety of literary techniques the very social context that I have inferred, from *other* sources, to be relevant in understanding their literary character and the motives for their creation.

To realize this dual purpose, the first chapter of *Romancing the Past* blithely sets forth in a traditional historical mode an account of the economic, political, military, and dynastic events that shaped the experiences of those for whom vernacular chronicles were composed. Succeeding chapters, however, are devoted to close readings of the texts that form the object of this study. The result is notable shifts in tone, style, and methods as the book moves between historical and literary sections, that is, from context to text and from text to context. This contrast in voice and analytical approach between the historical discussion in the first chapter and the literary discussions in the following chapters was unavoidable, given my resolve to examine both texts and their contexts in ways appropriate to each.

However laudable this resolve may appear, good intentions cannot hide the fact that it represents an epistemological nightmare—cavalierly assigning a communicative status to some medieval texts while simultaneously treating others as opaque, mise-en-abîme, and aporistic. As far as I am concerned, the problem of an adequate epistemology for history, one that could rise to what I have called in Chapter One the "semiotic challenge," is simply unsolvable. To me, the more interesting question is why we—or I—feel the need to preserve this dual perspective even when it so patently proves itself to be philosophically unsatisfactory and historiographically impractical. What are the investments, whether philosophical or political, that cause us to cling to the idea of an empirically verifiable, recoverable past even as we systematically undermine the very conditions of possibility for its realization.

This is a question I try in part to answer in the final, new essay of Part One, "In the Mirror's Eye: The Writing of Medieval History in America." And my answer is that this conundrum is itself symptomatic of a deeper, postmodern conundrum that is generated by the simultaneity of the desire for history and the recognition of its irreparable loss, a recognition that paradoxically nourishes the very desire it can never satisfy. What I call the desire for history not only represents the desire to recuperate the past or the other but also marks the inaccessibility of that absent other, an irony that seems to me to be the very figure of history in the late twentieth century.

The intellectual journey inscribed in the essays collected here, thus, traces the progressive dawning of an awareness of the need to confront a generation's profound loss of certainty in older ways of knowing, conceptualizing, and experiencing the past. Postmodernism has challenged us to elaborate new forms and new philosophies of writing history. If, as Lyotard argues, there are no longer any master narratives, still less are there any certainties about the nature and status of history itself, whether as an object of study or a subject of practice. Our confidence in the totality and ultimate unity of the greater historical enterprise is gone. Like so much else, history has been subject to the fracturing and fragmentation that has beset all aspects of postmodern thought. Not only are there no master narratives, there is no consensus even about the possibility of historical knowledge uncontaminated by the hermeneutic circle.

But it would be wrong to leave the impression that loss is the only sign under which we have labored. For the relinquishment of traditional models of historical writing has at the same time been exhilaratingly liberating and enormously productive, expanding, enriching, and deepening our historiographical practice while freeing it from its positivist illusions. If we have now abandoned the positivist certainties and foundationalism of the "old" historicism in favor of new and as yet unsettled historical practices, perhaps this is not cause for regret. A historiographical practice grounded in an awareness of its own philosophical and practical commitments will not diminish but rather strengthen our appreciation both of the past as the object of our study and of the present as the site of our investment in the past. It is my hope that the essays gathered here have contributed in some small way to reconfiguring the theory and practice of medieval historiography and will continue to play a part in the ongoing debates about the nature and meaning of history as we struggle to redefine the philosophical and disciplinary basis of our enterprise as historians.

PART ONE

Theory

1 ∎ *History, Historicism, and the Social Logic of the Text*

The study of literary texts appears at the moment to stand at a decisive juncture. Trends in critical thinking over the past decades have questioned the possibility of recovering a text's historical meaning. At the same time, there is a newly insistent plea for a return to "history" in the interpretation of literature. Before a rapprochement can occur, however, we need to have a clearer understanding of how both historians and critics understand "history" and of the ways in which postmodernist thought positions history and the role of the historian with respect to issues of literary interpretation at the forefront of contemporary critical debate. One thing is clear: the paradigms that have governed historical and literary study since the nineteenth century no longer hold unquestioned sway. The confident, humanist belief that a rational, "objective" investigation of the past permits us to recover "authentic" meanings in historical texts has come under severe attack in postmodernist critical debate. At stake in this debate are a number of concepts traditionally deployed by historians in their attempts to understand the past: causality, change, authorial intent, stability of meaning, human agency, and social determination. What place, then, does history have in a postmodern theoretical climate? What, if anything, can the historian contribute to the reconfiguration of both theoretical concerns and interpretive practices signaled by the very notion of postmodernism? My purpose here is to explore some of the issues in question from the historian's point of view, paying particular attention to trends in literary criticism that suggest a reawakened interest in history.

Looking at the current critical climate from the vantage point of a historian, one has an impression of the dissolution of history, of a flight from "reality" to language as the constitutive agent of human consciousness and the social production of meaning. The impulses promoting this "linguistic turn" have come from several directions.[1] Chief among them was the rise of structural linguistics, beginning with the publication in 1916 of Ferdinand de Saussure's *Course in General Linguistics* and continuing with the successive emergence of structuralism, semiotics, and poststructuralism, especially in its deconstructionist guise, whose principal impact has been felt in the period after World War II.

What unites these varieties of pre- and poststructuralisms is their common reliance upon a language-model epistemology, one that views language not as a window on the world it transparently reflects, but as constructing that world, that is, as creating rather than imitating reality.[2] Despite considerable differences among the polemicists and practitioners of poststructuralism, all begin from the premise that language is somehow anterior to the world it shapes; that what we experience as "reality" is but a socially (i.e., linguistically) constructed artifact or "effect" of the particular language systems we inhabit. A belief in the fundamentally linguistic character of the world and our knowledge of it forms the core of what I would call the "semiotic challenge." As a language-based conception of reality, semiotics has undermined materialist theories of experience and the ideas of causality and agency inherent in them. To meet the challenge of semiotics, we need to understand the full range of consequences entailed in its approach to both history and literature.

Post-Saussurean theory begins "from an analysis of language as a system of differences with no positive terms."[3] Far from reflecting the social world of which it is a part, language precedes the world and makes it intelligible by constructing it according to its own rules of signification. Since for Saussure such rules are inherently arbitrary, in the sense of being social conventions implicitly understood in different ways by differing linguistic communities,[4] the idea of an objective universe existing independently of speech and universally comprehensible despite one's membership in any particular language system is an illusion. Reality does not exist "beyond" the reach of language; it is "always already" constructed in language, which is itself anterior to our knowledge of the world. It follows that literature, as an instance of linguistic utterance, cannot transparently reflect a world outside itself, since that "world" is only a linguistic construct, and what it reflects, therefore, is merely another articulation of language, or discourse.

Like language, literature refers not to an exterior world but only to the operation of language itself. Structural linguistics rescues literature from its lonely island of privileged being by insisting that literary language is but one instance of a much broader or, more precisely, "deeper" system of linguistic practice, a system to which Saussure gave the name *langue*. For structural linguistics, literature is but an instance or index of *langue*, a determinate speech act (in Saussure's terminology, *parole*) that, like every other sort of speech act, derives its nature from the underlying deep structures of language governing a society's linguistic praxis. What literature offers is an index of socially construable meaning rather than an image of reality; it is to the construction of social meaning, rather than the transmission of messages about the world, that the exercise of literature is directed.

As developed by semiotics and deconstruction, Saussure's investigation into the properties of language systems was to have serious consequences for a historical understanding of both textuality and history by severing language from any intrinsic connection to external referents. Starting from Saussure's notion of words as "signs," conceived as arbitrary (because conventional) "signifiers" capable of producing multiple significations (or "signifieds"), semiotics focused attention on the performative aspect of language as the production of meaning, dependent upon the deployment of formal signs. Semiotics further insisted that meaning is produced by the internal relations of signs to one another, rather than by reference to extralinguistic phenomena. This means, as Raymond Williams has pointed out, that language "not only [is] not natural, but is a form of codification."[5] Language (pre-)exists in the form of available codes, and it follows that the creation of meaning is the work of rules relating signs to one another in the manner predetermined by the code's underlying system or *langue*. In that sense, John Toews perceptively notes, "the creation of meaning is impersonal, operating 'behind the backs' of language users whose linguistic actions can merely exemplify the rules and procedures of languages they inhabit but do not control."[6] Such a view of language as constituting impersonal codes governing individual expression radically disturbs traditional notions of the author as a centered subject, in conscious control and responsible for his or her own utterances. It is hardly surprising, therefore, that Roland Barthes declared all authors "dead." What remains as the literary work, from a semiotic perspective, is not an autonomous expression of a centered, speaking subject, but coded texts and the multiple readings to which they are susceptible.[7] What in positivism, historicism, and even New Criticism was deemed to be a text's coherent statement or point of view, ultimately discoverable through close reading, is fractured into a series of discontinuous, heterogeneous, and contradictory codes that defy interpretive unification except at the level of allegorical recodification, itself suspect as the ideological imposition of a false coherence where none in truth exists.

More detrimental for the historical consideration of literature than even this fracturing of the literary work into multiple and conflicting codes was the way in which semiotics inevitably dehistoricized literature by denying the importance of a historically situated authorial consciousness, a dehistoricization of the literary text that was tantamount to the denial of history. If authors are seen as bound by preexisting language codes rather than by social processes to which they give voice, and if those very social processes are themselves understood as linguistically constituted (are, in that sense, little more than alternative sign systems), then social life is essentially a play of discursive behavior, the interaction and combination of artificial, disembodied signs in unstable relationships with one another, cut off from any purchase on a world exterior to language and hence, in all senses of the word, immaterial.

It was deconstruction that was to carry the implications of post-Saussurean linguistics farthest in terms of the dissolution of the materiality of the sign, while at the same time moving the argument away from the consideration of speech to focus on *écriture* or textuality as the matrix of human linguistic consciousness. Once language was considered to be a system of arbitrary codification, the obvious response in the presence of codes was to decode and "deconstruct" them: to examine the specific processes at work in a given text's enactment of meaning in terms of the shifts and clashes of codes cohabiting within the literary work; to examine, that is, a text's mode of production rather than its referential content. Moreover, deconstruction came to focus on the surplus of significations produced by signs, a surplus that made it impossible to establish the stability of "intended" meaning in any act of speech or writing. The inevitable clash of codes coexisting within the text fractures the apparently continuous, harmonious surface of the work to reveal the contradictions and pluralities of meanings that it harbors. In the course of deconstructing a text, the reader is confronted, ultimately, by its final indeterminacy of meaning, its aporia, in the face of which the reader hesitates, unable to decide. For, once fractured, the multiplicity of differences inherent within the sign, differences that the text seeks to repress and/or negate, is exposed.[8] The goal of deconstruction is to unmask the varied and contradictory meanings that linger within the text's imposed silences. What this process of deconstruction ultimately discloses is the "inability of language to represent anything outside its own boundaries."[9] As Jacques Derrida explains it: "Through this sequence of supplements a necessity is announced: that of an infinite chain, ineluctably multiplying the supplementary mediations that produce the sense of the very thing they defer: the mirage of the thing itself, of immediate presence, of original perception."[10] Behind the language of the text stands only more language, more texts, in an infinite regress in which the presence of the real and the material is always deferred, never attainable. According to deconstruction, we are confined within a "prisonhouse of language" (to use the fashionable Nietzschean phrase) from which there is no exit, since, as Derrida proclaimed, "il n'y a pas de hors-texte."[11] Like semiotics, to which it owes its governing conception of language, deconstruction sees the operation of language as impersonal (language uses its speakers, Derrida claims, rather than the other way around), forming and reforming itself in the play of textuality (since even speech, for Derrida, can be construed as a form of writing, an "archiécriture"), endlessly interposing itself between consciousness and the "world" it claims to describe but fails to grasp.

This dissolution of the materiality of the sign, its ruptured relation to extralinguistic reality, is necessarily also the dissolution of history, since it denies the ability of language to "relate" to (or account for) any reality other than itself. History, the past, is simply a subsystem of linguistic signs, constituting its object according to the rules of the linguistic universe inhabited by the historian.[12] Historical being becomes for deconstruction, as Lee Patterson has shown, "not a presence but an effect of presence created by textuality. There is no *hors texte*, and in trying to discover the historically real we enter into a labyrinthine world that not only forecloses access to history in its original form but calls into question its very existence as an object of knowledge. For Deconstruction, writing absorbs the social context into a textuality that is wholly alienated from the real."[13] This is a problem not limited, moreover, to literary texts, for there is no sound epistemological reason, within a poststructuralist universe, to distinguish between literary and other uses of language. If the literary text is denied the ability to represent reality, so also are all texts, and the distinction traditionally drawn between literature and "document" becomes meaningless, since both participate equally in the uncontrolled play and intertextuality of language itself. If we cannot reach "life" through literature, we cannot reach "the past" through documents.[14]

In many ways, this is a surprising outcome to the structuralist enterprise, since one might have assumed that Saussure's emphasis on the arbitrary, conventional nature of *langue* as a social phenomenon would lead naturally to a historicist perspective emphasizing the variety and the historically determinate appearance of different linguistic systems. Even if one accepted Saussure's notion that reality is socially constructed, there is no implication in the *Course in General Linguistics* that it is constructed in all places and at all times in the same way; to the contrary, the Saussurean insistence on language as a system of difference without positive terms strongly militates against this conclusion. If language is an implicit social contract that binds members of the linguistic community to prescribed usages, without which communication and the production of meaning would be impossible, then any given language is necessarily a historically specific occurrence, for the investigation of which historicism appears to hold out the best hope. It is not surprising, then, that the principal adaptations of structuralist and poststructuralist principles within the domains of anthropology and history have attempted to restore the historicist posture more or less implicit in Saussure's formulations by focusing on the social construction of meaning in historically determinate cultural discourses. But, as I shall try to argue, while cultural anthropology and cultural history (together with the New Historicism, with which it entertains such rich relations) have successfully reintroduced a (new) historicist consideration of discourse as the product of identifiable cultural and historical formations, they have not been equally successful in restoring history as an active agent in the social construction of meaning.

Without doubt, the dominant figure in promoting the use of semiotic models for the study of culture and history on the Anglo-American scene has been Clifford Geertz. Although his first, enormously influential collection of essays, *The Interpretation of Cultures*, probably owed more to Northrop Frye's theory of archetypes than to semiotics proper, Geertz clearly grasped and argued for a semiotic concept of culture as an "interworked system of construable signs,"[15] which was to be the object of an interpretive, rather than functionalist, anthropology. In his classic essay "Deep Play: Notes on the Balinese Cockfight," Geertz put to anthropological use Frye's insistence that the meaning of literary texts is expressive and formal, not instrumental, by treating the Balinese cockfight as a "sustained symbolic structure," a way "of saying something of something," whose meaning was to be understood as a problem not of social mechanics (how cockfights functioned within Balinese society to reinforce status, deploy power, advance interests, etc.) but of social semantics. And he went on to propose that culture be examined as "an assemblage of texts" and that specific cultural forms "be treated as texts, as imaginative works built out of social materials."[16]

Geertz's brand of interpretive anthropology, as he later claimed, was "preadapted to some of the most advanced varieties of modern opinion,"[17] which he defined as "the move toward conceiving of social life as organized in terms of symbols (signs, representations, *signifiants, Darstellungen . . .* the terminology varies), whose meaning (sense, import, *signification, Bedeutung . . .*) we must grasp if we are to understand that organization and formulate its principles."[18] Annexing, within this definition, hermeneutics along with semiotics, Geertz powerfully argued for the application of what he called the "text analogy" to the study of culture, in which social action would be seen as a "behavioral text" and the goal of anthropology the "systematic unpackings of the conceptual world" of other cultures.[19] That Geertz's notion of symbolic anthropology was also compatible with (if consciously distinguished from) structural anthropology as practiced by Claude Lévi-Strauss was not the least of its benefits.[20] Where Geertz studied social behavior as symbolic texts, Lévi-Strauss studied texts as symbolic action, the resolution in the structure of the imaginary of real political and social contradictions. For both, access to the processes at work in the construction of symbols came via the formal patterns that a culture employed in the creation of its social texts. Thus, although texts were described as imaginative works built out of *social materials*, it was the formal patterns, the modes of representation rather than the social conflicts whose symbolic expression and resolution they served, which tended to become the object of investigation. The result, inevitably, was an aestheticizing of culture and its absorption into the ever-widening category of "textuality" as poststructuralism came to view it.[21] The promise of Geertz's semiotic approach to the study of culture lay in its desire to redirect anthropological explanation towards connecting "action to its sense rather than behavior to its determinants,"[22] avoiding thereby the determinism into which functionalism tended to fall. This promise was never quite realized, as the primacy of textual modes of analysis increasingly blurred the active nature of the "social material" that Geertz took as his texts. As in literary criticism, so too in ethnography: discursive models of the social construction of reality effected a separation of language and "reality," and the growing concentration on language became, as Nicole Polier and William Roseberry have remarked, "a centerpiece of the postmodern ethnographic project."[23]

Perhaps it should not (and certainly would not) disturb us that cultural anthropology has become progressively saturated with poststructuralist concepts of textuality, were it not for the extraordinary impact that Geertz's "text analogy" has had on the practice of social history and more especially on the emerging field of cultural history. In the hands of social historians, the appropriation of anthropological models, primarily by historians of early modern Europe, was a relatively straightforward affair. It was not confined to the use of Geertzian models, but drew as well from the anthropological work of Victor Turner and Mary Douglas, and Marcel Mauss and Arnold Van Gennep. Led by the groundbreaking work of Natalie Davis, social historians learned to study the ritual life of past societies: charivaris, carnivals, ceremonies of social inversion, and popular cults, even the massacre of cats, were studied as symbolic expressions of a social order that was both enacted and tested through ritual life.[24] As a consequence, the historian's field of inquiry and vocabulary were enormously enlarged; terms like *liminality, communitas,* and *ritual antistructure* became commonplace in the rhetoric of the new social historian. Although North American medievalists were not as quick as their colleagues in early modern European history to take up the anthropological standard, the work of Peter Brown on the cult of the saints, of Stephen White on arbitration practices, and of Patrick

Geary on the ritual humiliation of saints' relics, as well as Victor Turner's study of pilgrimage as a "liminoid" phenomenon, showed the potential that such work had for medieval history. At the same time, in France the group associated with Jacques LeGoff and Jean-Claude Schmitt (whose study *The Holy Greyhound* rapidly became something of a classic in medieval ethnography) organized the resources of the Ecole des Hautes Etudes en Sciences Sociales for the development of an ethnographically oriented medieval historiography.

In the main, social historians who employed ethnographic models were interested in the place of ritual in social life and were less apt to implement in any thoroughgoing sense Geertz's "text analogy." Although ritual was treated as a form of symbolic expression, it was not subjected to a genuinely literary analysis, nor did such historians rely in any systematic way on the conceptions of language that had grown out of Saussurean linguistics. Only with the emergence of cultural history were the assumptions built into the use of a discursive model for the analysis of sociocultural phenomena consistently developed and applied. Cultural history took as its domain the study of forms of social behavior and cultural production, both of which were now consciously recast in a semiotic mode and made permeable to the influence of recent trends in literary criticism and theory, including large doses of poststructuralism.

A good example of the way in which cultural history conceives of and repositions the text within a history of society that focuses upon cultural production is provided by Jonathan Culler's essay, "Literary History, Allegory and Semiology" (1976). Culler proposed that

> the best way of imagining a relationship between literature and society which could form the basis of cultural history and hence of literary history is to think of both literature and the culture of which it forms a part as institutions composed of symbolic systems which enable actions or objects to have meaning, among them literature and genres, whose conventions are devices for the production and organization of meaning.

For Culler and cultural historians generally, both literature and society are to be construed as systems of signs whose relationship to one another takes the form of commensurability or "homology." In such analyses, the critical foci of interpretation are directed not to the content of social life or literature but rather to the "operations which produce social and cultural objects, the devices which create a world charged with meaning."[25] These "operations" are the linguistic codes that constitute social and discursive formations. Given this, it is impossible to establish the priority of one to the other, to say that society determines or "causes" in any mechanistic sense the cultural production of meaning, or that there is an ontological difference between the imaginative and the "real" (between, for instance, literature and extralinguistic events, actions, or institutions), since what is construed as the "real" is itself the product of imaginary, that is, discursive construction. Thus Geertz, with characteristic clarity, declares: "The real is as imagined as the imaginary."[26] So also Roger Chartier, arguing on behalf of the substitution of sociocultural history for more traditional forms of intellectual history, insisted in his early work that "the relationship thus established [between the text and the real] is not one of dependence of the mental structures on their material determinations. The representations of the social world themselves are the constituents of social reality."[27]

It is at this point that the historian (perhaps naively) feels compelled to query: what, then, is the "real"? To this question Chartier provisionally answered: that which the text itself poses as real in constituting it as a referent situated beyond itself. But not only the reality aimed at by the text, for Chartier added to this definition the further qualification that what is real is, in a new meaning, "the very manner in which the text aims at it [reality] in the historicity of its production and the strategy of its writing."[28] In other words, what are real are the semiotic codes that govern the representation of life both in writing and in incorporated social structures.

What cultural history achieves by this equation of the imaginary and the real within the structures of discourse is a radical foregrounding and reconceptualization of the problem of text and context. If the imaginary is real and the real imaginary and there are no epistemological grounds for distinguishing between them, then it is impossible to create an explanatory hierarchy that establishes a causal relationship between history and literature, life and thought, matter and meaning. The context in which a text is situated is itself composed of constituted meanings, as "texts of everyday life," so to speak, and the connections between them are essentially intertextual.[29] It becomes impossible, on this basis, to identify aspects of social, political, or economic life that somehow stand apart from or make up a "reality" independent of the cultural constructions that historically conditioned discourses generate; text and context are collapsed into one broad vein of discursive production. Moreover, while cultural history has proven itself adept at treating discursive production in terms of historicist perspectives of epochal variation, its historicism is not accompanied by what most historians would understand as a historical explanation of the relationship between the production of meaning and social reality. From the point of view of the traditional literary or social historian, then, the achievement of cultural history lies in its reintroduction of a historicist consideration of literature; its failure lies in its refusal to differentiate between text and context or to establish an intelligible relationship between them that does not lead to their mutual implication in a textually conceived universe. The problem becomes even more severe when we remember that so-called documentary representations of reality (charters, laws, fief-lists, economic data, accounts of trade, or wars, not to mention cat massacres and cockfights) are equally included within the compass of the social construction of reality and equally understood as the result of "historically contingent discursive formations."[30] In the starkest terms, cultural history seems to recognize no acts other than speech acts, no forms of being which are not assimilated to textuality and thus made accessible to the workings of the text analogy.

The consequences of this way of looking at the problem of text and context for both historians and literary critics are far-ranging and serious. To begin with, as has occurred in symbolic anthropology following Geertz, it leads inexorably to an aestheticizing of culture in which the term *society* is implicitly emptied of its normal significance and reinscribed as *social text*.[31] Textuality absorbs the social into its own linguisticality; semiotic modes of literary interpretation expand their scope to include all and any manner of social texts, which now are treated as semiological systems. In this way, the deconstruction of the traditional distinction between representation and reality opens the way for the deconstruction of reality *as* text, a practice at which the New Historicists, using Michel Foucault to great effect, are expert. What began as a method of literary interpretation and grew into a generically textual interpretation has metamorphosed into social analysis. But, as Murray Krieger has cogently pointed out, one can argue that it remains a literary mode throughout: "It is only that this interpretation now ranges far beyond the literary and even beyond the textual realm in search of objects it makes available to itself, even if it treats them as if they were literary."[32] Thus, what may have begun as an attempt to rescue literature from its privileged being and New Critical self-enclosure has paradoxically extended the boundaries of the literary to include social and material reality, thereby dissolving the material into "meaning." Paradoxically as well, what began as a revolt against formalism appears to have reinstated formalist concerns, since, if language constitutes meaning (discursively and socially), then, as Martin Jay indicates, historians of society and literature "will have to pay attention to the linguistic dimension of the texts they examine,"[33] whether those texts are purely literary/intellectual or social texts.[34] Sociocultural history begins to look not so much like a substitute for traditional intellectual history as its modulation to another key, one that makes room for the new view of textuality engendered by post-Saussurean linguistics and, in particular, deconstruction. It is New Historicism that has been most alive to the possibilities emerging from this approach to cultural history.

Like cultural history, New Historicism takes as its point of departure a broadly symbolic and semiotic view of cultural production which seeks, in the words of Louis Montrose, "to resituate canonical literary tales among the multiple forms of writing, and in relation to the nondiscursive practices and institutions of the social formation in which those texts have been produced." At first glance, this formulation of the New Historicist project appears to rehabilitate the existence of "nondiscursive" practices and institutions as autonomous material realities, but Montrose quickly goes on to acknowledge "language as the medium in which the Real is constructed and apprehended."[35] Hence, as do cultural historians, New Historicists point to the culturally specific nature of texts as products of particular periods and discursive formations, and they view reality—history—as itself mediated by linguistic codes that it is impossible for the critic/historian to bypass in the recuperation of past cultures. Characteristic of New Historicism's conceptualization of the text-context conundrum (that is, as Lee Patterson succinctly defines it, the problem that the text is at once constituted by and constitutes history) are statements such as Montrose's claim that New Historicists are concerned with "the historicity of texts and the textuality of history" and Stephen Greenblatt's program "to examine the relation between the discourse of art and the circumambient discourses of society."[36] What such statements intend is the elaboration of a "cultural poetics," as Greenblatt calls it, in which a wide variety of social, institutional, and political practices are submitted to the same interpretive procedures as other, more recognizably discursive artifacts such as literary or nonliterary texts. Just as cultural history tacitly reinscribes society as "social text," so New Historicism treats political, institutional, and social practices as "cultural scripts."[37]

The debt here to Foucault is clear, and as with Foucault, the goal of New Historicist criticism is to demonstrate the power of discourse in shaping the ways in which the dominant ideology of a period creates both institutional and textual embodiments of the cultural constructs governing mental and social life. What perhaps differentiates the New Historicists from the practice of cultural historians, with whom they are otherwise so closely allied, is their skillful employment of the poststructuralist belief in the heterogeneous, contradictory, fragmented, and discontinuous nature of textuality, to which "social texts" are likewise assimilated. In this vein, New Historicism refuses unproblematical distinctions between "literature" and "history," "text" and "context," and emphasizes instead "the dynamic, unstable, and reciprocal relationship between the discursive and material domains."[38] But as should be all too clear by now, it is difficult to discover in what the materiality of the material domain consists, or how history is distinct from literature or context from text, in light of New Historicism's insistence on the symbolic foundation of all social constructions—textual and otherwise—and its persistent deployment of deconstructive readings in the interpretation of cultural artifacts of all kinds. Yet again, the elaboration of a (new) historicist approach to cultural production is not necessarily accompanied by a return to historical explanation as (old) historicism traditionally conceived of it. Instead, a global view of textuality and its shaping force in the constitution of social and literary formations has closed off access to a "reality" whose dubious status is figured by the persistent use of quotation marks. Yet I would argue that if we want to contextualize texts, we cannot achieve this merely by textualizing the context. New Historicism, like cultural history, appears to gloss over the problem of the text-context relationship by the adoption of a semiotic mode of analysis which occludes the issue altogether by treating culture, institutions, ideology, and power as merely interworked sets of symbolic systems or codes.[39]

It might be argued that cultural materialism, as advocated by Raymond Williams and other Marxists, successfully addresses this problem through its insistence on the materiality of thought and writing as actions-in-the-world, with real consequences comparable to those produced by what historians normally call "events." Thus Williams, in contrast to conventional Marxist views on the superstructural character of literary production, begins by seeing "language and signification from the beginning as indissoluble elements of the material social process itself, involved all the time both in production and reproduction." Moreover, like the cultural historians, Williams insists that "language is not a medium [transparently communicating thought]; it is a constitutive element of social practice." Just as cul-

tural history and New Historicism seek to abolish the distinction between a reified "language" and "society" by subsuming both within
textuality, so Williams rejects the same distinction in the name of an
encompassing materialism, in which language is an active social agent
in the workings of what he calls "practical consciousness" through
and by which reality is grasped.[40] Cultural production is, therefore,
one mode of material production, commensurate in its materiality
with other varieties of material production by means of which societies strive to sustain and reproduce themselves. And like them, it is
constitutive of social reality, a position that establishes Williams's
connection to the "cultural" (semiotic) component of cultural materialism.

It is not at all clear, however, how this shift from textuality to materiality, from discourse to "practical consciousness," and from the
impersonal operation of linguistic codes to the active agency of "social language" solves the problem of the relation of literature to society, that is, of text and context. To state that literature is also "real"
does not answer the question of how literature is associated with reality while remaining avowedly imaginary. Williams here comes close
simply to inverting Geertz's view that the "real is as imagined as the
imaginary" by the counterassertion that the imaginary is as real as reality, but we are no nearer a solution to the problem of their reciprocal interaction as distinct forms of social activity. Moreover, by seeing
language as constitutive of the real, Williams appears to come full circle and rejoin the semiotic view of culture held by cultural historians,
against which his materialism is directed. If Marxist criticism holds
some attractions for historians, even for those by no means Marxist,
it is because of its recognition of a crucial difference of order between
text and context, and of the necessity of theorizing their relation.

It is striking that, apart from Marxism, few strands of contemporary
criticism have managed to preserve a sense of history as a relatively
autonomous realm of human experience, unaffected by the prefiguration of linguistic construction. Literary theory in particular seems
to have entered a labyrinth of "textuality" from which there is no exit.

For most schools of critical theory, textuality has become, as Edward Said has pointed out, "the exact antithesis and displacement of what might be called history."[41] Even cultural historians and New Historicists, committed in principle to the reintegration of a contextualist perspective in the interpretation of literature and culture, have resolved the problem of how to effect such a reintegration by textualizing contexts, drawing social behavior and political power inexorably into the orbit of a critical stance that assumes the cultural construction of reality in and through language. At a time when one increasingly hears cries for a return to considerations of "history" and "power" in the interpretation of literary and cultural phenomena, it seems appropriate for the historian to ask why history as traditionally conceived appears to be so fragile.

In part, the ability of semiotics to sweep the theoretical field is testimony to the power of its challenge to traditional epistemologies, to the technical virtuosity of its practitioners, and to the underlying coherence of its theory, against which those advocating a return to history rather weakly invoke collective "common sense" or individual, subjective experiences. But it is unlikely that the semiotic challenge can be met simply by an appeal to individual sense and experience. If recent criticism is any indication, a historically grounded view of literary and cultural production is extremely difficult to theorize in the wake of the semiotic challenge, and the obstacles to doing so have thus far loomed large.

To some degree, those obstacles have arisen from the rather one-sided nature of the discussion, which has largely been in the hands of literary critics rather than historians. One of the problems has been a need on the part of literary critics for a stable term against which to play off the complexity of their textual readings. The more complex, fractured, and heterogeneous the critic's view of literary language has become, the greater the necessity for a "lucid" historical context against which to develop and, ultimately, adjudicate interpretive positions. The focus of structuralist and poststructuralist theory on discursive "codes," ironically, implies the existence of the same messages "in clear,"[42] and history has been cast in the role of repository for such "clear" communications from the past, offering a master narrative under whose aegis the occult meanings of texts can be solicited and allegorically rewritten.[43] For their part, historians have been left with the menial task of providing a lucid, accessible—above all, knowable and known—context while critics take their leisure in exploring the productive enigmas of textuality. Literary critics have been accustomed to get their history secondhand and prepackaged and have tended, in practice if not in theory, to treat it as unproblematic, something to be invoked rather than investigated. Yet if texts bear within them layers of discursive displacements and heterogeneous meanings, so too does history. Events are not necessarily any more logical, less ridden with contradiction and hidden intentions, than speech or writing. It is interesting that the notion of play, inconsistency, and difference so subtly deployed in the analysis of textuality never seems applicable to the treatment of history, although surely this is one place where the "text analogy" might prove useful to historians and certainly would be salutary for critics. And this remains a problem, in the end, only for those literary critics and historians who have not pursued the path of the "text analogy" to its logical conclusion in the collapsing of text and context within a single aestheticized understanding of culture.

Another difficulty has been a tendency to bracket the problem of causality. Among the indubitable attractions of anthropological models of the Geertzian sort is that they permit one to bypass issues of causality, thereby providing a way out of the reductive fallacies and determinism that had beset positivist and old-style historicist criticism. A discursive model of culture is well suited to the needs of literary critics, for whom the complexity of causal explanation should not be underestimated. As René Wellek and Austin Warren point out, causal explanation is highly overrated as a method of literary exegesis, for in the analysis of a literary work "cause and effect are incommensurate: the concrete result of extrinsic causes—the work of art—is always unpredictable." Cause-governed, extrinsic schools of interpretation tend to be, in their cutting phrase, "ergocentric," committed to isolating a few among the host of possible social factors re-

sponsible for shaping the literary work, hence inevitably reduction-
ist.[44] What is most striking, however, is the degree to which the rejection of causality has overtaken history done in the cultural vein as
well. Thus Robert Darnton, in *The Great Cat Massacre*, proclaims
that "cultural history is history in the ethnographic grain . . . ; its aim
is to read for meaning."[45] But it might be argued, as Toews does, that
while the history of meaning has successfully asserted the reality and
autonomy of its object, "a new form of reductionism has become evident, the reduction of experience to the meanings that shape it."[46]
What gets lost in the concentration on meaning in place of experience is the sense of social agency, of men and women struggling with
the contingencies and complexities of their lives in terms of the fates
that history deals out to them and transforming the worlds they in-
herit and pass on to future generations. These are the questions that
have always engaged historians on the deepest level of their commitment to understanding the past, and it seems unlikely that a literary
history informed by semiotic principles will be able to evade the issue
of causality—of "*why* and *how* a given form of literary work appeared as it did, where it did, and when it did"[47]—and still satisfy
even sympathetic historians' demands for a historical, and not merely
historicist, conception of cultural production.

In the final analysis, however, the difficulties encountered in resolving the text-context conundrum do not arise from the fact that as
professional scholars we are limited by or locked into disciplinary
competencies that we fear to transgress. They stem, rather, from technical problems that have gone largely unacknowledged in the theoretical literature. Primarily, they are due to a series of unrecognized
incommensurabilities among the objects, tasks, and goals facing historians and literary scholars that make the achievement of a genuinely integrated *literary history* extraordinarily troublesome.

There is, to begin with, an incommensurability in the object of
investigation. Literary text and historical context are not the same
thing, and if one should not be reduced to the other, neither should
they be held up as identical foci of the scholar's gaze. While the text
is an objective given, an existing artifact (in its material existence if

not in its constitution as a specifically "literary" work), the object of historical study must be constituted by the historian long before its meaning can begin to be disengaged. Paradoxically, in that sense the text qua text is materially "realer" than "history," and any attempt to adjudicate the interpretive meaning of a literary text by recourse to history as "reality" begins to look like an exercise undertaken backwards. History as given chronicle or unproblematic "truth" simply does not exist and so cannot serve as a master narrative for criticism into which the enigmatic codes of literary discourse can be transcoded in clear.

Moreover, since the historical text is not given but must be constructed, the historian of texts is a writer in his or her function of constituting the historical narrative, but a reader of the already materially extant text. The task facing the one is broadly constructive; the other, broadly deconstructive. It is not hard to see why few literary critics or historians of texts have given equal attention to both undertakings. The advantage of collapsing text and context, from this perspective, emerges not only as a response to the semiotic challenge, but as a means to avoid the apparently contradictory maneuvers involved in doing literary history as the doing of history and literature. And this does not even begin to take account of the problems arising from the differing nature of the texts one is required to read for each enterprise, commonly distinguished as "literary" (self-reflective) and "documentary" (in theory, transparent). No historian would argue that history is present to us in any but textual form. But whether this necessarily means that history is "made up," foreclosing access to any past other than that we interpretively impose on texts, remains, one hopes, an open issue. The problem, of course, is not whether there is a past "out there" (or, as Nancy Partner wittily observed, if, once we get there, there is a "there" there),[48] but how we reach it and what procedures permit us to do so in ways that respect its integrity. A historicist appreciation of the difference between then and now is surely a sine qua non of historically oriented studies. But this in itself does not vouchsafe an approach to the past that addresses explanatory issues of primary concern to historians, as the widespread application of the "text analogy" makes only too clear.

Arguably, as well, critics and historians will possess different goals in their respective inquiries, even when reading the same texts. While literary critics will perhaps be more concerned with the affective functions of a text, with its ability to startle, to confront the reader with new aesthetic and ethical forms, the historian is possibly more interested in a text's ideological function, the way it represents a broad complex of social relations. The growing attention to ideological formations in the study of literary discourse, in part stemming from the influence of Louis Althusser and Pierre Macherey, and particularly marked (in a Foucauldian tenor) in New Historicism, indicates that the distance separating literary critics and historians on this question is not, however, very great. Indeed, ideology, which once occupied a somewhat modest place in intellectual history, primarily among the sociologists of knowledge, has now become a virtual obsession with theorists of discourse, suggesting that the absorption of history into textuality is itself an ideological gesture with distinct ideological consequences, a by-product, perhaps, of the "hubris of word-makers who claim to be makers of reality."[49]

How, then, are we to resolve the question of the relation of text to context, of literature to life, while still acknowledging the full force of the challenge that semiotics has posed to our understanding of material and cultural production. It is clear that the massive dehistoricization to which the literary text has been subjected in recent decades cannot be overcome simply by reverting to the methodological status ante quo of prestructuralism, according to which "documentary" evidence is radically protected from the vagaries of textuality and history serves as a testing ground for vying schools of critical interpretation. Semiotics and deconstruction have too thoroughly implicated all forms of discourse within their epistemologies and too successfully demystified the privileged status of literary language for a simple return to old-style historicism to be persuasive. What is needed is the elaboration of a theoretical position capable of satisfying the demands of both literary criticism and history as separate yet interdependent disciplinary domains with a common concern for the social dimensions of textual production in past times. Just as we rightly reject the reduction of literature to a reflection of the world, so also must we reject the absorption of history by textuality. We need to rethink the issue of text and context in terms of a critical posture that does justice equally to textual, historicist, and *historical* principles of analysis and explanation.

As a starting point in the fashioning of this sort of critical stance, we can begin by remembering that texts represent situated uses of language.[50] Such sites of linguistic usage, as lived events, are essentially local in origin and therefore possess a determinate social logic of much greater density and particularity than can be extracted from totalizing constructs like "language" and "society." The advantage of this approach to literary history in terms of the social logic of the text is that it permits us to examine language with the tools of the social historian, to see it within a local or regional social context of human relations, systems of communication, and networks of power that can account for its particular semantic inflections and thus aid in the recovery of its full meaning as cultural history seeks to understand it. This meaning, I would argue, while it may be viewed as an instance of the larger social discourses that govern it, is not ultimately reducible to an articulation of a preexisting system of linguistic codes, or *langue* in the Saussurean sense. All texts occupy determinate social spaces, both as products of the social world of authors and as textual agents at work in that world, with which they entertain often complex and contestatory relations. In that sense, texts both mirror and generate social realities, which they may sustain, resist, contest, or seek to transform, depending on the case at hand. There is no way to determine a priori the social function of a text or its locus with respect to its cultural ambience. Only a minute examination of the form and content of a given work can determine its situation with respect to broader patterns of culture at any given time. What this means is that a genuine literary history must always to some extent be both social and formalist in its concerns, must pay attention to a text's "social logic" in the dual sense of its site of articulation and its discursive character as articulated "logos."

The critical stance I have in mind begins from the premise, already well stated by Mikhail Bakhtin, that form and content in discourse are one, once we understand that verbal discourse is a social phenomenon—social throughout its entire range and in each and every of its factors, from the sound image to the furthest reaches of abstract meaning.[51] It therefore assumes that particular instances of language use or textuality incorporate social as well as linguistic structures and that the aesthetic character of a work is intimately related (either positively or negatively) to the social character of the environment from which it emerges, requiring the critic to be sensitive to the content as well as form of the work. Material reality, as Judith Walkowitz has recently remarked, always exists as a certain pressure, a destabilizing force on cultural production, forcing representation to be reworked, shored up, deconstructed.[52] Moreover, the power of any given set of representations derives in large part from its social context and its relation to the social and political networks in which it is elaborated. Thus, as Carroll Smith-Rosenberg has written, language subtly mirrors the social location and relative power of its speakers, and words assume different meanings depending upon which symbolic dialect is being spoken.[53] Further, even if we accept the poststructuralist argument that language constitutes the social world of meaning, we must also insist, as she states elsewhere, that "language itself acquires meaning and authority only within specific social and historical settings. While linguistic differences structure society, social differences structure language."[54] Texts, as material embodiments of situated language use, reflect in their very materiality the inseparability of material and discursive practices and the need to preserve a sense of their mutual involvement and interdependence in the production of meaning.

The most fruitful means of investigating this material and discursive mutuality, I would suggest, is to focus analysis on the moment of inscription, that is, on the ways in which the historical world is internalized in the text and its meaning fixed. This process of "inscription" (or the fixation of meaning) is not to be confused with written in the traditional sense of "recorded." Rather, it represents the moment of choice, decision, and action that creates the social reality of the text, a reality existing both "inside" and "outside" the particular performance incorporated in the work, through the latter's inclusions, exclusions, distortions, and stresses. In force in shaping a literary text is a host of unstated desires, beliefs, misunderstandings, and interests which impress themselves upon the work, sometimes consciously, sometimes not, but which arise from pressures that are social and not merely intertextual. Historians must insist, I think, on the importance of history itself as an active constituent of the elements that themselves constitute the text. As Macherey indicates, the writer does not manufacture the materials with which he or she works, but neither does the writer stumble across them haphazardly. Every work possesses certain particular conditions of possibility and is produced in determinate situations; in seeing how a book is made, we see also what it is made *from*.[55] Macherey formulates the text-context problem in terms borrowed from psychoanalysis, describing history as the text's absent cause, its latent unconscious, the forces and texts against which it constructs itself, incorporating not a single meaning but layers of contested and conflictual meanings and silences that bind the work to reality. The psychoanalytic framework of Macherey's treatment of literary production may prove troublesome for some historians. But his view of the literary text as the site of multiple, often contradictory, historical realities that are both present and absent in the work (and in both capacities constitutive of its form and incribed meaning) offers a suggestive way of looking at the inextricably interrelated nature of social and discursive practices, of the material and linguistic realities that are interwoven into the fabric of the text, whose analysis as a determinate historical artifact in turn grants us access to the past. And it is by focusing on the social logic of the text, its location within a broader network of social and intertextual relations, that we best become attuned to the specific historical conditions whose presence and/or absence in the work alerts us to its own social character and function, its own combination of material and

26

discursive realities that endow it with its own sense of historical purposiveness.

A literary history that begins with a focus on the social logic of the text, then, incorporates yet modifies existing features of current historical and critical thought. It is akin to current social history in that it will tend to look at local or regional social structures and processes rather than at society as a global whole. It preseves the emphasis of cultural history in seeing textuality as both arising from and constitutive of social life, which it seeks to endow with meaning. It shares with deconstruction the notion that texts often perform elaborate, ideological mystifications of which it is proper to be suspicious and which the text itself inevitably will betray through its ultimate fracturing of meaning. But such a program remains distinct from current versions of cultural history and poststructuralism in its desire not to collapse text and context, language and reality, to the same phenomenological order. It acknowledges that "reality," "context," "social structure," and the like appear to present historians only through past texts that are interpretively reconstituted and that history as the object of our knowledge is, inevitably, absent and knowable only through textually mediated representations.

Yet it seems necessary, in light of poststructuralism's dissolution of history, to insist that context is not simply another text, if only for heuristic purposes. In analyzing the meaning of texts, we need to do more than juxtapose them beside the "circumambient" cultural "scripts" of the period in the fashion of New Historicists, a procedure that inevitably aestheticizes culture and transforms text and context into a species of intertextuality. We should, rather, seek to locate texts within specific social sites that themselves disclose the political, economic, and social pressures that condition a culture's discourse at any given moment. Involved in this positioning of the text is an examination of the play of power, human agency, and social experience as historians traditionally understand them. Only after the text has been returned to its social and political context can we begin to appreciate the ways in which both language and social reality shape discursive and material fields of activity and thus come to an understanding of a text's "social logic" as situated language use. In the end, what this means is acknowledging that cockfights are something more than symbolic gestures. It does not deny that the Balinese cockfight also possesses symbolic dimensions, but its full meaning as a social activity is not exhausted in its symbolic significance. Those who bet on the cocks are not only expressing their peculiar understanding of the nature of Balinese social culture (its "sociomoral hierarchy") but are also hoping to profit materially from the animal violence that ensues. In its particular mixture of symbolic and material negotiations, the cockfight serves as an apt metaphor for the kind of literary history that we need to begin to elaborate. No less than the violent scene of the cockfight, texts inscribe the variegated motives and interests, material desires and imaginary dreams that motivate human behavior, and we cannot deny to them and their readers the same involvements in contests, side bets, social aspirations, and wish fulfillments that characterize this now famous Balinese pastime. To see the past merely in its discursive dimension is like looking at the Balinese cockfight as a purely symbolic activity. Perhaps the time has come for us to place our bets elsewhere.

2

Orations of the Dead /
Silences of the Living

The Sociology of the
Linguistic Turn

Areas of formal study, Hans Kellner recently argued, are complexes of defenses against particular anxieties.[1] I would like to suggest that history's anxiety now hovers over the status and meaning of the word *reality*, whose power to signify—to stand for and mean something—is thought to be radically diminished. This is, of course, simply another way of posing the postmodern dilemma, the hallmark of which has been a growing awareness of the mediated nature of perception, cognition, and imagination, all of which are increasingly construed to be mediated by linguistic structures cast into discourses of one sort or another—the famed "linguistic turn" that has raised such troubling problems for the study of history and literature alike. In this, poststructuralism participates in what Ihab Hassan has described as the much broader pattern of postmodernism, which he defines as

> indeterminacy and immanence; ubiquitous simulacra, pseudo-events; a conscious lack of mastery, lightness and evanescence everywhere; a new temporality, or rather intemporality, a polychronic sense of history; a patchwork of ludic, transgressive or deconstructive approaches to knowledge and authority; an ironic parodic, reflexive, fantastic awareness of the moment; a linguistic turn, semiotic imperative in culture; and in society generally the

violence of local desires diffused into a terminology of seduction and force.

In short, what Hassan sees as a "vast revisionary will in the Western world, unsettling/resetting codes, canons, procedures, beliefs—intimating a post-humanism."[2]

Whatever else one thinks of it, the anxiety that subtends this postmodern "linguistic turn" is palpable, undeniable, and begs for explanation. And I trust that you will excuse me if, in attempting to offer an explanation for one possible source of our postmodern angst, I indulge in a characteristic historian's gesture and turn first to the past. Not to the distant, medieval past, but to one that is both far more and far less accessible—to a past that I will argue forms and informs the postmodern turn. For it seems to me that we cannot come to terms with the challenges that postmodernism poses for historical study (and thus relieve our anxiety about its continuing viability) without understanding postmodernism's own historical context, its social logic, if you will, the relations it entertains with the social world from which it emerges and with which it conducts its most intense, inner debates.

My concern in this chapter is not so much with the "linguistic or postmodern turn" per se—semiotics, structuralism, and the varieties of poststructuralisms they have spawned—as with the particular spin placed on the "linguistic turn" by deconstruction, thus inevitably with the work of Jacques Derrida. I begin with an assumption: namely, that there is something counterintuitive about the way deconstruction envisages the relationship between language and reality, signifier and signified, at least when viewed against the long-term philosophical and historical traditions of Western thought from Plato to the present. Counterintuitive in the sense that deconstruction's understanding of these relationships interposes so many layers of mediation—indeed, proffers little *but* mediation—that one is left enclosed within a linguistic world that no longer has a purchase on reality; a world where, furthermore, it is no longer possible to believe that language means what it says or can be made to say what it means. Deconstruction proposes an inherent instability at the core of language that places the determination of meaning ultimately beyond our reach. Every linguistic act, in Derrida's view, whether spoken or written, harbors unseen, silent, but powerful alterities that fatally unbalance and decenter its intended significance, leading it to transgress its own system of values. Sooner or later, every instance of language use—every text, in the broad sense that deconstruction understands that term—founders on its own indeterminacy, its aporia, the "impasse beyond all possible transaction," as Derrida defines it, "which is connected with the multiplicity of meanings embedded within the uniqueness of textual inscription."[3] Rather than conveying univocal meaning or representing the world, language sinks into an abyss created by its endlessly regressive system of self-referentiality (is mise-en-abîme, as the French goes). In Derrida's lapidary phrase: "il n'y a pas de hors-texte." There is no "outside" of textuality. Behind the language of the text stands only more language, more text, forming and reforming itself in the play of textuality, forever mediating, and thus deferring, the material presence towards which it appears to be destined but at which it never arrives.

The psychic destabilization produced by such a problematizing of the relationship between *res et verba*, together with the decentering of language and thus, perforce, of those who author and authorize it, suggests that deconstruction represents not only a rupture in the traditions of Western philosophy and history, but a psychic response to those traditions that is itself founded in rupture. It is this psychology of deconstruction that interests me, and I would argue that the psychology of deconstruction has a sociological—which is to say, historical—basis of deep particularity, which I would like to outline briefly here. And since my concern is centered (if one can still say that) in Derrida, let us begin with a few biographical and intellectual facts, all the while acknowledging that Derrida himself would never authorize (or author) such a beginning.[4]

Jacques Derrida was born in 1930 in Algiers, to a family of French Sephardic Jews. He was a schoolchild during the war and was prohibited as a Jew from attending regular school for eleven months between October 1942 and the spring of 1943, at which point he returned to lycée in Algiers. Subsequently, after three years of preparatory work at the Lycée Louis-le-Grand in Paris, he entered the Ecole Normale Supérieure. He taught at the Sorbonne between 1960 and 1964 and after 1965 at the Ecole Normale Supérieure and at the Ecole Pratique des Hautes Etudes. He is currently Président of the Collège Internationale de Philosophie and associated with the Groupe de Recherches sur l'Enseignement Philosophique. His first major work appeared in 1967, in which year he published three seminal books: his translation of and extensive commentary on Husserl's "Origin of Geometry" in *Speech and Phenomena*; *Writing and Difference*; and *Of Grammatology*. Numerous books and articles have continued to pour forth, all of them dedicated to demonstrating and working through the critical concepts first elaborated as the "science of writing," or grammatology, in the publications of 1967. And because they will prove crucial to the argument I wish to make, it is perhaps useful to look quickly at those key concepts, or master terms, around and through which Derrida's thought flows.

The first is the notion of "grammatology" itself, as a science of language consciously distinguished from, albeit indebted to, semiotics. Where semiology takes as its focus the operation of the sign (and the sign preeminently in its phonic dimension, i.e., in speech), grammatology is, in contrast, the science of the written trace, of the *grammè*. Of the *trace*, not of the thing itself. For Derrida, all writing (hence all thought) takes place *sous rature*, under erasure, and what is effaced according to deconstruction is the Western world's metaphysical illusion of presence. The trace—the *grammè*—does not represent the world of being; it is, rather, a mark of the absence of a presence, an always already absent presence, which for Derrida stands for the lack of origin or of any founding humanist significance that constitutes the very condition of human thought and experience. While marking the space of the absent thing, the trace yet keeps it legible, and the name of this double gesture at once effacing and retaining presence in Derrida's lexicon is "writing." Small wonder that, in "Plato's Pharmacy," he speaks of writing as metastasy, the displacement and multiplication of an original disease site, that disease site being the entire logocentric mirage of Western philosophy: the pretense of language's self-presence, of transcendent meaning, of Being, of metaphysics as such—understood as the philosophy of presence.[5]

Although Derrida acknowledges his profound debt to semiotics for its recognition of the sign as a place of difference (and of language generally as a system of differences), he breaks with Saussure over what he considers to be the latter's nostalgic allegiance to the possibility of a transcendental signified (that is, of a concept existing independently of the sign that signifies it).[6] Instead of difference, Derrida offers us *différance*—with an *a*—signifying the endlessly deferred presence of the absent origin. For Derrida, the absent origin is indifferently associated with the concept of a "decentered structure,"[7] that is, of a structure whose decentering, as he explains, is the result of "the event I called a rupture," itself, in turn, an effect of the coming into consciousness of the "structurality of structure":

> Henceforth it became necessary to think both the law which somehow governed the desire for a center in the constitution of structure, and the process of signification which orders the displacements and substitutions for this law of central presence—but a central presence which has never been itself, has always already been exiled from itself to its own substitute. The substitute does not substitute itself for anything which has somehow existed before it. Henceforth, it was necessary to begin thinking that there was no center, that the center could not be thought in the form of a present-being, that the center had no natural site, that it was not a fixed locus but a function, a sort of non locus in which an infinite number of sign-substitutions came into play.[8]

Moreover, this coming into consciousness of the "structurality of structure" is synonymous in Derrida's mind with the "moment when language invaded the universal problematic, the moment when, in the absence of a center or origin, everything become discourse," which he defines as, precisely, a system in which the transcendental signified is never absolutely outside a system of differences (in contrast to Saussure's retention of the possibility of a signified independent of the sign that created it). It is the absence of the transcendental signified that extends the domain and play of signification infinitely, since thought can never be stabilized or cut off from the infinite chaining of signification through the play of signifiers, whose movement is always that of supplementarity.[9]

In the postmetaphysical universe that Derrida inhabits, language works by means of this infinite series of substitutions; it is a sterile act of *dissemination* (another master Derridean term), in which writing is conceived as "a nonviable seed, everything in sperm that overflows wastefully (i.e., masturbation), a force wandering outside the domain of life, incapable of engendering anything,"[10] and most especially, incapable of engendering meaning. *Différance* betokens not only the deferral, the postponement, of presence and meaning; it is the symptom of their indefinite loss.[11]

Deconstructive reading strives to unmask this absence, this silence, this indeterminacy of meaning, at the heart of all language, in order to reveal the radical "otherness" that the trace effaces via the displacement effected by writing. Thus Derrida proclaims: "The sign is the place where the completely Other is announced as such . . . in that which it is not"; "The sign under erasure is always already inhabited by the trace of another sign which never appears as such."[12] Once dismantled (*déconstruit*), the multiplicity of differences inherent within the sign, differences that the text seeks to repress and/or negate, is exposed. The aim of deconstruction is, precisely, to make manifest the hidden meanings that continue to lurk within the silences and absences that the text attempts, in vain, to impose. And what this unmasking reveals, ultimately, is the "inability of language to represent anything outside its own boundaries."[13] Deconstruction at its most fundamental level is the philosophy of these ruptures, absences, displacements, and silences.[14]

At this point, one may surmise, one hardly requires additional evidence of deconstruction's counterintuitive character. Yet it is the very illogic of deconstruction that seems to compel a consideration of its sources, of the circumstances and impulses that led Derrida to break with the philosophical traditions with which his thought is most tightly bound up and upon whose margins he meditates: Plato, Hegel, Nietzsche, Husserl, and Heidegger. I would like to propose that we view Derrida's thought in the context of a post-Holocaust world. To do so, certainly, entails an analytical move that deconstruction itself seems to disallow if not wholly disable: a recourse to contextualization that foregrounds issues of history, biography, and the tensed relation between thought and reality (text and context) that inevitably raises the specter of authorial intentions, whether conscious or unconscious. In arguing that Derrida's writings can, and should, be viewed in light of the as yet unassimilated impact of the events of the Holocaust, and the rupture in Western European consciousness that those events effected, I am not arguing that the Holocaust "caused" deconstruction in any mechanical or determinative sense. Nor do I believe that a philosophy of the depth and sophistication of Derrida's can be simplistically viewed as a "reflection" or "representation" of a reality somehow existing independently of the thought by which it is known and transmitted, that is, in any transparent sense. Yet it is my firm conviction that all knowledge is situated knowledge, that it exists within a social and historical domain with which it sustains often indecipherable relations of which, nonetheless, the traces remain in the form of writing, itself to be understood as a performative act that constitutes as much as it is constituted by the field of discourses in which it resides.

To speak of "situated knowledge" is to invoke, however surreptitiously, the active presence of an authorial consciousness, of the knower as agent existing within a historical and textual world defined by place and time, all the while eschewing the claim that such knowledge, and its embodiment in textuality, is fully self-aware. In other words, one can retain the idea of an authorial consciousness without necessarily asserting that the sources and goals of its acts as agent are conscious, that is, that the text produced by the author is wholly present to itself in all its intentions and meanings. In this, I share with Macherey the belief that history functions as the text's unconscious, and that the relation between intention and product is never commensurate.[15] An analogous attempt to theorize the relation between biography and history, reality and textuality, with particular relevance for the present inquiry, is Shoshana Felman and Dori Laub's recent work *Testimony: Crises of Witnessing in Literature, Psychoanalysis and History*, and in particular Felman's discussion of the writings of Paul de Man as inextricably bound up with his wartime journalistic experiences, from which, she argues, de Man's participation in the elaboration of deconstruction cannot be severed, however occulted that relationship remained throughout de Man's lifetime.[16] As preface to the book, Felman and Laub proclaim their desire to

> suggest the first stage of a theory of an as yet uncharted, nonrepresentational but performative, relationship between art and culture, on the one hand, and the conscious or unconscious witnessing of historical events, on the other. This is a book about how art [and culture] inscribes (artistically bears witness to) what we do not yet know of our lived historical relation to the events of our times. In considering literature and art as a precocious mode of witnessing—of accessing reality—when all other modes of knowledge are precluded, our ultimate concern has been with the preservation both of the uniqueness of experience in the face of its theorization, and of the shock of the unintelligible in the face of the attempt at interpretation; with the preservation, that is, of reality itself in the midst of our own efforts at interpreting it and through the necessary process of its textualization.[17]

Similarly, it is my belief that Derrida has alchemized into philosophy a psychology deeply marked by the Holocaust—marked by, but not part of its experiential domain, in which the Holocaust figures as the absent origin that Derrida himself has done so much to theorize. This is to argue that, living at a moment burdened with the inescapable consciousness of the Holocaust, Derrida emerges into the history of philosophy as a theoretician of linguistic "play," and that the articulation of "play" is central to that process of alchemization that makes writing "after Auschwitz"—in the famous phrase of Adorno[18]—possible. Indeed, in a highly displaced form, this is precisely the starting point of Derrida's critique of what he calls the "structuralist thematic of broken immediacy":

This structuralist thematic of broken immediacy is therefore the saddened, *negative*, nostalgic, guilty, Rousseauistic side of the thinking of play whose other side would be Nietzschean *affirmation*, that is the joyous affirmation of the play of the world and of the innocence of becoming, the affirmation of a world of signs without fault, without truth, and without origin which is offered to an active interpretation. This affirmation then determines the non center otherwise than as loss of the center. And it plays without security. In absolute chance, affirmation also surrenders itself to *genetic* indetermination, to the *seminal* adventure of the trace. Thus there are two interpretations of interpretation, of structure, sign, of play. One seeks to decipher, dreams of deciphering a truth or an origin which escapes play and the order of the sign, and which lives the necessity of interpretation as an exile. The other, which is no longer turned toward an origin, affirms play and tries to pass beyond man and humanism, the name of man being the name of that being who, throughout the history of metaphysics or of onto-theology—in other words, through his entire history—has dreamed of full presence, the reassuring foundation, the origin and the end of play.[19]

Derrida belongs both by birth and by self-conscious identification to that "second generation" of the post-Holocaust world,[20] on whose psyche has been indelibly inscribed an event in which it did not participate, but which nonetheless constitutes the underlying narrative of the lives of its members. Theirs was, first and foremost, a world of silence, a "silence," as French psychoanalyst Nadine Fresco tells us in her brilliant evocation of the psychology of the "second generation," "that swallowed up the past, all the past."[21] The parents of these children

> transmitted only the wound to their children, to whom the memory had been refused and who grew up in the compact world of the unspeakable . . . [amid] litanies of silence, which outlined an invisible object enclosed in an impossible evocation. What the Nazis had annihilated over and above individuals was the very substance of a world, a culture, a history, a way of life. . . . Life was now the *trace*, molded by death. . . . Those Jews who have come late upon the scene, burdened with their posthumous life, infatuated by an irreparable nostalgia for a world from which they were

excluded on being born, feel a vertigo when confronted by the "time before", the lost object of a nameless desire, in which suffering takes the place of inheritance. The past has been utterly burnt away at the center of their lives. (420–21)

Born after the war, often to substitute for siblings who died in the war, they feel their existence "as a sort of exile, not from a place in the present or future, but from a time now gone forever, which would have been that of identity itself." As one interviewee declared: "Sometimes I feel that it is us who have been deported. Not because we are like them, but because on the contrary we came after them, and our lives no longer have any meaning." They feel themselves to be "Jews deported from meaning, their resident permits withdrawn, expelled from a lost paradise, abolished in a death in turn dissolved, dissipated, disappeared . . . deported from a self that ought to have been that of another. Death is merely a matter of *substitution*."[22] Or again:

> We were orphaned by a history that was not even our own, and that was the worst of it. . . . What we suffered from were things we did not, could not know, could not remember, and yet were somehow crucial to our identities. In place of the world for which we had been destined there was only a blank page, unwritten upon, unshared by those who had witnessed its demise, blanketed in white snows of silence, yet for all that an unspoken threat. You cannot master the unknown, and so the world—that world from which we had been disbarred by history—became an absent place of origin in which the death of the self was already prefigured. History had taken away our rightful legacies of memories, and left in its place not the sharp pain of terror and violence, to which we were not privy, but the numb deadness of silence. For us the past is a foreign place, for it contains no living voices, only scratches on the page, relics of spoken words, icons of distanced memories. Why bother to remember a personal history that has been so misplaced, so unrooted (not even uprooted) in the very experiences that have most powerfully shaped it, so distorted by the sound of unvoiced tales?[23]

It is a generation lost between the "orations" of dead bodies piled up at Auschwitz, which spoke tellingly but tragically, and the silences imposed by its elders, who literally could not "speak" the Holocaust (which was, in any case, in all senses of the word unspeakable). From their parents, this generation received only, in Erika Apfelbaum's words, "un héritage en forme d'absences" (a legacy in the form of absences).[24] And linked to the notion of absence in the work of French writers of the second generation, as Ellen Fine has demonstrated, are repeated evocations of void, lack, blank, gap, abyss. "La mémoire absente" in the novels of Henri Raczymow is "la mémoire trouée": hollowed out, fragmented, ruptured.

Perhaps most striking of all in the work of these writers is the sense of the utter inadequacy of language. "The world of Auschwitz," in George Steiner's famous remark, "lies outside speech as it lies outside reason."[25] Language "after Auschwitz" is language in a condition of severe diminishment and decline,[26] and no one has argued more forcefully than Steiner the corruption—indeed, the ruin—of language as a result of the political bestiality of our age.[27] And yet, for those who come after, there is nothing but language. As the protagonist in Elie Wiesel's novel *The Fifth Son*, states: "Born after the war, I endure its effects. I suffer from an Event I did not even experience. . . . From a past that has made History tremble, I have retained only words."[28]

Both for those who survived and for those who came after, the Holocaust appears to exceed the representational capacity of language, and thus to cast suspicion on the ability of words to convey reality.[29] In the writings of perhaps the greatest poet of these years, Paul Celan, language stutters on the edge of silence, words choke, the voice suffocates. Holocaust literature in general is a literature "of fragments, of partial and provisional forms."[30] And for the second generation, the question is not even how to speak, but, more profoundly, if one has the right to speak, a de-legitimation of the speaking self that, turned outward, interrogates the authority, the privilege of all speech.[31] (Which, of course, is precisely what Derrida does in his attack on logocentrism.)

Moreover, the "Auschwitz model," Jean-François Lyotard concludes, "designates an experience of language that brings speculative discourse to a halt. The latter can no longer be pursued 'after Auschwitz.' "[32] Thus intimately bound up with the paralysis of language is the death of metaphysics, itself, perhaps, merely the displaced sign of the death of God in "*l'univers concentrationnaire.*" As Steiner, again, has argued:

> The Holocaust took away those metaphors which made it possible for human words and human syntax to speak about God. It may be that after the gassing, the burning, etc. we no longer have cause or need to "speak" to a God whose . . . overwhelming attribute became that of absence, of nothingness.

What the Holocaust wrought, according to Steiner, was "the exit of God from language."[33] In Celan's poem *Psalm*, God is apostrophized as "No One." "No One bespeaks the dust of the dead."[34] The absence of God from the Holocaust is also His silence. "After Auschwitz," metaphysical presence became, like writing itself, a term *sous rature*, under erasure.

The connection I am trying to draw between the experience of Jews and Derrida's notion of grammatology—of writing—let me hasten to say, is a connection that Derrida himself has repeatedly made. Derrida comments on Edmund Jabès' *The Book of Questions* in his essay "Edmund Jabès and the Question of the Book," by elaborating on Jabès' claim that "Judaism and writing are one and the same waiting, one and the same hope, one and the same wearing down." Judaism, in Jabès' argument, "is the product of the desert, the desert seen essentially as a land desolate with silence and listening . . . listening with all the sounds caught at the heart of this silence."[35] Derrida complements Jabès' theme, arguing that the situation of the Jew "is exemplary of the situation of the poet, the man of speech, and of writing." And, like Jabès, he sees writing as the desert, that is, as separation, as an infinite anchoritism, an eternal exile from a lost paradise of vocal presence that was the garden of speech. For both, the Jew is the alien outsider, detached from society, hence symptomatic of life on the abyss. Similarly, says Derrida: "writing is also an exile from Being. . . . The Poet and the Jew are not born here but elsewhere. They wander separated from their true birth. . . . Writing is the moment of the desert as the moment of separation."[36] It is absence, privation, from which language sets out and which then constantly shapes it. And to the extent that language is inherently unstable, writing is also an exile from meaning, and thus a kind of death. "Death strolls between letters," says Derrida; "it goes without saying that the god of writing [Thoth] must also be the god of death."[37]

The strategy of deconstruction, as Derrida describes it in "Shibboleth," is a cut, an incision, a *circumcision* into language, that inaugurates the process of dismantling. A circumcision that Derrida defines as a "reading wound."[38] And it precisely a wound, a scar—trace of the wound erased—that I believe lies at the root of the deconstructive gesture, a psychic scar of guilty belatedness: the guilt of absence, of nonparticipation, of nonpresence that haunts the second generation as it struggles with its "héritage en forme d'absences." Deconstruction is often falsely accused of nihilism. But since it is elaborated in the shadow of death and annihilation, perhaps it bears the unconscious trace of its own absent origin.

It is not hard to see the parallels between this psychology of the "second generation" and the basic tenets of postmodernism: the feeling of life as a trace, haunted by an absent presence; its sense of indeterminacy; its belief in the ultimate undecidablity of language (its aporia, in Derrida's sense); its transgressive approaches to knowledge and authority; and, perhaps most powerfully, its conviction of the ultimately intransitive, self-reflective character of language, which seems to have lost its power to represent anything outside itself, hence to have lost its ability, finally, to signify. In its profound commitment to a fractured, fragmented, and endlessly deferred, hence displaced, understanding of language and the (im)possibilities of meaning, postmodernism shares with the "second generation" the anguish of belatedness, the scars of an unhealed wound of absent memory, and the legacy of silence.[39]

While we should, I believe, reject deconstruction's dissolution of history, its absorption of history into textuality, we can and should learn to appreciate and employ what deconstruction teaches us by and in its enactment of the complex tensions that shape the post-modern world. Deconstruction, I have argued, at its most fundamental level is a philosophy of rupture and displacement. Insofar as the emblematic figure of the postmodern world is the displaced person—and I believe that it is—then we are all displaced persons in some profound sense. It is hardly surprising, in this light, that the two obsessions of postmodern thought are bound up with language and the body, for the displaced person carries with him or her these, and these alone.[40]

Moreover, the tension between our sense of the past's erasure through the annihilation of memory and our desire for history is the same tension that inhabits deconstruction as it strives to liberate itself from a lingering nostalgia for presence, a presence that it simultaneously acknowledges is always already absent and, thus, like the past, an unattainable object of desire. Like the members of the "second generation" (which is, in the end, our own), we live at a moment of great cultural instability and uncertainty. Like them, we struggle to know the absent and the other, to affirm a right to words and to speech. We, too, waver between a sense of helplessness and loss of agency and aspirations for self-empowerment, all the while admitting the difficulties that accompany these efforts and the impediments that make their full achievement impossible. We, like Derrida, are "trying to write the question: (what is) meaning to say?"[41] and are willing to risk the possibility of meaning nothing in a world without claim to metaphysical guarantees.

However this moment of historical (or ahistorical) consciousness will ultimately be "worked through," to borrow Freud's terminology, and whatever the manner in which it will reshape forever our understanding of history and the ways in which we set about representing it, this much seems clear: we cannot escape the past nor evade the responsibilities that it imposes upon us. For us, especially, as professional historians, we must accept the burden of confronting it, even if we suspect in the depths of our being that we may never achieve mastery over it. But history is, in the end, more about humility than mastery, entails more struggle than success, is motivated much more by loss than by gain. What we do not confront today will, like all things repressed, return to haunt us tomorrow.

Moreover, there is one thing that deconstruction teaches us, more powerfully than any other strategy of reading that I know of. And that is to listen to silence. If Jabès strains to hear the sound enclosed within the silence of the desert, Derrida has taught us to heed the silences within language. As historians of the past, we are constantly engaged in attending, as Paul Zumthor wrote recently, "to the discourse of some invisible other who speaks to us from some deathbed, of which the exact location is unknown. We strive to hear the echo of a voice which, somewhere, probes, knocks against the world's silences, begins again, is stifled."[42] Our most fundamental task as historians, I would argue, is to solicit those fragmented inner narratives to emerge from their silences. In the last analysis, what is the past but a once material existence now silenced, extant only as sign and as sign drawing to itself chains of conflicting interpretations that hover over its absent presence and compete for possession of the relics, seeking to invest traces of significance upon the bodies of the dead.

3 ∎ Towards a Theory of the Middle Ground

Milan Kundera, in *The Unbearable Lightness of Being*, has as one of his major characters a painter named Sabina, who during her school days, a period when the strictest realism had been required of all students so as not to sap the foundations of socialism, had tried to be stricter than her teachers and had painted in a style concealing the brush strokes. But, one day, she happened to drip red paint on a canvas. The trickle looked like a crack; she began playing with the crack, filling it out, wondering what might be visible behind it. And thus she began her first cycle of paintings, called *Behind the Scenes*. On the surface, there was always an impeccably realistic world, but underneath, behind the backdrop's cracked canvas, lurked something different, something mysterious or abstract. "On the surface, an intelligible lie; underneath, the unintelligible truth."[1] And thus the goal of her art became to penetrate the false intelligibility of the surface to reach the unintelligible truth below.

History, Kundera seems to be telling us throughout *The Unbearable Lightness of Being*, like Sabina's realist canvases, is the illusion of an intelligible reality, that intelligible surface that cloaks the presence of an unintelligible truth. *Einmal ist keinmal*, Kundera insists. Once is the same as never. Linear time, the fortuity of event, cannot germinate meaning, for it lacks the inhering significance of the cyclical, the ever-returning—in effect, the mythic. Therefore, history, in its particularity and in its telling, is only the illusion of an intelligible reality—but perhaps a necessary illusion, since without it there would be no hope. Kundera's profound suspicion of the lies that realism proffers—and thus necessarily that historical writing, the final refuge of realism, enshrines—might be attributed to his experience of a Soviet world in which the rewriting of the past routinely attained Orwellian dimensions,[2] were it not for the fact that this suspicion participates in the much broader pattern of cultural revisionism that we have come to call postmodernism.

Whatever else one thinks of it, the anxiety that subtends the postmodern turn is palpable and heard in every corner of the world. "Temps d'incertitude," "crise épistémologique," "tournant critique," Roger Chartier reports of the current "temps des doutes" in French historical thought, betokening a widening circle of pessimism about the very possibility of historical knowledge, which Chartier attributes to postmodernism's effacement of traditional models of understanding and intelligibility in the search for the past, itself the result of what Foucault once called history's liberation from the "bien maigre idée du réel."[3] And nowhere has this epistemological crisis in the writing of history been more insistently sounded than in the United States, where publications and debates on the philosophical entailments of postmodernism with respect to historical praxis are proliferating at an extraordinary rate. Indeed, in the view of one recent commentator, "postmodern literary criticism has become so powerful and influential across such a broad range of disciplines, and it has raised so many troubling questions about the conceptual foundations of history itself, that historians can no longer ignore it."[4]

Even if this jeremiad for history is premature, it remains true that the paradigms that have governed historical and literary study since the nineteenth century no longer hold unquestioned sway. The old positivist dream that an "objective" science of history was possible, allowing the historian to recover an authentic knowledge of the past, has come under severe attack in postmodernist critical debate. The hallmark of this debate has been a growing awareness of the mediated nature of perception, cognition, and imagination, all of which are increasingly construed to be mediated by linguistic structures cast into discourses of one sort or another—the famed "linguistic turn" that has raised such troubling problems for the study of history and literature alike. As John Toews has eloquently summed up, if we take postmodern theory seriously,

> we must recognize that we have no access, even potentially, to an unmediated world of objective things and processes that might serve as the ground and limit of our claims to knowledge or nature or to any transhistorical or transcendent subjectivity that might ground our interpretation of meaning.[5]

Semiotics, especially, has argued for a linguistically determined epistemology, viewing language not as a reflection of the world that it captures in words, but as constitutive of that world, that is, as generative, rather than "mimetic." As a language-based conception of reality, semiotics has disrupted traditional literary and historical modes of interpretation by its denial of a referential and material world, a material reality we formerly believed could be known and written about scientifically. Until recently, the writing of history depended on a concept of language which, as Nancy Partner puts it,

> unhesitatingly asserts the external reality of the world, its intelligibility in the form of ideas, concepts, phenomena or other mental things and a direct connection between mental things and verbal signs.

But postmodernism has shattered this confident assumption of the relation between words and things, language and extralinguistic reality, on the grounds, as she states, that language is the "very structure of mental life, and no meta-language can ever stand outside itself to observe a reality external to itself."[6] To the degree that language is understood within a semiotic perspective as a closed system of signs in which meaning is produced by the relations between words themselves, rather than between words and their referents, an irreparable rupture between verbal signs and material referents is created and

language is cut loose from any necessary or fixed system of represen-
tating the world of things. It was, of course, Saussure who first set
forth these principles of semiotics in his *Course in General Linguistics*
(1916), insisting that language is a system of differences with no positive terms, a system that precedes—and thus constitutes—the world,
making it intelligible by constructing it according to its own rules of
signification. For Saussure, such rules are inherently "arbitrary" in the
sense that they are socially agreed-upon, conventional meanings.
Thus, while Saussure retained a notion of the referentiality of signs,
the ultimate reference is implicitly understood in different ways by
different linguistic communities. Given this, it is impossible to argue
that objective knowledge of the universe unmediated by language can
be attained, since there is no way to reach reality except through discourse. Hence historiography, a subset of a larger linguistic community, cannot transparently reflect the world; instead, it merely articulates with its own inflections the postulates made possible by the
broader discourse of which it is a member and from which it derives
its competence. This problem becomes doubled, so to speak, when
we remember that historians rarely apprehend a past world as such,
but merely the textual remnants that have survived the ravages of
time. If historical documents themselves do not reflect past realities,
then the historian is inescapably immersed in a series of discursive
and textual enactments constituted by the linguistic systems of the
past, which cannot vouchsafe access to its realities.

Such a view of the closed reflectivity of language—its radically intransitive character—necessarily jeopardizes historical study as normally understood. Where once we confidently asserted the capacity
of language to grant an essential and foundational stability at the core
of identity, language, and belief, postmodernism posits the essentially
hybrid nature of the world, rejecting the possibility of pure types of
any sort. It is a world of "mixed marriages": between words and things,
power and imagination, material reality and linguistic construction.
At its furthest reach, deconstruction articulates our sense of the discontinuous, fractured, and fragmented nature of reality, whose dubious status is figured by the persistent use of quotation marks. To cite

Foucault again, our current practice of history "disturbs what was previously considered immobile . . . fragments what was thought unified . . . shows the heterogeneity of what was imagined consistent with itself."[7] Fragmented and decentered as well is the very notion of the individual self, the entire humanist concept of "man" who, in the famous closing lines to *The Order of Things*, Foucault predicted "would soon disappear like a face drawn in sand at the edge of the sea."

How are we to accept the challenge that semiotics and postmodernism pose to historical writing and at the same time preserve *some* of the traditional goals that have always engaged historians? Are we to believe that our representations of the past are no more than illusory realist canvases, intelligible lies we tell ourselves and others in order to mask our fear that what lurks behind is the unintelligible truth of human experience, which defies any and all attempts to apprehend it in the now fractured artifice of our words? Is illusion our only hope for the past, as well as the future? If we accept that history is always a written account of the past that is itself based on the mediatory texts left by the past—hence irreducibly linguistic at both its termini—how do we understand the process by which the texts bequeathed by the past are transformed into a historical narrative that purports to tell the truth about that past? These are not small or insignificant questions, and the answers to them are not easily procured.

In seeking to answer these questions, we would do well, I believe, to refocus our attention on the question of mediation, for it both stands at the crux of the "linguistic turn" and yet may offer a way of connecting our current preoccupation with language to theories of historiography and the historian's function as conventionally understood. At the same time, the obvious links between the notion of mediation and the intermediate may lead us to a theory of the middle ground as the place of mediation, the only ground on which, I believe, history and postmodernism can hope productively to interact. If one of the major moves in poststructuralist thought has been to displace the controlling metaphor of historical evidence from one of reflection to one of mediation (that is, has been a shift from the notion that texts and documents transparently "reflect" past realities, as positivism believed, to one in which the past is captured only in the mediated form preserved for us in language), then we need to think carefully about how we understand mediation and how that understanding affects our practice.

The classical concept of mediation views it as an analytical device that seeks to establish a relationship between two different orders or levels of phenomena that are the object of scrutiny, between, say, a work of literature (or any linguistic artifact) and its social ground. Because the objects of analysis are phenomenologically distinct, they can only be compared against the background of some more general identity, and mediation, as Jameson explains, represents "the intervention of an analytic terminology or code which can be applied equally to two or more structurally distinct objects or sectors of being."[8] In that sense, mediation is a term that describes, in Raymond Williams's definition, "an indirect connection or agency between separate kinds of act."[9] And this definition holds both for the operation of mediation in the past (that is, for example, as embodied in a discourse that mediates between a social world and its literary or discursive consciousness of its own nature) and for the historical analyses that we undertake of that world, allowing historians to comprehend historical experience via the linguistic evidence—whether literary or documentary—by which we come to know and understand the past. The critical aspect of the classical notion of mediation is that it keeps analytically separate the dual phenomena that at the same time it seeks to relate, that it functions, therefore, as a middle term that mediates *between* two disparate yet analytically relatable domains of inquiry.[10]

The modern concept of mediation, such as articulated by the Frankfurt school, insists, to quote Adorno, that "mediation is in the object itself, not something between the object and that to which it is brought," a concept of mediation that attempts to abolish (or overcome) dualism altogether.[11] In this view, mediation is an active process that constructs its objects in precisely the sense that poststructuralism conceives of the social construction of reality in and through language. Rather than functioning as a middle term relating two disjunct phenomenal orders from which it stands apart, mediation is intrinsic to the existence and operation of the reality that it actively produces. In studying history, then, what we study are the mediatory practices of past epochs which, then as now, constructed all being and consciousness. Moreover, the performative nature of such discourses—preserved and thus available to us only in texts of a literate, if not precisely literary, nature—prohibits our access to any reality other than the codes inscribed in such texts.

One could restate this in simpler fashion by arguing that what we study in the past are discourses, which represent identifiable units of a given society's mediated and mediating practices and beliefs. The result of this focus on discourse, I have argued, is to collapse text and context into a single, aestheticized understanding of culture, a procedure characteristic of New Historicist criticism, with its self-avowed elaboration of a cultural "poetics" and, to a lesser extent, of new forms of cultural history, both of which tend to treat texts and their contexts as equally part of one broad vein of discursive production characteristic of a given epoch. Thus Lynn Hunt, herself an exemplar and advocate of the new cultural history, poses what seems to me to be the relevant and trenchant question that arises from New Historicist and cultural history's focus on the social practices of any given society as discursively homologous artifacts:

> where will we be when every practice—whether it is economic, intellectual, social or political—has been shown to be culturally determined? Or, to put it another way, can a history of culture work if it is shorn of all theoretical assumptions about culture's relationship to the social world, if indeed, its agenda is conceived as the undermining of all assumptions about the relationship between culture and the social world?[12]

To be sure, for historians and literary critics alike, whichever definition of mediation one chooses, the mediating function will be constituted by language because language, by definition, is that which mediates human awareness of the world we inhabit. Moreover, it is late in the day to have to insist that all historians, even of positivist stripe, live and breathe in a world of texts, or that knowledge of the past is primarily present to us in textual form. But our understanding of the implications of this "always already" textualized character of historical data, their inevitably mediated state as made up of language, depends to a high degree on what concept of mediation we adopt and, by logical inference, what view of language we deploy. Just as there are multiple models of mediation, so also are there various ways of viewing language: the fashionable, postmodern performative idea of language as constitutive of the world, hence inherently self-reflective; an instrumentalist or constative view of language, in which language describes and explicates as well as "invents" reality and, in that sense, constitutes an "instrument of mediation between human consciousness and the world it occupies."[13] This second concept of language is normally employed in scientific discourse or in any discipline concerned with purveying information about the world rather than with the construction of social meaning. One of the features of the "linguistic turn" in the humanities has been to replace the classical notion of mediation with the modern and to undermine our faith in the instrumental capacity of language to convey information about the world. But must we really choose between these two conceptions of language and mediation? Must we limit language's power to the reflexive, or is there not room in our historiographical practice, as there clearly is in our everyday linguistic habits, for a constative (i.e., descriptive) as well as performative use of language, even when that language is embodied in past texts (including documents) and thus possesses something of the literary character that poststructuralism has taught us to apprehend? The alternative between seeing language as either perfectly transparent or completely opaque is simply too rigidly framed.[14] Without in any way creating a hierarchy of discourses, can we not differentiate among forms of language use and kinds of texts, some of which—the literary—obviously belong in the realm of the self-reflective while some others— what we normally think of as the documentary—may at least in part be usefully categorized under the rubric of instrumental. And, to extend the argument, though the majority of the first sort of texts, in their literarity, almost certainly work in the performative fashion that poststructuralism suggests, and thus constitute mediations in Adorno's sense, is it not possible to be persuaded of this and, *at the same time*, to grant that instrumental uses of language are capable of conveying to us positive knowledge of history, inferentially derived from records of all sorts, and thus to mediate between us and the past?

Obviously, the question of instrumental language is more of an issue for historians than for literary critics, whose positive knowledge of their material is given to them ready-made, as it were, in the form of literary texts. Historians, however, have no givens—no ready-made chronicle of events or histories—and must construct their narratives on the basis of some positive (if ideologically impressed)[15] vision of the past. It is precisely this incommensurability in the objects of investigation distinguishing historical and literary study which seems to me to require a much more highly differentiated analysis of their respective aims and obstacles than they have yet received in debates on postmodernism. The goal of this analysis would not be to return to or reproduce traditional dualisms; it would be to create a more productive and reciprocal duality in our approach to the past and a keener sense of the heterogeneous nature of the material available for its study.

The duality of perspectives that I am arguing for would allow us to maintain these distinct issues in a more clearly delineated and fruitful tension, with implications for our understanding of the character of representation as well as of "reality."[16] I do not wish to contest the "linguistic" character of even instrumental language as preserved in documentary records. The archive is as much the repository of written traces as the literary text. However, because our knowledge of the past comes to us in documentary representations, we need not confuse the problems entailed in our access to the past with the past itself. Moreover, as Martin Jay points out, "because certain social forms can be read as if they were languages, there is no reason to suppose their linguisticality exhausts their being."[17] I do want to insist that language functions in many registers and in many modes (often at the same time), not all of which are mise-en-abîme. The polarized character of the debate over poststructuralism has tended to insist that we align ourselves on one or the other side of the semiotic divide, as if we were somehow in a zero-sum linguistic game. But in opting for the middle ground, I would also opt for a mixed and potentially richer understanding of language and its mediatory possibilities, in the interest of a more highly differentiated analysis of past texts and their social contexts. The middle ground that I am seeking to demarcate would allow both concepts of mediation and language to be put into play simultaneously.

A duality of perspectives in the investigation of texts (literary *and* documentary) and their social contexts is what I have elsewhere tried to convey by the phrase "the social logic of the text," a term that combines an insistence on seeing language as socially generated with an equal insistence on understanding the discursive character of all texts as literary artifacts. My emphasis on the text's social site stems from my belief that the power and the meaning of any given set of representations derive in large part from their social context and their relation to the social and political networks in which they are elaborated. Even if one accepts the poststructuralist argument that language constitutes the social world of meaning, it is possible to maintain that language itself acquires meaning and authority only within specific social and historical settings.

Implicit in the notion of the "social logic of the text," then, is the belief that we are capable of recovering some sense of the material world of the past, a belief that in turn commits us to at least a partial acceptance of language's instrumental capacity to convey information about historical forms of life, for without that capacity we could never know in even a partial sense anything about history. This is not an attempt to smuggle positivism in through the back door. It *is* an attempt to argue for an understanding of semiotics that retains a conception of the sometimes referential (if always "arbitrary" because conventional) function of signs as part of socially shaped systems of human communication organized by languages, as Saussure himself understood semiotics. It is only by acknowledging the irreducibly semiotic character of our historical practice, I believe, that we can respond to the challenge semiotics has posed to traditional historiography. But a semiotic conception of language does not commit one to a belief in the intransitively self-reflective character of *all* linguistic acts and artifacts. Indeed, it was over this very point that Derrida ultimately broke with Saussure's theory of language, accusing him of a lingering nostalgia for a "transcendental signified" (i.e., a concept existing independently of the sign that signifies it). As successor to semiotic theory, Derrida wishes to install a view of the endlessly ludic and mediatory play of language unconnected to any ground exterior to itself. In granting the force of semiotic conceptions of language, we do not necessarily have to concede the Derridean spin that deconstruction places on it. We must refuse, as Chartier has recently argued, to "postulate an identity between the logocentric and hermeneutic logic that governs the production of discourse, and the 'logic of practice,' which rules behaviors that define social identities and relations. . . . To concentrate on the concrete conditions and processes that construct meaning is to recognize, unlike traditional intellectual history, that minds are not disincarnated, and, unlike semiotics, that the categories which engender experiences and interpretations are historical."[18]

Moreover, even an acceptance of a semiotically based view of language and of deconstructive modes of reading does not compel us to abandon our effort to enrich our understanding of the past as more than a complex of discursive strategies and events. It is a relational reading of text and context, of overt and suppressed meanings, of implied and articulated purposes, together with the variety of literary and discursive modes in which they are given voice, that I believe we need to pursue if we are to achieve a genuinely historical understanding of textual production. This means occupying a theoretical "middle ground" and practicing a "mixed" kind of reading, attentive to the differential linguistic practices and registers of past languages. Thus I would agree with Dominick LaCapra's desire to "elaborate a critical and self-critical historiography that remains open to the risks Derrida explores but also insists upon certain constraints in the manner that engages the disciplinary conventions of professional historians."[19] These "disciplinary conventions" comprise a respect for empirical-analytic techniques of research—that is, a belief in the referential, constative possibilities of language—along with a new and theoretically informed appreciation of the literary nature of all historical documents and their mediating and supplementary role in all historiography.

Postmodernism challenges us to develop such complex strategies of research and reading, despite the fact that they are not easily theorized. Moreover, it is clear that many historians have already taken up this challenge and are implementing it in practice, even if they have not yet fully voiced their theoretical stances. In addition to the broadly diverse works that range themselves under the label of cultural history, feminism in particular has been at the forefront of an attempt to meld traditional forms of social history with strategies of reading and analysis borrowed from critical theory, not least from deconstruction. Because it has always been important to feminists to retain a sense of women's distinctive historical experience, yet at the same time to deconstruct the conventional implications of sexual difference by demonstrating how gender is itself a socially and culturally constructed category of experience, feminist historiography has produced in recent years some of the most sophisticated studies combining both perspectives. One thinks, for example, of Judith Walkowitz's books *Prostitution and Victorian Society: Women, Class and the State* (Cambridge, 1980) and *City of Dreadful Delight: Narratives of Sexual Danger in Late Nineteenth-Century London* (Chicago, 1992), both of which investigate Victorian discourses on sexuality in relation to the regulation of women's social lives and the social and public space they occupied in London at the end of the nineteenth century. In American history, a comparable, and exemplary, *combinatoire* of social and discursive analyses can be found in Carroll Smith-Rosenberg's *Disorderly Conduct: Visions of Gender in Victorian America* (Oxford, 1985), but these are only a few among a host of studies that could easily be cited. They have shown that a historiographical practice located in the middle ground can be at once innovative, coherent, and telling, enriching our understanding of the intricate dance of discourse and experience in past times.

Although the precise connections between thought, language, and action may be difficult to explain, it is not helpful to deal with them in terms of what Brian Stock has called "textual gnosticism."[20] A flexible appreciation of the ways postmodernism can aid in redefining the nature of historical investigation and enhance historiographical practice would surely represent a healthy appropriation of its tenets, without necessarily consigning us to its more extreme, and polarizing, forms. The middle ground is rarely a comfortable terrain to seek to occupy, since one is by definition always (already) outflanked on both sides. But any contemporary historiography that hopes to be successful will inevitably have to integrate theory and practice—to make compatible a practice of theory and a theory of practice—and that will mean negotiating the middle spaces and grounds that currently divide theory *from* practice. Historians have traditionally shied away from such questions, preferring to leave them to the airy speculation of philosophers and critics. It is a mark of how unusual our own enagement with history has become that we feel compelled to confront them now. But this is scarcely cause for regret. A historiographical practice grounded in an awareness of its own philosophical and practical commitments will not diminish but rather strengthen our appreciation both of the past as the object of our study and of the present as the site of our investment in the past.

4

In the Mirror's Eye

The Writing of Medieval History in North America

The title of this chapter derives from the name of the most prominent journal dedicated to medieval studies in North America, the journal *Speculum*, edited and produced by the Medieval Academy of America, and from the image that traditionally adorned its cover. In the inaugural issue, E. K. Rand, the first editor, explained the sense that guided the choice of name:

> *Speculum*, this mirror to which we find it appropriate to give a Latin name, suggests the multitudinous mirrors in which people of the Middle Ages liked to gaze at themselves and other folk— mirrors of history and doctrine and morals, mirrors of princes and lovers and fools. We intend no conscious follies, but we recognize satire, humor and the joy of life as part of our aim. Art and beauty and poetry are a portion of our medieval heritage. Our contribution to the knowledge of those times must be scholarly, first of all, but scholarship must be arrayed, so far as possible, in a pleasing form.[1]

For Rand and his co-founders of the Academy and what they aspired to make its leading journal, medieval studies in North America were thus consciously directed at overcoming the prejudices and ideological contamination that the very term *medieval* had acquired over the centuries, connoting a dark, backward, superstitious, "Gothic" age, what Karl Marx once called mankind's "zoology," his animal history. Instead, the image that the *speculum* of medievalism in America should display was, whatever its ultimate shape, above all, as Rand's prefatory remarks indicate, to be comely, a portrait of the attractive state of the profession it served. To represent this goal, the founders placed on the front cover a picture of a hand holding up an empty mirror, devoid of any image, to the viewer/reader's gaze. As icon of both the journal and the studies it hoped to promote, *Speculum*'s barren mirror thus invited the medievalist to cast his or her own image upon its vacant specular face. To do so, however, required a willed investment of the self (in effect, a narcissistic self-involvement) in order to generate those images by and through which to contemplate the meaning of the past. In the choice of name and iconographic gloss, the founders of the Medieval Academy unconsciously underlined what was and remains the determinative condition of possibility for the study of medieval history in America: absence. For alone among the countries claiming a Western European birthright, America lacks a medieval past. Any attempt to argue the importance and relevance of medieval history, therefore, must first overcome its evident "otherness," its utter alterity and lack of connection to any visible, shared national or cultural "American" past.

The "alterity" of the Middle Ages, of course, is hardly unique to the American consciousness of the era. Indeed, as Lee Patterson has repeatedly insisted, the Middle Ages has from the beginning served postmedieval Western historical consciousness as one of the primary sites of otherness by which it has constituted itself.[2] As constructed by Renaissance humanists, the Middle Ages comprised the West's shadowy "other," against which the Renaissance and modernity itself were defined, a modernity delineated above all by its difference from the premodern Middle Ages. As Patterson conveniently sums up:

> Humanism, nationalism, the proliferation of competing value systems, the secure grasp of a historical consciousness, the idea of the individual, aesthetic production as an end in itself, the conception of the natural world as a site of colonial exploitation and scientific

investigation, the secularization of politics and the idea of the state—all of these characteristics and many others are thought both to set the Renaissance apart from the Middle Ages and to align it definitively with the modern world.[3]

From this perspective, the Middle Ages is precisely that, a millennium of middleness, a space of empty waiting and virtual death until the reawakening of the West to its proper nature and purpose in the period of the Renaissance.

For Europeans, the Middle Ages, if not modern, is at least "there," evident in the monuments it erected and the traditions that stand presumptively at the origin of the modern European national states. It is, in fact, one of the peculiarities of medieval study everywhere that it constantly hovers between the dual consciousness of the Middle Ages as a place and time of non-origin (i.e., the dark, deathly period constructed in and by the Renaissance) and of origin (the origin of the modern state). Caught in this double bind of non-origin and origin, lack and plenitude, the Middle Ages, Kathleen Biddick has argued, can be "everywhere, both medieval and modern, and nowhere, sublime and redemptive."[4] It is, in part, this alterity—this "otherness"—of the Middle Ages that has given medievalists their sense of professional legitimacy, since the very strangeness and "difference" signified by the distant past suggests a special virtue required for its study. In the United States, however, the paradox of presence and absence common to medieval studies generally is incommensurably more acute, and precisely to the degree that the Middle Ages constituted an "absent other" there, just so did the first scholars of the era insist, in a highly overdetermined fashion, on its relevance as the origin of the modern, hence American, world. To overcome absence and otherness, the original students of the medieval past construed alterity rather as identity. Given this, it is hardly surprising that the study of medieval history in the United States has from the beginning been marked by inherent paradoxes.

To begin with, although medieval civilization represented the triumphal past of "Catholicism" and "Gothic culture," a world organized according to the dictates of a deeply traditionalistic outlook on life and social customs, in North America its first historians tended to be Protestant, enlightened, and revolutionary founders. Jefferson and other early American revolutionaries were immersed in myths of Anglo-Saxon democracy, whose laws and chronicles, they believed, foreshadowed their ambitions for democracy. So indebted did Jefferson feel to Anglo-Saxon culture and what he took to be its legacy of social democracy that he planned to put two Anglo-Saxon heroes, Hengist and Horsa—invited by Vortigern into Britain, according to Bede's *History of the English Church and People*, to aid in the defense of the country against enemies to the north—on the Great Seal of the new Republic, whose obverse side would bear an image of the pillar of fire that led the Chosen People into the Promised Land (Exodus 13:21–22). According to John Adams, to whom he had communicated his wishes, Jefferson saw Hengist and Horsa as representing "the form of government we have assumed,"[5] thereby tracing American democratic institutions to their origins in the social practices of the pre-Christian Germanic peoples.[6] Jefferson cannot have read his Bede very carefully, though, since the latter made it clear that although Hengist and Horsa arrived in the guise of England's protectors, "nevertheless, their real intention was to subdue it," which, having done, Hengist became the founder of a *royal* line.[7] More ominous still was the link with the Old Testament pillar of fire, signifying not guidance or protection, but an emblem of conquest, a vivid illustration of the young country's territorial ambitions.[8] The underlying contradictions that marked such use of medieval figurations of American destinies would remain a characteristic feature of the American search for identity and origins in an absent and displaced medieval past.

To be sure, Henry Adams ushered in a new era by embracing with emotional intensity what was in some sense—at least from the perspective of Enlightenment thinkers—medieval history's most offensive aspects, but his passionate, slightly irrational celebration of the medieval past was not to be incorporated even into his own teaching of medieval history at Harvard. Adams illustrates a split in the approach to medievalism that was to continue for some time. In his writing he used the Middle Ages and what he saw as its vital, collective, organic culture as an exemplary counterpoint to the "anomic, dehumanized industrializing world that he himself inhabited."[9] His *Mont-Saint-Michel and Chartres*, a work F. N. Robinson character-ized as "that sensitive, poetic tribute of a skeptically minded, some-times disillusioned modern to the spirit of the Middle Ages,"[10] turned to the Middle Ages as warrant for medievalism's antimodern agenda. In this, Adams participated in a burgeoning Romantic ideal-ization of the Middle Ages in late-nineteenth-century America among those who, like Adams, sought in the medieval world an ide-alized vision of an alternative social model against which the defects of the modern world could be judged.[11] In a famous chapter of *The Education*, Adams contrasted the spirit of the Virgin, to whom so many of the artistic and intellectual products of the High Middle Ages were dedicated, to that of the modern dynamo, image of the materialistic, dehumanizing greed and technology of the modern age.[12] For Adams, what was attractive about the Middle Ages was precisely its alterity; it was, he observed, "the most foreign of worlds to the American soul."[13] The New World, Adams believed, had not inherited medieval institutions, patterns of social organization, or re-ligious beliefs; the study of medieval history, therefore, could offer no great truths or lessons for the guidance of American life.[14] Its utility, by implication, lay merely in the escape that it provided from the in-creasingly harsh realities of the modern world, a realm of fantasized otherness in which to locate the antimodernist self.

Thus, in 1877, when Harvard president Eliot invited the young Adams to teach the Middle Ages, Adams could think of little to offer his students but the dry facts of political and legal history, learned during his two years of advanced historical training in Germany, where he had been taught to read documents in the new, philologi-cally oriented manner of the German seminar. For seven years, as lec-turer in History 2 (forerunner of the modern Western Civilization course), Adams taught the stuff of history with all the discipline and purposelessness of antiquarian research.[15] Adams's legacy to the study of medieval history in America was thus a double and divided one: his writings articulated a conservative strain in American medievalism which would serve as a refuge for those wishing to retreat into a world of preclass, preindustrial society.[16] His teaching, on the other hand, inaugurated what was to become, under the leadership of Charles Homer Haskins, an almost exclusive concern with the political and institutional development of the monarchical states of northern Europe, in particular England and France, that persisted virtually to the present time.

If Adams was the first to teach mediéval history professionally in America, Haskins was America's first true professional medieval historian.[17] Moreover, if Adams represents American medievalism's antimodernist agenda, Haskins was the first and most powerful figure in promoting its modernist agenda. And like his Enlightenment forebears, to whom as a progressive Democrat he was heir, Haskins resolutely stressed the continuity of the American present with past medieval institutions. Haskins came from an affluent, Protestant family in Pennsylvania. A child prodigy, he learned Latin and Greek from his father before he was seven, and at the age of fifteen he entered a local college. He transferred to Johns Hopkins in his second year and earned a B.A. in 1887 and a Ph.D. in American history in 1890. From Johns Hopkins, Haskins went to Wisconsin to teach American history; but after a few years, he determined to become a medievalist, and so, as required for aspiring medievalists at the turn of the century, he decamped for Europe, entering France's prestigious Ecole des Chartes, designed to train the country's archivists and (in that period) historians in the scientific investigation of medieval documents that goes by the name of diplomatics. After a half-dozen years spent in study at the Ecole des Chartes and travel to various archives in England, France, and Sicily, Haskins accepted a professorship at Harvard in 1910. At Harvard he subsequently became dean of the Graduate School of Arts and Sciences, which delayed his major publications until the last half of his academic career, roughly the period from 1918 to 1929. In 1928, three years before the stroke that would incapacitate him, he found his successor in Joseph Reese Strayer, a graduate of Princeton who came to study with him at Harvard, before returning to Princeton to teach for the remainder of his career. Between them, Haskins and Strayer were to direct and dominate the practice of medieval history in North America from the 1920s down through the late 1980s.[18]

Haskins's formation at Hopkins was to have an enduring impact on his career and ideas. The Department of History had graduated Woodrow Wilson but a few years earlier, and throughout his life Haskins would prove an ardent Wilsonian progressive, sharing with Wilson a deep faith in progress, rational reform, and the benefits of government, beliefs that significantly shaped his historical practice. Like Wilson a profound patriot, Haskins similarly partook of the president's admiration for the British constitution and political achievement. Not content to implement his views in the classroom, Haskins accompanied Wilson to the Paris Peace Conference in 1919 and 1920 as one of three principal advisors. With Robert Lord, he helped to create Czechoslovakia and Yugoslavia, states carved from the Austro-Hungarian Empire.[19] On returning to Cambridge, he assumed the directorship of the American Council of Learned Societies, from which position he helped to found and finance the Medieval Academy of America in 1925 and its new journal, *Speculum*,[20] both intended to signal the coming of age of American medieval studies by rivaling in seriousness, exacting standards of scholarship, and formal (not to say deliberate) dullness the great academies of European learning, on which these American institutions were consciously modeled.

Medievalism's modernist agenda that Haskins sought to implant on American soil in its broadest sense took the form of an alliance among positivism, Idealism, naturalism, and objectivity, many of whose components derived, ultimately, from the German scientific historiography of the late nineteenth century, but which Haskins was to cast in a distinctly American, early-twentieth-century, progessivist mold. To do so, however, Haskins had first to cover the absence of a medieval past in America, to guarantee the relevance of medievalism to precisely the vision of continuity and progress that informed his activities both as a professional historian and as an advisor to President Wilson. Few American historians have argued the relevance of medieval history to Americans as eloquently or with as profound conviction as Haskins. While recognizing, as he said, that "American history is our first business," it was not, he believed, "our sole business," and in any case, the two were ultimately part of the same story. European history, Haskins argued in an essay entitled "European History and American Scholarship" (1923), is

> of profound importance to Americans. We may at times appear more mindful of Europe's material indebtedness to us than of our spiritual indebtedness to Europe; we may in our pharisaic moods express thanks that we are not even as these sinners of another hemisphere; but such moments cannot set us loose from the world's history. Whether we look at Europe genetically as the course of our civilization, or pragmatically as a large part of the world in which we live, we cannot ignore the vital connections between Europe and America, their histories ultimately but one.[21]

And of all the available European pasts, Haskins signaled America's natural affinity with that of England, for, he declared, "English history is in a sense early American history."[22]

This insistence on continuity and relevance was institutionalized subsequently in the founding of the Medieval Academy and *Speculum* in 1925, whose embracing purpose was to promote American study of the Middle Ages in all its varieties and subdisciplines in order to help Americans, wrote George R. Coffman in the official report of the foundation, "to comprehend our medieval ancestors." Help was needed, he confessed, given the obscure and complex nature of medieval civilization, and it would require the "cooperation and the creative energy of students of art, archeology, folk-lore, government, law, literature, medicine, philosophy, theology and all other branches" of knowledge to elucidate.[23] Thus, from its inception, the professional study of the Middle Ages in America disclosed a durable structure of paradox in American medievalism—the sense of the absolute remove of the medieval past, its strange, difficult, occult nature, combined with any equally absolute sense of filiation with it.

Haskins was not unaware of this paradox and in his books and essays sought to resolve it in directions that would promote the modernist agenda for which his appropriation of the medieval past stood. His enduring tribute to the modernity (hence, simultaneously, Americanism) of the medieval past was his work *The Renaissance of the Twelfth Century* (1927), in which he contested the master narrative of Western civilization according to which the modern world began in the Renaissance. But, Haskins insisted,

> the continuity of history rejects such sharp and violent contrasts between successive periods, and . . . modern research shows us the Middle Ages less dark and less static, the Renaissance less bright and less sudden than was once supposed. The Middle Ages exhibit life and color and change, much eager search after knowledge and beauty, much creative accomplishment in art, in literature, in institutions. The Italian Renaissance was preceded by similar, if less wide-reaching movements; indeed it came out of the Middle Ages so gradually that historians are not agreed when it began, and so would go so far as to abolish the name, and perhaps even the fact, of a renaissance in the Quattrocento.[24]

Thus, far from having the Quattrocento constitute Western civilization's modernity, Haskins pushed the beginnings of modernism back to the twelfth century, thereby strengthening at one and the same time the continuity of the Middle Ages with the present and the centrality of its study as the seedbed or parent civilization of the modern West. Although little read today except for its genuine contributions to the history of science,[25] Haskins's argument in *The Renaissance of the Twelfth Century* for the modernity of the Middle Ages began that "revolt of the medievalists"[26] which sought a new legitimacy for the medievalist's professional identity against charges of obscurantism, irrelevance, and technical virtuosity that continually haunted the practice of medievalism in America in the face of its clear lack of connection with the national identity.

Making a virtue out of necessity, Haskins argued that America's lack of direct connection with the Middle Ages cultivated detachment on the part of its scholars—"one of America's great advantages as regards many aspects of European history . . . enabling the historian to trace [the history of European civilization] without those national prejudices from which his European confreres cannot wholly emancipate themselves"[27]—thus reinforcing the scientific character of scholarship done in the German, positivist mold. In that sense, the very alterity of the Middle Ages abetted the entrenchment of positivism as *the* scientific form of scholarly method in American medieval historiography, whose counterpart in literary study was an equally fervent espousal of philology,[28] both part and parcel of the specific kind of "source criticism" (*Quellengeschichte*) that American scholarship generally learned during its early tutelage in the German seminar.

Translated into the realm of historical practice, Haskins's positivist objectivity and German-style historicism took the form of a search for the rational basis of the political and administrative development of monarchical institutions in Europe, especially those of the Anglo-Normans and the French. Like Wilson an admirer of the British constitution and political achievement, Haskins focused his attention on the Normans, whose governmental genius he believed had reconstituted the British political system after the Norman Conquest (1066), bringing to the disordered and backward Anglo-Saxon realm the peculiarly systematized and centralized form of feudalism that the Normans had first developed in France. The fruits of this research had begun to appear in articles after Haskins started teaching at Harvard, but his magisterial work *Norman Institutions* was not published until 1918, thus favoring a more widely based reorientation in American medievalism away from the study of German/Anglo-Saxon history after World War I.[29] Hence one effect of Haskins's concentration on Norman institutions was to maintain the traditional orientation of American scholars towards British history but at the same time subtly to redefine what was best in Britain as "French" (or Anglo-Norman), thus permitting American scholarship to evade any possible stigma attached to German history as a result of the war, a move more than validated (and strongly reinforced) by the outcome of World War II.

Norman Cantor has persuasively argued that Haskins's achievement as a medieval historian lay in applying the basic tenets of Wilsonian progressivism to the study of medieval history. Those tenets rested, Cantor asserts, on the belief in "an educated middle class seeking to gain power and extend its learning and code of rationality and efficiency to every walk of life. Wilsonianism's fundamental dogma was that centralizing power in the hands of an educated and professional elite was the salvation of the country."[30] In Haskins, the influence of Wilsonianism can be seen in his focus on the inherent rationality of the Norman brand of feudal organization, with its tendency to centralize, and hence place power in the hands of a court elite at the expense of an anarchic barony, and its establishment of political and judicial order to bring peace and stability to the realms under Norman sway, in Sicily as well as England. The lesson that medieval monarchies thus bequeathed to the American present was the power of government to effect unity and consensus out of fragmentation and discord. And no one was to sound this lesson more clearly than Haskins's premier student, Joseph Reese Strayer.

Strayer shared with his mentor a dedication to the investigation of what he called "the medieval origins of the modern state,"[31] in particular by studying the growth of royal bureaucracies, governmental powers, and the legal and constitutional principles by which medieval kings were able to secure not only the ability to rule through force but the affection and loyalty of their subjects. As in the case of Haskins, the focus on monarchy was more or less accidental, and Strayer's real concern was for the elements that promoted governmental stability and effectiveness and allowed the state to protect its subjects, a concern that earned him decades of employment as a consultant to the CIA.[32]

Strayer's Harvard dissertation for Haskins, *The Administration of Normandy under Saint Louis* (Cambridge, Mass., 1932), continued his mentor's focus on the Normans, but in a Normandy reintegrated into the French realm as a result of its reconquest by Louis's grandfather, Philip Augustus, in 1204. Once again, the questions Strayer posed were Haskins's questions concerning the impact of a specifically Norman style of government, now upon the French monarchy. In particular, he wondered if Norman customary law had tempered the activities of the Roman lawyers of the French crown in the thirteenth century, while teaching them how to develop their own systems of administration and taxation.[33] Behind this question stood the desire to reinterpret French monarchical institutions in such as a way as to make them compatible with American democratic principles, to divest the French monarchy (at least in the Middle Ages), that is, of the charge of absolutism, a form of political governance that Strayer found personally distasteful and historically irrational and ineffective, since he fervently believed that totalitarian regimes were naturally weak by virtue of their inability to win their subjects' adherence.

Strayer's attempt, in effect, to "Americanize" royal history in the Middle Ages proceeded along three lines. The first, which owed most to Haskins's influence, was to argue for the innovative, ameliorative impact of the centralizing monarchies in twelfth- and thirteenth-century England and France, whose actions brought order out of chaos and national unity out of feudal fragmentation. Government, as such, was a "good" thing, securing for its subjects the necessary peace and stability that enabled them to prosper. Moreover, and most important, medieval kings, such as Henry II of England and Philip the Fair of France, achieved these results not through violence but by instituting a legal system able to deliver cheaper and more effective forms of justice to their subjects. Royal centralization, therefore, far from tending to absolutism, was the first step in the implementation of Western constitutionalism, a rational system for the adjudication of national issues and a style of government beneficial to the king's subjects. Strayer devoted a lifetime to demonstrating that this, *not absolutism*, represented the true achievement of medieval monarchies. The result of this work was his monumental book *The Reign of Philip the Fair* (1980), in which Strayer argued, against the grain of previous scholarship, that Philip the Fair, instead of representing a capricious, tyrannical king who used a rising class of lawyers brandishing the principles of Roman law to argue for the status of the king as beyond the reach of law (*rex legibus solutus est*), was a "constitutional" king, who used legal principles to ensure the welfare and security of his realm to the benefit of his subjects.[34]

Strayer was aware, of course, that in France the monarchy ultimately took an absolutist turn, for which he offered a basically "geographical" explanation. In a series of interesting essays,[35] Strayer argued that the reason that England became a true constitutional
monarchy, with effective parliamentary government, was its restricted
size and early centralization. Because the realm was small and highly
organized by English monarchs, who drew upon their subjects' services in the administration of the law, it fostered unity among the
barons who, when the monarchy turned capricious under King John,
were able to band together to oppose royal power and to institution-
alize that opposition in the creation of Parliament. France, in contrast, was too large and too late in developing habits of centralized
consultation for this to occur. Because the king had been so weak for
so long, the barons had little motive to unite against him, and once
the monarchy became powerful, as it did beginning with Philip the
Fair, the "barons" could not develop those habits of cooperation and
concerted action that in England combined to produce a parliamentary form of government. Instead, French kings, when they needed
to consult their subjects over questions of taxation, tended to do so
by individual region rather than in a unified assembly, promoting
fragmentation and particularization among the nobility, which
worked to the monarchy's advantage. For this reason, the Estates-
General in France never developed in the same way as Parliament in
England, and France took an absolutist turn that would, to be sure,
call forth its corresponding opposition in the French Revolution
(thus confirming Strayer's deeply held belief that totalitarian regimes
never finally succeed). The effect of this "geographical" argument was
to exculpate the king of any charge of tyranny, since it represented a
historical constraint that medieval monarchs simply did not have the
resources to overcome. The "moral" upshot of this argument was to
preserve the "virtue" of the French king as a legitimate, constitutional
ruler, who held true to the principles of rational, just government,
even if in the end he was betrayed perforce by the recalcitrant conditions of the realm he governed.

The "virtuous" character of medieval monarchy—an analogue, no doubt, of the American virtue that both Haskins and Strayer sought to extol and promote—can best be seen in the second of Strayer's main lines of research, a series of articles dedicated to demonstrating the ideological means by which royal government in the Middle Ages was able to procure and maintain the loyalty and affection of the governed, affirming along the way Strayer's conviction that no government could rule by violence alone. In articles such as "Defense of the Realm and Royal Power in France," and "France: The Holy Land, the Chosen People and the Most Christian King,"[36] Strayer argued powerfully that French kings had succeeded in winning the devotion of their subjects by successfully articulating the legitimate basis of their rule and, especially under Saint Louis, by presenting themselves as rulers worthy of affection and obedience, producing a cult of kingship in France that was centered on the person of the ruler. It was this ideological legitimacy, a mystique of monarchy that encouraged "Frenchmen" to look to the king as the focal point of an emergent sense of national identity, and not the deployment of powers of coercion, that fundamentally explained the success of the French medieval monarchy. So effective were the administrative systems put in place by medieval governments, and so secure the loyalty of their subjects, that the emerging national states of Europe, Strayer argued in his presidential address to the American Historical Association,[37] were able to withstand the crises of the fourteenth century, in sharp contrast to the Roman Empire, doomed to succumb to the vagaries of the fourth century precisely because it lacked the bureaucratic mechanisms and affective legitimacy that medieval kings had successfully brought into being.

The precondition for these developments, and the third vector of Strayer's research, was what he termed the *laicization* of society in the thirteenth century.[38] By this term Strayer meant something close to Weber's "disenchantment" of the world, a tendency to place faith in human rather than divine figures, and the human figures who became the repository of that faith were, of course, kings. In claiming that the thirteenth-century medieval world was increasingly secular in outlook and in sentiment, Strayer challenged the core image of that "greatest of centuries" (the title of Catholic historian Walsh's book on the period) and the assumption that what made medieval monarchs powerful were the sacral (not the judicial) powers that they exercised.

It would be difficult to overestimate the impact of Strayer's long career of teaching and research on the writing of medieval history in North America. Beginning in the 1930s, for half a century Strayer trained generations of students whom he sent out across the country, populating centers of medieval study from coast to coast. If one includes Haskins, between them they span virtually the entire length of professional medievalism in America, shaping it with their notions of scientific methodology, rationality, and progressive ideology. A parallel consequence of their dominance, Cantor has argued, was to leave medieval studies in America firmly in the hands of "a small, enclosed world of determined, middle-class WASPs, ruling unchallenged (before the German-Jewish emigration of the late thirties) on the history of Roman Catholic Europe."[39] And it was precisely a sea change in the recruitment of medievalists in the 1960s and 1970s that was to change the face of American medievalism almost beyond the point of recognition. This new generation, entering graduate school in the 1960s and the profession in the mid-1970s, completely reoriented the study of medieval history in America, creating a new landscape of concerns that could hardly have been anticipated. In this, medieval history was scarcely alone. The changes it experienced were part of a much broader movement which, from the perspective of the 1990s, can be seen as the importation and adaptation of postmodernism[40] into the heart of American scholarship in all fields.

In some ways, medieval studies might have been thought to be ideally placed to exploit the historicist strain in postmodern thought, since it had always insisted on difference ("alterity") as the privileged category defining the relationship of the Middle Ages to the modern world of scholarship. Given that a dominant impulse in postmodern criticism is precisely the attempt to "think" difference—that is, as Eric Santner explains it, "to integrate an awareness of multiple forms of otherness, to identify . . . across a wide range of unstable and heterogeneous regionalisms, local knowledges and practices"[41]—medievalists were in principle predisposed to the hermeneutic posture that postmodernism demanded of its practitioners. Moreover, the vaunted complexity of medieval documents, the necessity for highly technical approaches to them, implied that meaning in medieval texts was *not* naturally accessible and that such texts were, by nature, opaque, at least to the modern reader. In that sense, philology—the principal technical apparatus in the medievalist's arsenal of interpretation—might have seemed compatible with the emerging sense of the opacity of all writing (of writing as *différance*, in Derrida's sense) and with the turn to textuality as the matrix and condition of possibility for all forms of knowledge. Similarly, the sense of marginality, and the quest for it, that haunts the postmodern era should be equally congenial to the American medievalist, whose object of study lies outside the master narrative of Western modernity and whose own relationship to the profession is often considered to be, if not marginal itself, at least of marginal utility in a national environment committed to innovation and relevance.

And yet, American medievalists—and among them, historians in particular—have been slower than almost any group in the academy to take up the challenge of postmodernism. In part this was due to the highly overdetermined nature of the discourse of continuity and progress that had marked the American relation to its patently absent past virtually from the time of Jefferson on, and which had subtended the modernist agenda of the profession in its very formation. In part, and somewhat paradoxically, it was also due to the conservatism of some who joined the profession, for whom the Middle Ages retained its appeal as an alternative model of social being, belief, and intellectual elitism. (It was, after all, hard to do, demanding a mastery of languages that few Americans naturally commanded.) And in part, it may also have been due to the sensed implication that the very disarray of modernism that *post*modernism by definition portends, threatens to deprive the Middle Ages of whatever *negative* interest it once had as the refuge of the unenlightened, irrational, and "other."[42] In all these ways, the arrival of postmodernism may have

seemed to undermine the unstated but nonetheless powerful investments of self that medievalists brought to their work and in which
they mirrored their professional identities. It was, therefore, not until the late 1970s at the earliest, that there began to appear those currents of thought in medieval historical scholarship in America that
can be linked to the influence of postmodernism.

In my view, there were three dominant trends in historical work in
the late 1970s and 1980s that made themselves felt in the domain of
medieval historiography and that, in sum, constituted a virtual "revolution" in the American (and, in the Haskins-Strayer sense, "Amer-
icanizing") writing of history. The first was a rejection of the positivist certainties and foundationalism of the "old" historicism
—together with its implicit, universalizing humanism—in favor of a
"new" historicism that took its lead from the creation of "discourse"
studies written under the sign of Foucault (at least initially) and
which resulted in a social "constructionist" approach to the past that
would issue, ultimately, in the practice of "cultural history."[43] Another way of characterizing this shift is as a transformation in the idea
of history from a narration of, in the old Rankean formulation, *wie
est eigentlich gewesen*, to history as representation, a recognition that
the investigation of the past occurs only through the mediatory and
mediating texts that it bequeaths and that, therefore, what is "recovered" is not so much the "truth" of the past as the images of itself that
it produced, images conditioned, indeed determined, by its ambient,
and historically determinate, discourses.

Second, and closely allied to this shift was the so-called linguistic
turn, or what might, in its most general sense, be termed a transformation in the understanding of documents as texts rather than
sources. For medievalists, this shift, conducted under the impact of
both symbolic anthropology of the Geertzian sort and semiotics
(and, in part, Derridean deconstruction, though Derrida's influence
was felt primarily in the field of criticism, not history), contested the
positivist and philological center of all medieval studies, and is perceived by the older generation of medievalists in the United States as
a threat to their very enterprise. This because, in treating documents

as texts rather than sources, it suggests the instability and opacity of all and any knowledge of the past, while at the same time (perhaps more important?) attacking the very foundations on which medievalists had constructed their professional legitimacy, involved as it had always been with mastery of highly technical (rather opaque) fields such as paleography, diplomatics, codicology, and so on, not to mention all those "dead" languages. Together, these two movements are creating a "new medievalism" (in the title of a recent collection of essays) that is, in Eugene Vance's words, "a science not of things and deeds but of discourses; an art not of facts but of encodings of facts."[44]

The third (chronologically earliest) transformation came about as a result of the emergence of American feminist historiography and, ultimately, gender studies, whose impact was to shift attention away from precisely the "public" sphere that had engaged the work of American medievalists in the Haskins-Strayer tradition to the private, domestic, and, increasingly, carnal (that is, bodily) spheres. Although feminist historiography initially concerned itself with demonstrating the presence of women in the Middle Ages, making them "visible" as actors upon the historical (if not public) stage—a strategy of *inclusion*, of reading women into the then dominant historical discourse—it quickly developed into a much broader interrogation of the very basis of a practice that claimed "truth" while omitting from its purview fully half the population, a result of which was to demonstrate the ways in which patriarchy itself (especially in its highly misogynist, medieval variant) relied upon a gendered view of nature and power for its success.[45] From there it was but a short step to an exclusive concern with women themselves, a concern that has been especially prominent in the field of medieval spirituality[46] and literary study,[47] where the search for authentic women's "voices" is producing highly paradoxical uses of poststructuralist interpretations of the extant texts.

Although these changes have characterized American historiography in general from the 1970s on,[48] in the field of medieval history, what might, for the sake of symmetry, be here called medievalism's postmodernist agenda required a prior, and double, analytical move:

first, a "demodernization" of medievalism's modernist project that had stood at the core of virtually all medieval disciplines since the late nineteenth century and had endowed American medievalists especially with a professional purpose and identity; second, a (postmodern) "defamiliarization" of the resulting—demodernized—cultural artifacts, an analytical gesture that at the moment appears to entail a certain "demonizing" of the Middle Ages, the corollary of which is what Paul Freedman has called "the return of the grotesque in medieval historiography."[49] What is taking place, therefore, is not so much the product of the unearthing of new texts (although, inevitably, it has led to the discovery of them) as a massive interpretive shift in the meaning of the Middle Ages that has emerged as a consequence of a complete refocusing away from the normal to the contested, from an optimistic and "progressive" decoding of the past to a reappropriation of its otherness,[50] an alterity now construed not merely as the boundary demarcating the premodern from the modern, but as a radical form of "otherness" that almost defies comprehension.

The three directions of change I have indicated might all be seen as aligning themselves beneath the Foucauldian banner: *inquiéter tous les positivismes* (to disrupt all forms of positivism). I am not trying to suggest that Foucault has been the determinative influence on the development of American medievalism's postmodern agenda. Indeed, if one takes literary studies and their impact on historians into account, equal if not greater weight must be given to semiotics and deconstruction. But since Foucault committed himself to working through the implications of postmodernism within history, it has to some extent been easiest for medieval historians to absorb the principles of postmodernism via his writings.

Foucault's work has been especially influential within the domain of historicism, where he has argued that in a postmodern age the problem of history "is no longer one of tradition, of tracing a line, but one of division, of limits; it is no longer one of lasting foundations, but of transformations that serve as new foundations";[51] which is to say that history is a form of archeology. To take Foucault's notion of archeology seriously, therefore, meant abandoning the master narrative of continuity and progress that had informed historical practice at least since the nineteenth century (indeed, earlier) in favor of a fractured, discontinuous, and ruptured sense of the past. As a practical matter, it has promoted a concentration on micro-histories which are no longer assumed to reside within a larger, lineal network of continuous relationships. If genealogy once meant for historians the tracing of direct lines of descent from past to present, under the sign of Foucault it now stands for all that is contingent, invasive, aleatory in history, the constant irruptions and disruptions, misalliances and failures that mark familial relations over time.

At the same time, the implications of a Foucauldian notion of discourse make a belief in objectivity, positivism's ethical twin, virtually untenable, since no thought (or thinker) can escape the knowledge-power systems of its own historical, archeologically disjunct era, thus problematizing in fundamental ways the transactions between past and present required for genuine historical understanding, creating a seemingly unbridgeable hermeneutic gap. Within the domain of textuality, Foucault's archeological metaphor points to the treatment of documents as "monuments," that is, as "mute" artifacts, which no longer "speak" to us clearly and directly from the past, but must be submitted to an intrinsic analysis (like the silent stones of the archeological site) before they can be made to yield up their secrets.[52]

Within women's history, Foucault's constructivist view of discourse, when applied to issues of sexuality, has powerfully abetted the feminist view that sexual categories that were once thought to be natural, universal, and given, the very bedrock of identity and being, are instead historically produced under determinate, discursive conditions and in the service of specific material (patriarchal) interests and power relations. Thus gender differences have themselves been revealed as part of a master narrative that, in unmasking, feminist historiography seeks to dethrone. While few medievalists have followed feminists such as Judith Butler in affirming a wholly performative notion of gender, the very instability, lability, and obscurity of medieval notions of sexuality have lent themselves readily to this kind of treatment.[53] In particular, Caroline Bynum's work on late medieval spirituality has disclosed the centrality of the body and bodily practices to a form of asceticism that is peculiarly female, both in its recourse to food as a central symbol of transcendence (in particular, through consumption of the Eucharist) and in its highly penitential, self-punishing mode of bodily deprivation (fasting, self-flagellation, etc.).[54]

Finally, Foucault's attack on the normalizing mechanisms of modern epistemological regimes has promoted a sensitivity to ways in which knowledge-power systems marginalize and exclude—silence, in effect—some while valorizing others, and has led medieval historians to take a fresh look at the operations of the Church and its systematic theology in the High Middle Ages as well as to seek out those elements of medieval society that contest and thus seem to escape their power. The result of this view of the "normalizing" tendencies of all discursive formations and the desire to undermine their efficacy has been, within medieval history, a complete reinterpretation of the thirteenth century as witness to what has been called "the rise of a persecuting society."[55] Thus, the "greatest of centuries" is seen no longer as the center of a modern, rational progressive movement but as a Foucauldian panopticon of discipline and colonization, seeking out in order to tame and punish all those perceived as dissenting from the Church's regime. This has encouraged, as its obverse, new interest in heretical groups,[56] in Jews and in Jewish-Christian relations,[57] in children, in popular culture, in gays and other marginalized groups.[58] If recent meetings of the Medieval Academy are to be trusted, multiculturalism, postcolonialism, "orientalism," and "sodometries" are soon to follow.

What is particularly striking about medieval work done in this vein, moreover, is the degree to which it focuses not only on the marginal but on the grotesque. Thus Bynum trains her eye on extraordinary acts of asceticism among the women she treats, who routinely drank seeping pus from wounds, fasted to the point of starvation, and submitted to horrifying acts of self-deprivation, all in the name of spiritual transcendence. Jewish historians have recently returned to the study of the massacres of 1096, with their images of piles of dead and mutilated bodies.[59] Even within the most traditional domain of feudal studies, there is a growing emphasis on violence as the engine that drives the feudal machine.[60] Indeed, the latest work on the Normans, Eleanor Searle's *Predatory Kinship and the Creation of Norman Power*, stresses the violent, ritualized nature of their exercise of power, in sharp contrast to Haskins's view of the rational, systematic nature of Norman feudalism. Thus violence, conflict, and marginality are producing similar effects in many fields of research: the "defamiliarizing of what previously seemed canonical, progressive, and modern in favor of the ironic and fantastic."[61]

If one inquires into the reasons for this sea change in the practice of medieval history in America, the answer, it seems to me, lies not so much in the impact of postmodernism per se but in the reasons for the American receptiveness to postmodernism's agenda. And to understand these reasons it is necessary to return to the social recruitment of American medievalists in the 1960s and 1970s. In addition to the entrance of women and blacks into the American academy for the first time, there was also a new wave of participation among classes and what, for lack of a better word, can be called ethnic groups, among them Jews, all of whom entered the university in newly massive numbers in the early 1960s, thus constituting a clientele whose interests needed to be addressed and a pool from among which future professionals could, and would, be recruited. Hence, John Van Engen, in seeking to understand the motivations that have prompted Americans to take up the study of the Middle Ages, in whatever aspect, in light of its absolute remove in space as well as time from their personal and/or familial experience, has pointed to the ambivalence with which these "new" groups of Americans have approached the study of European, and specifically medieval, history. Even for those with cultural roots in Europe, Van Engen believes, most came from among peasants, the unfree, or the dispossessed, retaining, therefore, "little personal stake in the old European order." Moreover, Van Engen insists, the sting of that removal was real . . . the heirs to those immigrants have never been able to decide whether they should spitefully keep their distance, avoiding the old corruption, or return to Europe with pent-up intensity, reclaiming or making space for all that was once denied them. The study of the European Middle Ages remains for Americans a continuing dialectic between connection and disjunction, the tug of social and cultural features still influential among us and the shimmer of something totally and yet perceptibly other.[62]

Surely this, together with the influence on American scholarship of the German-Jewish refugees and their children, provides one of the profound reasons for the current disorientation, or, to put it more positively, reorientation, in the study of the Middle Ages. For ours is the first generation of those immigrants, both from among the dispossessed of the "old European order" and the refugees from Hitler's Europe, to enter the American academy in large numbers, bringing with it all the ambivalence toward and desire for mastery over that world we have all, in some deep way, lost.

Given this, it is hardly surprising that the most powerful sense of the Middle Ages current in the academy is what goes under the name of its "alterity," for that hermeneutic alterity offers the best means of escaping from the model of total (and totalitarian) identification which was the chief mode of studying the Middle Ages in the past. In that sense, as Robert Stein recently suggested to me, "in its resistance to totalitarian identifications, the position of loss may well be a privileged position from which scholarship can proceed." Alterity, from this perspective, is the name we give to the recognition that the past inevitably escapes us, that words, names, signs, functions—our fragile instruments of research and scholarship—are at best only momentarily empowered to capture the reality of the past, the knowledge of which as a lived, experienced, understood repository of life is always slipping away, if indeed it was ever knowable to begin with.

What has changed in the postmodern understanding of medieval alterity, and serves sharply to distinguish it from the earlier modern construction of it, is the simultaneity of our desire for history and the recognition of its irreparable loss, a recognition that paradoxically nourishes the very desire it can never satisfy. This desire has, therefore, an elegiac component, in which it is transformed into a kind of mourning for the unpossessed (or lost) "other." In postmodern historiography, I would argue, the tension between our sense of the past's erasure through the annihilation of memory and our desire for history harbors a longing for presence, a presence we simultaneously acknowledge as always already absent, and thus, like the past itself, an unattainable object of desire. What I call the desire for history not only represents the desire to recuperate the past or the other but also marks the inaccessibility of that absent other, an irony that seems to me to be the very figure of history in the late twentieth century.

Our desire for the past is, therefore, borne alongside our recognition of its loss, a loss we no longer can, or care to, mask beneath the modernist guise of continuity and progress. If postmodernism has seemed to this generation a viable, indeed crucial, theoretical context out of which to work, this is so, I believe, because postmodernism invites us to mourn, as Eric Santner has written, "the shattered fantasy of the (always already) lost organic society that has haunted the Western imagination."[63] The "alterity" of the Middle Ages, it appears, is our own estrangement from that fantasy writ large. On the cover of *Speculum*, there is no longer a mirror.

PART TWO

Practice

5 ▮ Political Utility in
Medieval Historiography

A Sketch

Historians have long recognized the importance of law and jurisprudence in shaping political life in the Middle Ages, yet relatively little
attention has been paid to the political utility of medieval historiography, either as a source of political theory or as a determinant of political behavior. But history no less than law was, to borrow F. W.
Maitland's phrase, the place where life and logic met, the codification
of an intellectual confrontation with reality. And, like law, historiography played an important role in the politics of a traditional society ✓
dependent, as was medieval society, upon the past for legitimacy.

This chapter seeks to investigate the ways medieval chroniclers at
the Abbey of Saint-Denis in France viewed and used the past to explain and legitimate politics. The chronicles of Saint-Denis formed
the most extensive and consistently royalist historical corpus in medieval France, if not anywhere in the Middle Ages. From the twelfth
to the fifteenth century, the monks of the Abbey of Saint-Denis were
continuously engaged in writing history, producing an enormous
body of historical works, both Latin and vernacular, in which they set
forth the history of France from its putative Trojan origins.[1] In the
course of this task they became, in a very real sense, the historical
voice of France. This enormous collection, so valuable for an inquiry

into the historiographical mentality of medieval chroniclers has, unfortunately, never been systematically exploited. Concerned with the
chronicles as source material for other studies, both nineteenth- and
twentieth-century discussion of them has focused on the problem of
verifying their historical accuracy or exposing known instances of dis-
tortion or downright fabrication. Indeed, it is only recently that medieval historiography in general has begun to be investigated as an intellectual tradition that demands the same sympathetic attention to
its underlying beliefs and techniques of expression accorded other
genres produced by medieval intellectual life.[2] And that effort has not
yet extended to the chronicle tradition of Saint-Denis. But no less
than the scholastic or the poet, the Saint-Denis chronicler operated
with a set of philosophical assumptions and a literary tradition from
which he drew his understanding of his subject and his means of
communication. He belonged to an ancient and rich historiographical tradition that included the best works of both Christian and classical history. This tradition directed his inquiry onto specific paths,
molded his views and interpretative strategies, and provided a language of historical discourse through which he might impart his
findings. It gave him, in short, the tools of his craft.

Medieval historiography offers an excellent subject for investigating the function of the past in medieval political life, for surely few
complex societies have so clearly regulated their life in accordance
with their vision of history. Medieval social life was governed by
custom, that is, historical precedent, so much so that even innovations in social and legal practices were given the force of custom.[3] As
custom, social practice was both legitimized and made prescriptive:
because it was customary it was *ipso facto* good and, because good, to
be followed.

Politically, the situation was more complex. In theory medieval
government originated in the divine will of God, functioned at His
behest, and strove to do His bidding. This conception of the ex-
tratemporal dimension of medieval politics was summed up in the
lapidary formula *rex Dei gratia* and symbolized in the consecration
ceremony of the king. In a general way, divine right remained the

foundation of political legitimacy throughout the medieval period. The theological basis of medieval government was, in this sense, consciously unhistorical, for consecration asserted a right to rule *de novo*, irrespective of the past.[4] Nevertheless, consecration established only the legitimacy of rulership; it provided medieval kings with few guides to action and little in the way of explicit programs of political policy. These were drawn, instead, from the record of the past. Just as custom reigned supreme in social life, so history, the record of political tradition, determined the parameters of political activity. Along with divine right, medieval governments justified their dominion on the grounds of what Max Weber called the "authority of the eternal yesterday."[5]

It is only by appreciating how deeply this attitude of piety towards the past ran in medieval society that we can begin to understand the use made of history. It is a question not of the mindless repetition of tradition, nor of an inability to innovate or create, but of a compelling necessity to find in the past the means to explain and legitimize every deviation from tradition. In such a society, as Joseph Reese Strayer remarked, "every deliberate modification of an existing type of activity must be based on a study of individual precedents. Every plan for the future is dependent on a pattern which has been found in the past."[6] The eternal relevance of the past for the present made it a mode of experiencing the reality of contemporary political life, and the examples the past offered had explanatory force in articulating the true and correct nature of present forms of political action. The overall tendency of the chronicles of Saint-Denis was to assimilate past and present into a continuous stream of tradition and to see in this very continuity a form of legitimation.

In part, this explains the enormously rich use made of forgeries, historical legends, and myths in medieval political life. The legend of Trojan origins, the myth of the translation of empire from Roman to Frank, the legacy of Charlemagne, the Valerian prophecy, and a host of other quasi-historical traditions could be shaped to present needs. What is important here is to recognize the fruitfulness of the medieval approach to the past. Precisely because it was so little known in

? But then documentation would be a threat

any critical sense, the past could become a vehicle for change. All that was needed was to recreate it in the image of the present and then claim its authority for the legitimation of contemporary practices. Perhaps the most egregious example of this process is the fabrication of a crusading past for Charlemagne by the monks of Saint-Denis at precisely the time when French kings first took up the cross.[7] But this is only one among many illustrations of what is, in the end, a fundamental posture towards history. It means that the medieval chronicler utilized a very fluid perspective with regard to past and present. The search for the past was guided by present necessities; but so, too, the historical understanding of the past for its part determined the rhetorical presentation of contemporary events. Thus, in a reverse procedure, Philip Augustus's campaign against Otto of Brunswick in 1214, for example, is viewed as a renewal of Charlemagne's struggle with the Saxons, and draws its historical meaning from that context.[8]

Obviously, such a peculiar posture towards the past affected the nature of medieval historiography, shaping a vision of the past that could be manipulated to supply legitimacy to the present. Although it is difficult to prove that kings consciously sought to imitate the great deeds of history, one may at least assume that the general intellectual forces at work in medieval historiography influenced not only the writings of the chroniclers but events themselves.[9]

Although historians have long recognized that medieval chroniclers wrote according to rhetorical principles of classical historiography developed in the ancient world, it is worth examining these briefly, since they formed the literary basis of historical writings in the Middle Ages. To the Greeks and Romans, history is an operation against time, an attempt to save human deeds from the futility of oblivion.[10] It is also a struggle against Nature, whose cyclical permanence stands in imposing contrast to the transitoriness of human existence. To defeat time and gain the permanence of the natural universe would mean to enter into the everlasting, to insert the mortal into the realm of cosmic immortality.[11] History for the Greeks and Romans is essentially heroic, a way of measuring man's capacities against those of the universe. As the record of human greatness, it shields mankind from the destruction of time, bestowing on him eternal fame and glory. Once written down, memory preserves this immortality from generation to generation.

The chroniclers of Saint-Denis retained the memorializing impulse of ancient historiography without, perhaps, the intensity that a philosophy lacking belief in the afterlife invests in historical work. As Cassiodorus had already remarked, chronicles were "the mere shadows of history and very brief reminders of the time."[12] Still, the opening sentences of chroniclers' prologues recall this mnemonic function of history, embracing it as a principal cause for writing. Suger, for example, in writing the history of Louis VI, desires to raise to him "a monument more durable than bronze, whose memory no vicissitude of time can efface."[13] So, too, Guillaume de Nangis, in the Prologue to his *Vita Sancti Ludovici*, begins by extolling the value of history as a record of princely deeds:

> The effort and application of historians have endeavored to commit to literary tradition, as an example, the most memorable deeds of kings and princes who reigned in ancient times, lest we see them slip from human memory and be destroyed by devouring time.[14]

But as Guillaume's Prologue shows, the emphasis has shifted somewhat. Rather than a means of achieving immortality, no longer dependent upon human memory, the desire to create a permanent record of human deeds now has a primarily ethical function. For like Greek and more especially Roman historians, medieval chroniclers see the past as a school of moral instruction, a storehouse of examples of good and evil conduct that illuminate principles of behavior and teach men how to live. They repeat Cicero's famous definition of history as "the witness of the past, the light shed on truth, the life-giving force to memory, the guide to life" (*De oratore*, II, IX, 36). History is a form of moral exhortation and employs hortatory devices that move men to assent to its precepts. This ethical function ties history to rhetoric, for it is the orator's duty to guide the historian's expression so that he may achieve moral persuasiveness. To the extent that the medieval chronicler follows a canon of composition, it is derived from rhetoric.[15]

It is probably fair to say that the medieval historian honored rhetorical rules of composition more in the breach than in practice. But he was at least aware of them and strove to follow them with what little skill he possessed. The typical complaint of rude speech and lack of literary learning with which each writer began his work betrayed not only the inculcated habit of monastic humility but also a true sense of literary limitations that could not be overcome. Although such complaints were part of rhetorical convention, the poignant warning with which Rigord prefaces his *Short Chronicle of the Kings of France* has the ring of truth: "Do not expect in my small narrative the eloquence of Tully or rhetorical flourishes, since I will have done well if, from the confusion of facts, an orderly arrangement emerges which will escape the bite of censure."[16] While few writers were capable of literary greatness, all recognized the principles on which a true literary history should be written and those within their grasp they readily obeyed.

In conformity with the laws of *narratio* as developed by classical rhetoricians, the chroniclers of Saint-Denis sought to make their accounts brief, lucid, and truthful.[17] Although they rarely heeded the command of brevity, and not invariably that of lucidity, they did base their narrations as far as possible on eyewitness testimony or documents thought to be truthful. Rigord was probably more scrupulous than his monastic companions in claiming that he would omit things "unknown" to him, but his stated desire to rely on his personal knowledge of events or, failing that, information derived from his own inquiry of others, accords with principles of evidence in historical writing that go back as far as Herodotus and Thucydides.[18] Often this meant copying verbatim the histories of previous writers, who being closer to the event acquired a probable authority regarding it. But it revealed at least a rudimentary concern for evidence, despite the fact that critical method, whatever the claims of the historians for their works, remained weak throughout the Middle Ages. The closer the chronicler came to describing events of his own times, the more reliable he became, and many writers were conscious of and tried to control deficiencies in their sources.

In the same way, although lacking literary subtlety, sometimes even a grasp of grammar, the chroniclers sought to write in a simple manner that would make up in forthrightness what it lost in ornamentation. In place of elaborate classical *sententiae, loci communi*, and other rhetorical conventions, the Saint-Denis chronicler aimed at an open, unembellished style which could be understood by all. As Primat explained in the Prologue to the *Grandes Chroniques*: "Si sachent tuit que il tretera au plus briément que il pourra, car longue parole et confuse plest petit à ciaus que l'escoutent, mais la briés parole et apertement dite plest aus entendanz"[19] (Everyone should know that he [the author] will treat [his material] as briefly as possible, since long and confusing speeches little please those who must listen to them, while short and clear accounts delight the audience). No matter how attenuated the literary form of the medieval chronicle, it takes its point of departure from the essentially rhetorical conception of history as a means to persuade men to imitate good and avoid evil. The basic purpose of historical writing, then, is edification;[20] at least in theory, it is more concerned with the propagation of moral idealism than with a concrete analysis of reality. By setting forth the experience of the past, history, to use the favorite phrase of Renaissance writers, was "philosophy teaching by example."[21] Particularly in the realm of politics, history had long been thought of as a necessary education for rulers who were considered best situated to learn its precepts and translate them into action.[22] Dionysian authors urged kings to read their works so that, as Rigord wrote to Louis VIII in the Epistle Dedicatory to the *Gesta Philippi Augusti*, "you will always have before your eyes like a mirror the commendable acts of such a prince, as an example of virtue."[23] By their very adherence to the exemplar theory of history, the chroniclers expressed the belief that history had a moral and political utility beyond mere description of the deeds of the past.

One result of this approach to history was a willingness to reduce the complexity of human experience into stereotypes that could be utilized easily to make a moral point. Medieval chronicles even more than classical histories strike the modern reader by the thinness of their concern for individual personality. In the chronicles of Saint-Denis, it is obvious that the description of characters is largely conventionalized. W. J. Brandt has maintained that the lack of interest in human character and motive which appears in chronicles can be traced to the medieval scientific "mode of perception." Medieval science, he argues, denied coherence in human character and behavior, envisioning man simply as a collection of attributes with more or less independent status. This perceptual mode, in Brandt's view, made it impossible for chroniclers to consider character in its totality and thus to establish any workable approach to the problem of individual personality.[24] Without a theory of personality, the descriptive powers of chroniclers necessarily foundered, and any attempt to explore the relation between character and conduct was doomed to failure.

Similarly, Brandt and others have argued that medieval chroniclers lacked any concept of causation. The exemplarist and stereotypical use of historical events and persons meant the abandonment of a concern for causal process. It elevated these data into the realm of universal moral precepts, denying what a modern historian would consider their historicity, their relationship to a historical context. The result was an enormously weak sense of anachronism, an inability to distinguish the particularity of historical phenomena and separate them from universally valid moral principles.[25]

So, too, it is argued, the symbolic mentality of the Middle Ages obstructed causal thinking, since causal relations tended to yield to symbolic connections. Perhaps no one expressed this better than Marc Bloch when he wrote that "in the eyes of all who were capable of reflection, the material world was scarcely more than a mask, behind which took place all the really important things; it seemed to them also a language, intended to express by signs a more profound reality. Since a tissue of appearances can offer but little interest in itself, the result of this view was that observation was generally neglected in favor of interpretation."[26] From all sides, scientific, literary, and religious, medieval thought, it seems, conspired to deny the historian a basic tool of research: a disposition and a capacity for seeking out causal process beneath the variety of historical matter that came within his purview.

Without denying the truth of these assertions, I would like to modify their harsh implications somewhat. While the medieval historian may have lacked a specifically modern sense of causation, he nevertheless operated with a set of assumptions about the relationship between events in the past and present reality which, for him, functioned much as modern theories of causality do for us. In order to understand this, it is necessary to return to the use of *exempla* and reinterpret their possible function in medieval historiography.

To begin with, we might point out, as Nancy Struever has reminded us, that the *exemplum* in medieval literature "had not the humble status of fact, but . . . a quasi-religious prescriptive status as traditional material."[27] It not only illuminated universal moral realities, it commanded men to pursue them; like custom, it determined modes of behavior. It therefore asserted a relationship between behavior in the past and contemporary practice which, if not fully causal, nevertheless suggests something more than moral exhortation. If one tries to determine the source for this peculiar use of *exempla* in medieval thought, its similarity to biblical exegesis is immediately apparent. The typological interpretation of the Bible by medieval exegetes establishes precisely the same analogous relationship between genuine historical acts in the past and their fulfillment in later, also genuinely historical events. In typological exegesis the earlier event, analogous to the later, becomes a foreshadowing, a "type" of it. As Richardson has explained:

> The typological interpretation of the Bible differs from the allegorical in that it detects a real and necessary correspondence in the structure and meaning of the original or "typical" event or complex of events to the new application or fulfillment of it. Accordingly, the idea of the fulfillment of the Scriptures will mean . . . the fulfillment of history, the making explicit of what was implicit in the pattern of earlier historical events by the movements of the

later events, the deepening of the meaning of history itself as this meaning is revealed to the prophetic insight.[28]

By means of typological interpretation, the significance of the past is reaffirmed for the present; the old becomes a prophecy of the new and its predeterminant in the sense that its very existence determines the shape and the interpretation of what comes later. In this way, the past becomes an explanatory principle, a way of ordering and making intelligible a relationship between events separated by vast distances of time.

It seems obvious that monastic chroniclers, trained on the daily reading of the Bible, could easily have transferred this way of reading Scripture to the interpretation of history.[29] What is involved is the secularization of typology, its application to the material supplied by history rather than sacred events. As early as the second century, Christian writers began to view occurrences in their own lives as the fulfillment of Old Testament prophecies.[30] It is not hard to imagine, once this step was taken, how the present came to be viewed as a fulfillment not only of sacred prophecies but of other events themselves.

I would like to suggest that *exempla* as used by the Saint-Denis chroniclers were often intended to function like biblical types. Although the chroniclers' prologues suggest that their methods of explanation and expression differed insignificantly from classical rhetoric, the use of *exempla* in their narrative is informed by an exegetical tradition that owes more to the Bible than to Cicero.[31] When the chroniclers drew analogies between their rulers and David, Alexander, Constantine, or Charlemagne, they were not merely ascribing a particular list of attributes to their subject. They were affirming a positive, virtually causal relationship between what a David or a Constantine had done and the deeds of the "new David." The record of the past was seen as having a relation to the present that was more than prescriptive, if less than what we would consider as scientifically causal. In this way the past not only explains the present, it exercises an indirect influence over contemporary events. The sense of an implicit relationship to what had happened before made it unnecessary for these historians to investigate the immediate causes of occurrences. In the minds of the chroniclers, Philip Augustus acted as he did "because" Charlemagne had, and what Charlemagne did he, too, would do. While explaining the present, the past casts the shape of the future. Typological thinking sets up a complex field of influences which ties past and present, present and future into one essentially prophetic mode of analyzing history. For this reason a characteristic voice of history in the chronicles of Saint-Denis is prophecy; not in the Old Testament sense of decrying contemporary practice and foretelling better or worse days to come, but in its ability to establish genuine historical relationships between temporally distinct phenomena.

With the aid of such "typologies" the chroniclers could use figures and events of the past as explanations and as modes of legitimizing present political life. For example, the formulation by Dionysian chroniclers of the fiction known as the *reditus regni ad stirpem Karoli Magni*—the return of the Capetian realm to the heirs of Charlemagne in the person of Louis VIII, the biological descendant of Carolingian parents—engendered a typological relationship between the second and third *races* of French kings and thereby made available to succeeding Capetians the ideological claims embedded in the Carolingian topos (see Chapter Seven, below). It described a political future that would unfold as the realization of the potentialities of the past and thus implicitly legitimized the political programs and policies to which Capetian efforts in the thirteenth and fourteenth centuries were directed as an acting out of the dictates of history. For in such a scheme, the past was prophetic, determining the shape and the interpretation of what was to come and binding past, present, and future into a single, comprehensive historical matrix.

In a more immediate sense, the Carolingian typology was used to legitimate Capetian conquests under Philip Augustus and his successors as a return to the former imperium of Charlemagne, grounding present action in a mythical, but highly usable, past that held unchallenged authority in the minds of contemporaries. Such typologies were, moreover, multivalent. The Carolingian topos also endowed the

Capetians with a new identity articulated in the title Rex-Imperator, with its implied reference to the imperial past of Frankish kings. Although this identity was subject to shifting interpretation, it was to be a decisive factor in shaping French goals in the last Capetian century. The *reditus* doctrine, as applied to Philip Augustus and his successors, illustrates the underlying typological structure of the chronicler's thought, the utilization of historical topoi as explanatory principles of contemporary action, and the hortatory and legitimizing function of the past that enabled historical actors and writers to come to terms with their present reality.

Similar uses were made of the newly furbished crusading past of Charlemagne to supply historical precedent, and hence legitimacy, to royal crusading ventures; and of the conversion of Clovis, which demonstrated France's long-standing dedication to the fundamental principles of Christian society, and thus aided in the development of the notion of France as a "Holy Land,"[32] whose past achievements in service to the Church gave the nation a historical personality and argued assent to its aspirations for political leadership among the states of Europe.

Throughout the chronicles of Saint-Denis, legitimizing accounts of previous French kings as "good," "just," "pious," "benevolent," and "powerful" carefully build up an internal structure of historical relationships that is fundamentally typological. On the basis of these typologies, Dionysian chroniclers elaborated historical, ideological, and ethical themes that governed their presentation of Capetian kingship and created a national past that was a source of immense pride, exalting the kingdom as well as the dynasty. Precisely because such typological relationships fit so well with medieval modes of perceiving historical reality, both sacred and secular, the ideological elements arising from them were persuasive as political propaganda, justifying the monarchy's actions and programs. At the same time, they helped to clarify for the nation itself the inner meaning of French history, just as biblical typology clarified the meaning of Christ's new dispensation to mankind in relation to the historical preparation for His coming articulated in the prophetic teachings of Judaism. In this way, the royal myth, fostered and amplified by historical typologies that reaffirmed the continuity and the legitimacy of royal action, contributed to the formation of a national identity in France in the Middle Ages.

The typological nature of medieval historical thinking also helps to explain its weak sense of chronology. To date an event precisely in the past means fixing its significance as a distinct object, separated from the present. But typology wishes to break down the barriers between past and present, to draw events out of the past and make them live in present experience. It operates with what Driver calls the "principle of contemporaneity," in which "time and historical occurrence refuse to take their place in a chronology of the past. The event which *was* meaningfully enters the *now*." Because history is a mode of experience, and not merely ascertainable fact, it refuses to die, to remain chronologically fixed in the past.[33]

History utilized as a mode of experience constructs time as a continuum rather than as a series of distinct acts following one upon the other into the past. It functions like tradition, assuming a certain identity between what happens then and now. To the very degree that men in the Middle Ages sensed the reality of the past, they were incapable of perceiving with equal acuteness its distance. This does not mean, as Gaston Paris claimed, that they believed in the immutability and permanence of all things. On the contrary, they were philosophically and religiously conditioned to an appreciation of the transitoriness of mundane occurrences, so tellingly designated as the "temporalities."[34]

The act of writing history was in fact a means of preserving the reality of time. By capturing the moment in written memory, history, as Gilson points out, constructed a duration, "redeeming the world from the stream of becoming."[35] To put it somewhat differently, history creates a "time-space" that saves the things of the moment and establishes their relation to what has happened and will happen. And because of its concentration on politics, history creates above all a temporal "space" that sustains political life.

If one looks at the chroniclers of Saint-Denis from this perspec-

tive, their insistent concern with genealogy takes on a new importance. The creation of a historical traditioin required the demonstra-
tion of social continuity over time. It is instructive that the opening
lines of the *Grandes Chroniques* announce their concern with political continuity as established through genealogy:

> Pour ce que plusieurs genz doutoient de la genealogie des rois de
> France, de quel origine et de quel lignie ils ont descendu, enprist il
> cest ouvre à fere par le commandement de tel homme que il ne
> pout ne dut refuser.

> [Because several people express doubt concerning the genealogy of
> the kings of France, namely from what origin and from which line
> they are descended, he (Primat) has undertaken to produce this
> work at the command of a man such as cannot be refused.]

Similarly, the organizational frame of the entire work is supplied by
genealogy:

> Et pour ce que III generacions ont esté des rois de France puis que
> il commencierent à estre, sera toute ceste histoire devisée en III
> livres principaus: ou premier partera de la genealogie Merovée, ou
> secont de la generation Pepin, et ou tierz de la generation Hue
> Capet. . . . Li commencemenz de ceste histoire sera pris à la haute
> lignie des Troiens, dont ele est descendue par longue succession.[36]

> [Because there have been three generations of Kings of France
> since they began to exist, the whole history will be divided into
> three principal books: the first will speak of the genealogy of
> Meroveus, the second of the generation (i.e., descendants) of
> Pepin, the third of the generation of Hugh Capet. . . . The begin-
> ning of this history will start with the high lineage of the Trojans,
> from whom the kings of France are descended through a long suc-
> cession.]

Genealogy, even when largely mythical, asserts the temporal durability of a people. Because it considers rulers as the expression of social
continuity, whose own unbroken descent implies the political continuity of those they rule, it establishes a temporal dimension for the
consideration of politics.

At the same time it provides a framework for precisely the kind of enriching use of the past that medieval chroniclers essayed. Genealogy transforms the connection between the political past and present into a real one, seminally imparted from generation to generation. As evidence of historical continuity, it lends plausibility to the analogizing tendencies of medieval historical thought, allowing perceived relationships between historical figures and events in the past and present to be viewed as part of one continuous stream of history. It prevents these "typologies" from becoming purely symbolic connections and therefore saves history from allegory.

The extent of medieval allegorizing of history can be seen in a historian such as Joachim of Flora, for whom historical data are merely signs of the spiritual significance and tendency of history. Because the chroniclers of Saint-Denis grounded their works in a real, genealogical tradition, they never yielded to a purely prophetic treatment of history. Unlike Joachim, who uses genealogy for allegorical purposes, they remain bound to the human, biological significance of their genealogies. The record of the past, while prophetic in its ability to shape the course of future events, never lost its foundation in social and political reality.

Perhaps this explains the need to create genealogies when they were lacking, as in the case of the Trojan origins of the Franks.[37] Once this relation to an ancient past was asserted, everything between the mythical Trojan foundation of France and the present became historically relevant as part of French tradition. Without such a framework the attempt to aver desired connections to past events became highly subjective and open to interpretation. With it, an "objective" relationship to the past was maintained, to be explored and utilized for guidance and for legitimation of the present.

Genealogy also made it possible to organize history into a total plan around a central theme. In the case of the chronicles of Saint-Denis, that theme was for the first time a purely royal one.[38] The chronicles of Saint-Denis represent, in their totality, the first history of France, invoked to illustrate and sustain the royal myth. Once we become sensitive to the explanatory and legitimizing function of the historical "typologies" employed by Dionysian chroniclers, a whole new dimension to their historiographical techniques seems to open up. Beneath the flat, almost opaque surface of the political narrative, one senses the effort to establish a coherent system of historical relationships which both tell the story and convey its meaning for the present. The chroniclers of Saint-Denis were not particularly successful in this effort, or at least so it seems to the modern reader. But one wonders if the fault lies with them or with us. Just as any modern reader inevitably fails to catch the wealth of biblical allusion evoked in all medieval writings, by phrases, words, and surface details as well as direct references, perhaps we fail equally to catch the secular typologies evoked in much the same manner. There is no way to restore to the modern reader the historical imagination of a medieval audience, any more than most of us can become as fully conversant as a monk with the Bible. But we can perhaps agree that such a system of reference and explanation is implied in the structure and the methods of medieval historiography. If we agree on this, it should be possible to read medieval chronicles in a new way, no longer as quarries to be mined exhaustively for information whose historical status, by our standards, is difficult to verify. Rather, we might study them as vehicles for the expression of fundamental ideas concerning the nature of medieval political reality and its relation to the political past. Medieval chronicles might thus be made to yield a new understanding of the political utility of history in the Middle Ages.

6

Genealogy

Form and Function in Medieval Historiography

With a characteristically indulged pleasure in malice, Gerald of Wales tells the following story of a fellow Welshman, a certain Melerius who, under circumstances somewhat unusual, was gifted with the knowledge of future occult events. If the evil spirits oppressed him too much, the Gospel of Saint John was placed on his bosom, and, like birds, the spirits immediately vanished. But when the book was removed, and the *History of the Britons* by Geoffrey of Monmouth was substituted, the spirits instantly reappeared in greater numbers, and remained a longer time than usual on his body and on the book.[1] Despite its sardonic tone, Gerald of Wales's tale of his hapless compatriot, whose reading of Geoffrey of Monmouth oppressed him so mightily in body and soul, seems to me an apt figure for medieval historiography, for few phases of the Western tradition of historical writing have called forth so many critical demons. Indeed, medieval historiography is that rare phenomenon among scholars, a field often scorned as much by those who are acquainted with it as by those who are not.

It is hardly necessary to rehearse the litany of errors of which the practice of historiography in the Middle Ages stands accused: its philosophical alliance with theology, which evacuated from history its human purpose and meaning; its literary alliance with rhetoric, which made it inimical to the pursuit of truth; its exemplarist and stereotypical use of historical events and persons for moral teaching, denying them what a modern historian would consider their historicity, their relationship to a historical context; its concern with experience, custom, and repetition, rather than reason, individuality, and process; even its absence from the curriculum of medieval pedagogy, which meant, as V. H. Galbraith once remarked, that the serious study of history in the Middle Ages was "nobody's business."[2] To the above failings, one normally adds its low level of literary achievement, approaching at times narrative unintelligibility; a weak notion of historical evidence; lack of sense of anachronism; propagandistic intentions; substitution of symbolic interpretation for causal analysis; and vulnerability to invasion by fiction, forgery, myth, and miracle, not to mention genuine demons. In short, medieval historiography, by all critical odds, is inauthentic, unscientific, unreliable, ahistorical, irrational, borderline illiterate, and, worse yet, unprofessional.

This chapter does not seek entirely to dispel the critical demons that have plagued the study of medieval historiography. But I would like to offer some general observations on the way in which the medieval historian has approached his task and his text and, as a consequence, on how we might profitably consider medieval histories as both literature and fact, or, more nearly, as literatures *of* fact, and then to examine this problem with a narrower focus on one particular species of history in the Middle Ages—that of genealogically influenced vernacular narratives from thirteenth-century France.

The literary study of medieval historiography must begin with the recognition that for the medieval chronicler the events he recorded were also the structure of his history,[3] determining a priori the shape of his narrative. History, conceived in this manner, was the record of visibly perceptible events in which conformity to "facts" in the sequential order of their happening was the principal test of historiographic truth. The medieval chronicler thus began with a belief in the mimetic identity of his narrative to the events it recounted, with a belief, in other words, in the metaphoric validity of his text. From this flowed a concern with establishing correct order, not conjecture about causes or conceptual interpretation, as the chief task of the historian, and he was construed to be most faithful to that task when displaying, in their proper places, the plethoric variety and variability of human occurrences. That such a view of the historian's task tended to result in what appears, at least to us, to be an unfortunate narrative clutter was an unavoidable concomitant of an ethical commitment to mimetic accuracy. Moreover, the mimetic goals of the medieval chronicler affected the nature of his method as well as the style of his narration. I would like to suggest that the historian in the Middle Ages viewed his text as a transparency through which he sought to convey to his prospective audience of readers or auditors as direct and vivid an impression of past and present reality as possible. In considering his text as transparent, a lucid medium of transmission, the chronicler apprehended history itself as a perceptual field, to be seen and represented instead of constructed and analyzed, an object more of perception than of cognition. Taking written form, chronicles were, as Cassiodorus called them, *imagines historiarum*[4]—images of histories, likenesses, semblances, pictures. And, if one accepts this analogy, it seems logical to assume that the "images" residing in the perceptual field of history were perceived and transcribed in accordance with the prevailing techniques of pictorial illustration in pre-Renaissance Europe, that is, by a multifocal, "cyclic" method rather than as a unified field, the former a method which Robert, discussing manuscript illumination, interestingly calls *Chroniken-Stil.*[5]

There are several insights to be gained by considering medieval historiography in this way. It helps to explain, for example, the privileged status of eyewitness testimony as evidence; the virtual absence of epistemological concerns (*what* is seen and known being more important than *how*); the seemingly dispersed, paratactic construction of the narrative, as the chronicler shifts his gaze over the historical landscape; and the lack of explicit causal analysis, as modes of representation take precedence over modes of explanation.[6] Equally important, it explains what is perhaps the most distressing feature of medieval historiography to modern researchers—its extraordinary vulnerability to legend, fiction, and fable; in a general sense, the absence of source criticism. But this, too, is a natural consequence of the historian's conception of his text as a transparency. Facing the past, the medieval chronicler viewed himself essentially as a faithful conveyor of the written record and his text as a vehicle for transmitting segments of past texts conjoined. He was above all, as Bernard Guenée recently emphasized, a compiler, cloaking his authorial persona within the authoritative works of others, with which he tampered only at great moral risk.[7] By substituting compilation for research, the medieval chronicler became peculiarly a slave to his documents, whose errors he piously passed on. In the same way, facing the present, the chronicler would naturally, and with the same piety, incorporate into his account whatever legends, miracles, or fictions circulated in the world he was attempting with mimetic fidelity to record. In both cases, the "untruths" of past or contemporary observers easily entered the narrative without necessarily violating the chronicler's obedience to the first law of history—which was, of course, the pursuit of truth (*prima lex historiae veritas est*). Indeed, to leave them out would have been neglectful of that obligation to truth, for once such fictional elements became part of the received stock of stories, there was practically no sound theoretical ground for banishing them from the narrative, hence the widespread presence of *ut alii dicunt* (as some people say). Historical criticism, as we understand it, arose primarily when sources or testimony used by the chronicler disagreed on any given point, demanding resolution. Those medieval historians whom modern scholars admire most for their critical sensibilities are the ones who used a fairly wide variety of contradictory texts and reports in writing, and therefore were forced into making "critical" choices, although it is probably only fair to add that the most common strategy of determination found in medieval chronicles is simple juxtaposition of opposing views, a kind of primitive historiographic *sic et non*.

Anyone who has read more than a few medieval chronicles will, at this point, immediately object that if a medieval historical text is a transparency and history apprehended as a perceptual field, the chronicler must have operated with a rigidly exclusionary canon of permissible perceptions. Surely what strikes the modern reader most forcefully is not only the nearly universal existence of narrative disarray, but so much narrative disarray about the same things, a depressing redundancy of actions recounted and meaning extrapolated which lend to chronicles their air of dreary sameness. In response, I would argue that the very transparent nature of history as literary form led to the emergence of sets of historical canons which acted to delimit the historian's subject matter and to control its narrative presentation. For, just as history, being transparent, was susceptible to invasion by fictions circulating in the chronicler's sources, so also was it receptive to being shaped by structures already residing in the social reality which the historian perceived as the focus of his narrative. And, in keeping with my metaphors of perception, I would like to call these structures "perceptual grids," which directed the historian's glance at relatively fixed categories of human experience and governed both the nature of his perceptions and the manner in which he transmitted them. Depending on the chronicler's point of view, his ideological perspective, his traditional or individual historical vision, such "grids" came to him more or less naturally from the world in which he was embedded and, in the absence of theoretical assumptions about historical writing, provided the structural principles that guided his work.

Perhaps the clearest illustration of this process is the monastic application of typological exegesis to the interpretation of secular history (found, for example, in writers such as Bede), a clear result of the hegemony of biblical modes of thought in the intellectual life of the monastery. While typology is possibly the most common organizing "grid" in medieval historiography, it is by no means the only one, nor do they all originate in previously existing forms of thought. Another perceptual "grid," more social than intellectual in origin, yet important for the shape of vernacular history in thirteenth-century France, is the structure of the lineage family, which expressed its ex-

istence in written form as genealogy. It is to the form and function of
genealogy in historical narrative that I would like to devote the
remainder of my remarks.

Genealogy intrudes into historical narrative at precisely the time
when noble families in France were beginning to organize themselves
into vertical structures based on agnatic consanguinity, to take the
form, in other words, of *lignages*.[8] Genealogy was both cause and
consequence of this development, for its appearance as a literary
genre in the twelfth century signaled the lineage's consciousness of itself and, to a certain extent, as Duby has remarked, was able to create this consciousness and to impose it on members of the lineage
group.[9] Written above all to exalt a line and legitimize its power, a
medieval genealogy displays a family's intention to affirm and extend
its place in political life. As genealogies were amplified in the course
of the twelfth century, pushing out in every direction, filling in each
sequence with more detail, adding names of younger sons, daughters,
and ancestors not previously mentioned, the profile of the family tree
became a skeleton of aristocratic society, revealing the multiple
threads that crossed and recrossed, binding regional nobilities into
ever more integrated congeries of family relations. Raised to the royal
level, genealogy took on the overtones of a dynastic myth, synonymous in many respects with the central myth of French kingship as
the unbroken succession of the *trois races* of France. But whether aristocratic or royal, genealogies were expressions of social memory and,
as such, could be expected to have a particular affinity with historical
thought and, at least to a certain extent, to impose their consciousness of social reality upon those whose task it was to preserve for future generations images of society in the record of history—Cassiodorus's *imagines historiarum*.

Occasionally, histories expressly state their debt to genealogy as a
principle of narrative order, as in the case of Guillaume de Nangis's
Chronique Abrégée (1285–1300), which, in its initial Latin redaction,
now preserved at the Bibliothèque Nationale (lat. 6184), was composed "in the form of a genealogical tree," with the trunk and its
ramifying branches actually drawn on the outer margins of the man-

uscript.[10] But this is the least important and the least interesting manifestation of the ways in which genealogy provided structure to history, and in any case, later French amplifications of Guillaume's text so multiplied the discursive matter of the narrative as to obscure thoroughly the original genealogical format of the Latin text. Rather, it is genealogy as symbolic form, conceptual metaphor not marginal cartoon, that had the greatest impact on the patterning of historical narrative and the formation of its expressive meaning. Through the imposition of genealogical metaphors on historical narrative, genealogy becomes for historiography not only a thematic "myth" but a narrative *mythos*, a symbolic form that governs the very shape and significance of the past.

There are two principal ways in which genealogy as a conceptual metaphor affected historical literature in thirteenth-century France: first, as form, by supplying a model for the disposition of narrative material (in other words, as perceptual grid and narrative frame); second, as meaning, by reinterpreting historical events in accordance with the model of filiation suggested by genealogy. Both operate in texts, to cite only two examples, as different in character in other respects as the *Histoire des ducs de Normandie et des rois d'Angleterre* and the *Grandes Chroniques de France*.[11] The first of these, the *Histoire des ducs de Normandie*, is the work of the Anonymous of Béthune, an Artesian gentleman attached to the house and person of Robert VII of Béthune, whose fortunes he followed during the period when Robert served among the mercenary forces of King John of England. Completed in 1220, the Anonymous's *Histoire* is one of the earliest histories in French prose and may be said to represent the new literary trend of vernacular historiography among the French-speaking Flemish nobility of the early thirteenth century. Our second text, the *Grandes Chroniques de France*, is the multivolume vernacular history of the kings of France written at the Abbey of Saint-Denis as part of the official history of the French monarchy, to which the monks also devoted an extensive series of Latin chronicles. The first section of the *Grandes Chroniques* in Old French was completed by Primat in 1274. These two works, one aristocratic, the other royal, one lay in origin, the other monastic, nevertheless equally reveal the penetration of genealogical metaphors of historical form and function into the very center of their respective historical enterprises. And it is precisely the congruence of these phenomena in texts that are unrelated in terms of ideological impulse, exploitation of Latin sources, or patronage that sustains the notion that the rise of the *lignage* family as the fundamental social fact of thirteenth-century France was responsible for the new patterning of historical narrative discernible in both texts.

As a formal structure, genealogy deploys history as a series of biographies linked by the principle of hereditary succession,[12] which succession stands as much for the passing of time as for a legal notion of transference. From a strictly generic point of view, this manner of ordering history represents a conflation between the theoretically distinct genres of *vita* and chronography. Thus the Anonymous of Béthune's *Histoire des ducs de Normandie* traces the history of the duchy of Normandy and the kingdom of England from the time of the Norman arrival in France to 1220 by interlacing the family histories of the various ruling houses on both sides of the Channel, among which his own patron's house of Béthune figures prominently. Each ruler in the ducal and royal succession is given as full a *vita* as information permits and, throughout, the Anonymous shows extreme sensitivity to questions of legitimate birth, hereditary rights, and the actions of what he explicitly calls the *lignages*,[13] producing a braided narrative formed from the independent histories of each lineage grouping. In the less complicated dynastic history of the *Grandes Chroniques*, the single thread of Capetian descent organizes the narrative as a genealogy of the *trois races* of French history, reaching back to the legendary Trojans, from whom, Primat asserts, "the kings of France are descended by long succession."[14] Primat lays out the economy of his text to match the three main dynastic structures of French kingship, explaining in the Prologue that "because there have been three generations [*generacions*] of Kings of France since they began to exist, the whole history will be divided into three principal books: the first will speak of the genealogy of Meroveus [*la généalogie Merovée*], the second of the generation of Pepin, the third of the generation of

Hugh Capet."[15] Each reign is treated as coterminous with the life of the ruler, and every regnal segment of the *Grandes Chroniques* begins and ends with summary portraits of kings, an unmistakable trace of the biographical orientation.

In a vernacular chronicler such as the Anonymous of Béthune, notable for his impartiality, such portraiture veers towards realism, while in the ideologically committed *Grandes Chroniques*, the product of Capetian sponsorship, it achieves a highly iconic character. The result is a narrative gallery of kings in continuous succession not unlike the sculptural elements of the same name on the west facade of Notre-Dame. Indeed, the genealogical myth that underlies the *Grandes Chroniques*, presenting the history of French kingship as an unbroken, wholly legitimate succession of rulers from Priam to Pharamond, to Clovis, to Charlemagne, to Philip Augustus, and so on down the centuries, threatens to overwhelm the separate identities of individual kings with a mythic homogeneity imposed by the ideal pressure of such dynastic fictions. But the realism of the Anonymous and the iconism of the *Grandes Chroniques* are merely poles between which any chronicler might locate himself in the passage, in literary terms, from a low mimetic to a high mimetic mode.

What is more important is that both histories (and many others) share the essential principle of a narrative order based on genealogical succession in which the most significant structural divisions of history are supplied by generational change. In this sense, the royal myth of genealogical continuity becomes, in a work like the *Grandes Chroniques*, the historical *mythos* in Northrop Frye's meaning of narrative structure and emplots history as genealogy.[16]

Moreover, genealogy employed as a perceptual "grid" inevitably affected the chronicler's organization of the chronological time of his history, resulting in a narrative controlled by dynastic rather than annalistic or calendar time.[17] On a deeper level, genealogy functioned to secularize time by grounding it in biology, transforming the connection between past and present into a real one, seminally imparted from generation to generation. On a biological model, the *series temporum* which it was the duty of every chronicler to record becomes an interconnected succession of past moments in which time, because human, is historicized. It is here that the filiative model implicit in genealogically determined historiography had its second and greatest impact. For it suggested the human process of procreation and filiation as a metaphor for historical change. In this, it came very close to considering history as the "genealogy of events," which Robert Nisbet has identified as the principal Western tradition of historical thought about the past as historians, as opposed to philosophers (or, in his terminology, developmentalists) treat it.[18]

Whether such metaphors of procreation and filiation in medieval chronicles ever actually operated, as presumably they do in modern historiography, as forms of causal explanation, remains an open and probably insoluble question.[19] At the very least it can be said that genealogy restored the linear consciousness of history, which, as Auerbach so brilliantly demonstrated, was destroyed by the adoption of figuration as the basic strategy of historical interpretation in the early Middle Ages.[20] Genealogy necessarily fashions history as linear narrative, for what, after all, is a *lignage*, if not a line? Insofar as vernacular chroniclers remain faithful to the human, biological significance of their genealogies, they can perceive relationships between historical figures and events in the past as part of one continuous interrelated stream of history. The procreative process by which human beings engender successive generations is the human shape of history generating events over time, events that stand in a filiative relation to one another that mirrors the reproductive course of human life.[21]

Thus, beneath the apparent narrative disarray, the paratactic disjunction of episodic units, and the seeming logical incoherence which scholars have assumed to be the necessary by-product of narrative parataxis, lay a metaphor of procreative time and social affiliation that brought together into a connected historical matrix the essential core of the chronicler's material. In this way, genealogy enabled chroniclers to organize their narratives as a succession of *gestes* performed by the successive representatives of one or more *lignages*, whose personal characteristics and deeds, extensively chronicled in essentially biographical modes, bespoke the enduring meaning of history as the collective action of noble lineages in relation to one another and to those values to which their *gestes* gave life. It is as if the synchronic assemblage of meaningful acts which history can and should relate were diachronically projected onto the screen of the past, without at the same time losing their exemplary character.

What is particularly interesting about these genealogical chronicles—internally structured, we should remember, as agnatic lineages focused on the transmission of property, name, and status from father to son—and what connects them directly to the central generative myths of Christianity is the extent to which they replicate the patrilineal origin of mankind itself. As recounted in Genesis, God creates man (Adam), from whom alone woman (Eve) derives. This patrilineal generation, of course, is repeated in the regeneration of mankind through the creation of the (new) man, Christ, this time explicitly designated as a Son to God, also explicitly designated as God the Father. Genealogical histories are thus, from a structural point of view, narrative mimeses of the creation of life itself and as such acquire a genuinely paradigmatic character as imitations of the supernatural order upon which the social order of the human community is based. Historical myth and historiographical *mythos* are one and the same expression of an underlying Christian metaphysics which explains the generation of mankind in patriarchal terms, and which thereby seeks a supernatural foundation for the continuance of patriarchy as an exemplary structure of social order.

In closing, I contend that genealogy overcomes the conceptual parataxis suggested by, but not necessarily implicit in, medieval narrative form, and does so by providing an image of connected historical relationships fundamentally grounded in social reality, the very social reality history was meant transparently to display. If the chronicle's narrative matter was not explicitly linked by a syntax of relation, there is no reason to assume that a medieval reader could not have made the necessary connections in his own mind, particularly given the highly canonic nature of the subjects in any historical genre. This is to argue, of course, that narrative parataxis is not invariably a sign of logical incoherence. Because the writer does not explain connections, we need not suppose that the reader could not supply them, any more than we need suppose that the interrelation between iconographic elements of a stained glass window remains necessarily unintelligible to the viewer because they are set off from one another by lead frames.[22] Indeed, a serious investigation of medieval narrative technique from the point of view of pictorial methods of representation might go far towards resolving this problem, but that would require another, quite different, essay.

In conclusion, I would like simply to suggest that genealogy, as a complex of metaphoric structure, narrative "grid," and social context, represents one case, among many possible cases, of the sensitivity of medieval historical narratives to social realities and indicates how medieval chroniclers responded to those realities as well as to the aesthetic conventions of literary tradition. Clifford Geertz long ago proposed that we examine human culture as an assemblage of texts by treating social practices as imaginative works.[23] With all due humility, I would like to register my plea that we read medieval historical texts as cultural phenomena, by returning them to the social context in which they originated and from which they drew both form and meaning. In doing so, we can perhaps begin to appreciate the way in which the literary tradition of history in the Middle Ages was penetrated and modified by social change. For history is, even in the Middle Ages, a literature of fact, and as such its study cannot be isolated from those aspects of social and cultural process about which, in the end, it is the purpose of history to instruct us.

7 The Reditus Regni ad Stirpem Karoli Magni

A New Look

Ci faut le generation du grant Challemaine et decent li roiaume aus hoirs Hue le Grant que l'en nome Chapet . . . Mais puis fu ele recovrée au tens du bon roi Phelippe Dieudoné, car il epousa tout apenséement, pour la lignie le grant Challemaine recovrer, la roine Ysabel qui fu fille le conte Baudoin de Hanaut; . . . Dont l'en puet dire certainement que li vaillanz rois Loys, fiuz le bon roi Phelippe . . . fu du lignage le grant Challemaine, et fu en li recovrée la lignie.[1]

[Here fails the generation of the great Charlemagne and the realm descends to the heirs of Hugh the Great called Capet. . . . But afterwards it was recovered in the time of the good King Philip the Godgiven, because he married, intentionally, in order to recover the lineage of the great Charlemagne, Queen Isabelle, who was the daughter of Count Baldwin of Hainaut. . . . Hence one can say with certainty that the valiant King Louis, son of the good King Philip . . . was of Charlemagne's lineage, and that the line (of Charlemagne) was recovered in him.]

Thus begins the preamble to the Capetian section of the multi-volume history of the kings of France known as the *Grandes Chroniques*. Written by the monks of Saint-Denis in a continuous series from 1274 on, the chronicle attained a quasi-official status due both to its enormous popularity and to the monastery's close connections with the ruling house. Acting simultaneously as an instrument of Capetian propaganda and, in its own right, as the most comprehensive interpreter of French history, the *Grandes Chroniques* served to shape and transmit to the nation at large a dominant image of Capetian kingship and its role in the destinies of France.

A critical aspect of the Dionysian conception of royal history was the belief, enthroned in the preamble to the fifth volume cited above, that the three dynasties[2] to whom the realm had been entrusted were linked by ties of blood, thus providing an example of dynastic continuity enjoyed by no other peoples in Western Christendom. French royal history was, so to speak, a seamless web of legitimate rule.

The historiographical fictions that made this view possible, the political context in which they appeared, and the purposes to which they were put are the subject of this chapter. While it is certainly true, as all commentators on the passage agree, that the idea of the return of the Carolingians to the throne represents "a phenomenon of dynastic thinking of the first order,"[3] it is my belief that the doctrine technically known as the *reditus regni ad stirpem Karoli Magni* was not originally aimed at dynastic legitimation. Rather, it took its impulse from the momentous events occurring during the reign of Philip Augustus and the consequences, both territorial and intellectual, of his stunning conquests. By situating the origins of the *reditus* in this political context, I hope to discover its meaning and function.

The preamble to volume five of the *Grandes Chroniques* is a summary of a much more detailed exposition of Capetian genealogy and the relation of the *troisième race* to their Carolingian predecessors found in volume seven in the introduction to the reign of Louis VIII. Here the recovery of the Carolingian line in the person of Louis VIII, and hence the "return" of the Carolingians to the throne, is treated not only as a matter of dynastic succession but in the broader context of the political events surrounding the *mutatio regni*—the transferral of the crown of France from the house of Charlemagne to the house of Hugh Capet.

The full development of the theme comprises three distinct elements that have been brought together to create the classic form of the *reditus* as it was subsequently known in the Middle Ages. Although this conflation of texts was the work not of the monks themselves but of their sources, for convenience' sake I shall cite it as it appears in the *Grandes Chroniques* and momentarily reserve discussion of the textual tradition.

The chapter begins with an abbreviated genealogy of the kings of France and their descent from the Trojans, already given twice before in the course of the chronicle.[4] Proceeding through the Merovingians, the passage telescopes the Carolingian epoch and broaches the advent of Capetian rule with the following account:

> Laquelle lignie de Pepin et Challemaine son fils regna et tint le royaume jusques à l'an de l'Incarnation IXc et XXVI anz. Lors en ce temps avint que Hue dit Chapet, conte de Paris, envai et prist le royaume de France à soy, et aussi fu transporté la seigneurie du roiaume de France de la lignie des Sesnes; c'est à dire de ceulz de Saissoigne.

> [This line of Pepin and Charlemagne, his son, ruled and held the realm until the year of the Incarnation 926. Then it happened that Hugh called Capet, count of Paris, invaded and took the realm of France for himself, and in this way the lordship of the realm of France was taken away from the lineage of the Saxons, that is, from those of Saxony.]

The chronicle then breaks off the narration of the succession and inserts the well-known story of Saint Valery's prophecy to Hugh Capet of his elevation to the kingship. The author relates that he has read in the deeds of Saints Richer and Valery how their bodies were taken from their churches to the church of Saint-Bertin for safekeeping at the time of the Norse invasions. When, however, the Normans were converted and the monks requested the return of their relics, the monks of Saint-Bertin, aided by the violence of Arnulf, the Carolingian count of Flanders, refused to relinquish them. Saint Valery appeared to Hugh Capet, then count of Paris, to enlist his aid in the recovery of the bodies: "Go to Arnulph, the Count of Flanders, and tell him that he must send back our bodies from the church of Saint-

Bertin to our own churches; for we delight in our places more than in any other." Hugh, obedient to the dictates of God and his saintly messenger, promptly fulfilled Valery's demands. In return, Valery appeared once more to Hugh and prophesied: "Pour ce que tu as fait ce que tu fu commandé de par nous, tost et isnelement, nous te faisons assavoir que tes successeurs regneront le royaume de France jusques à la septième ligniée"[5] (Because you have done what we commanded you to do, each and every thing, we can let you know that your successors will rule the kingdom of France until the seventh line).

Returning to his subject matter, the author announces the accession of Louis VIII as the literal fulfillment of Valery's prophecy and supplies the genealogical evidence to support this contention:

> Selon ce qui est dit et ordoné, nous poons conter entièrement du temps Hue Chapet qui fu filz Hue le grant de Paris jusques au roys Loys, de qui nous traitons, VII generacions et VII degrez descenduz de lignage Hue le Grant conte de Paris. Hue Capet fu le premier roy et engendra le roy Robert . . . [to Louis] . . . qui fu engendré en noble dame Ysabiau fille Baudoin jadis conte de Henaut; lequel Baudoin descendi de noble dame Esmengart jadis contesse de Namur, laquelle fu fille Charle le duc de Lorene oncle Loys le roy de France qui mourut le derrenier de la lignie Charle le grant sans hoir.

> [According to what is said and ordered, we can count in its entirety from the time of Hugh Capet, who was the son of Hugh the great of Paris, until king Louis, of whom we now speak, seven generations and seven degrees descended from the line of Hugh the Great count of Paris. Hugh Capet was the first king and engendered the king Robert . . . (to Louis) . . . who was born of the noble lady Isabelle, daughter of Baldwin the former count of Hainaut; which Baldwin descended from the noble woman Ermengarde, formerly countess of Namur, and she was the daughter of Charles, duke of Lorraine and uncle of Louis the king of France who died as the last of the line of Charles the Great without heir.]

Louis, son of Elizabeth of Hainault, who was descended from Charles of Lorraine through a (fictitious) daughter Ermengart,[6] bore within him the Carolingian seed. No mere Capetian but a "Caro-line," with his succession "il apert donc que l'estat du royaume est re-tourné à la lignée de Challemaine le Grant. Et puet l'en veoir l'avi-sion des II corps saint Richier et Saint Valeri que la translacion du royaume fu faite de la volenté Nostre Seigneur"[7] (it thus appears that the state of the realm has been returned to the line of Charlemagne the Great. And hence one can see in the prophecy of the two bodies of Saint Richer and Saint Valery that the transferral of the realm was done by the will of Our Lord).

The three elements included in the narration are easily separated: (1) the account of Hugh Capet's accession and the displacement of the Carolingians from the throne; (2) the Valerian prophecy; and (3) the Carolingian descent of Louis VIII, which effects the *reditus regni ad stirpem Karoli*. They are artfully combined to convey an impression of divinely directed inevitability, and the total message of the passage clearly heralds the legitimacy of Capetian rule. By letting Valery's prophecy and its fulfillment follow Hugh's usurpation, the blame for this illegitimate action is deflected from Hugh himself. Any last suspicion of usurpation is wholly effaced by the return of the realm to the heir of the very Carolingian from whom Hugh had rapaciously grasped it. The *reditus* thus seemingly performs two vital functions: justification of Capetian rule against the background of its violent beginnings and the elevation of the royal house through proof of its Carolingian heritage.[8]

The textual tradition of the *reditus* has been masterfully worked out by K. F. Werner. The wording of the passage as it appears in the *Grandes Chroniques* shows that the monks are translating the anonymous *Gesta Ludovici Octavi, Franciae Regis*,[9] which in turn derives from chapter 126 of book 31 of Vincent of Beauvais's *Speculum Historiale* (1244).[10] For a long time, historians believed Vincent was the creator of the doctrine, but the fact that he reports the demise of the Carolingians in 926, although in other places he knows better, establishes beyond doubt in Werner's opinion that "this part of the *Speculum Historiale* is not Vincent's own."[11]

Werner has traced the *reditus* back to Andreas of Marchiennes, a

Flemish historian, who wrote at the latest in 1196 his *Historia suc-cincta de gestis et successione regum Francorum*.[12] Since Andreas could not know at this time whether Louis would in fact reign, the *reditus* clause appears in conditional form: "Si iste [sc. Louis] post patrem regnaverit, constat regnum reductum ad progeniem Karoli Magni"[13] (If he [Louis] shall reign after his father, it will constitute the return of the realm to the heirs of Charlemagne). The genealogical refer-ences in the *reditus* text essential to its development can already be found between 1180 and 1184 in the genealogies of Anchin, a neigh-boring monastery of Marchiennes, and Werner has established that Andreas was the author of these genealogies as well.[14]

The Valerian prophecy that appears in all the versions, however, belongs to a much older tradition. It is recounted around 1040 in the *Historia Relationis Corporis S. Walarici*[15] and, in a variant form, in the *Cronica Centulensi sive S. Richarii*, written by the monk Hariulf in 1088.[16] From this time until its incorporation into the *reditus* text, it is continuously cited, notably by Ordericus Vitalis in his *Historia Ecclesiastica*.[17]

The *Historia Relationis* states that the *regnum* shall be given to Hugh's heirs *usque ad septimam generationem* (147) and the *Cronica*, *ad septem successiones* (275). Although a verse narration of the *Relatio-nis* makes clear that the prophecy envisaged only seven generations,[18] Vincent reports that "in some books where we say *septimam*, we find *sempiternam*."[19] The temptation to transform the prophecy's limited delegation of rule into an eternal right may have been strong in Capetian circles and even at the end of the thirteenth century Guil-laume de Nangis simply says, "septimam, id est in perpetuum."[20]

It is quite clear, in any case, that in its original form the prophecy in no way implied the necessity of a Carolingian restoration. It is tan-talizingly silent on the course of post-Capetian history and could, as we shall see, as easily be turned against as towards the legitimation of the *troisième race*. The genius of the *reditus* as a legitimizing fiction, if indeed it was intended as such, is that it combines prophetic and ge-nealogical strains in a way that satisfies many of the most deep-rooted currents of medieval dynastic thinking. It wipes away the stain of usurpation and transports the *mutatio regni* into the realm of God's wondrous workings; and it reinforces the Germanic feeling for blood-right (*Geblütsrecht*) to the throne, according to which the Carolingian claim to rule remained imprescriptable throughout the Middle Ages.[21] In Louis VIII, the Carolingian *stirps* through both his mother, Elizabeth of Hainault, and his father, Philip Augustus,[22] medieval chroniclers found the ideal object for reconciling the actuality of Capetian rule with the imperatives of historical legitimacy.

It should come as no surprise, then, that the *reditus* has been universally interpreted as a device intended to legitimize Capetian possession of the French crown. The literary evidence that it was later employed for this purpose is overwhelming. Nevertheless, this interpretation rests on two assumptions that are open to question. First, it assumes that Capetian kings after nearly two hundred years of rule still needed the support of such fictions to sanction their government; second, that identification with their Carolingian predecessors could be achieved only by means of a full reintegration with the dynasty through bloodlines. Sufficient evidence exists, I think, to cast some doubt on the validity of these assumptions. A brief excursus on these questions is necessary before continuing an analysis of the *reditus*.

The elevation of a non-Carolingian to the crown was not unprecedented in France. Before Hugh Capet, the Robertian dukes of France had temporarily mounted the throne thrice. Nothing suggests that Hugh's election was either planned or recognized as the installation of a new dynasty. Nevertheless, from certain perspectives the change in ruling houses could be considered illegitimate. At Pepin's consecration in 754, Pope Stephen had conveyed the realm to him and his heirs and forbade, under pain of excommunication, the election of any member outside the line.[23] And there persisted, as I have noted, the Germanic sensitivity to kin-right. The advent of the Capetian line in 987 constituted, in this view, a "*prima facie* break with the dynastic principle."[24]

Despite these considerations, there is a surprising absence of polemic directed against the new rulers. Nor are there any signs of actual dynastic strife, although Charles of Lorraine's sons eventually escaped imprisonment and lived on as witnesses to the persistence of the Carolingian line. Almost immediately upon the cessation of the struggle between Hugh Capet and Charles of Lorraine (991), chroniclers and nation alike seemed to accept their new Capetian rulers.[25]

The earliest accounts of the *mutatio regni*, such as Aimoin of Fleury's widely known *De Regibus Francorum*, emphasize the dying out of the direct Carolingian line and Charles's disqualification from rulership because of his marriage, and relegate Hugh to the role of duly elected king for a people destitute of rulers.[26] Odorand of Sens, a monk of Saint-Pierre le Vif and near contemporary to the events of 987, even claimed that Louis V had given Hugh the realm (*donato regno Hugoni Duci*) to govern.[27] This story was later elaborated by Gervais of Tilsbury to include a marriage alliance between Louis's widow, Blanche, and Hugh as the condition for the voluntary transfer of the realm.[28] Such fictions were, in actuality, unnecessary, for Hugh's wife did indeed possess Carolingian blood, a fact already known in the early eleventh century by the monks of Saint-Magloire, who recorded it in their *Translatio Sancti Maglorii*.[29] The marriage of Robert the Pious to Constance of Arles was similarly brought forth to support Capetian legitimist claims, since Constance's mother, Adelaide of Anjou, had as her second husband Louis V. That Constance was the fruit not of this marriage, but of a later one, was conveniently overlooked.[30] In fact, with the exception of Anne of Russia, every Capetian spouse up to Elizabeth of Hainault could aver a connection with Carolingian lines.[31] Official opinion projected the Capetians as legitimate heirs of the Carolingians, referred to them in all their documents, and adopted all their rights.

Naturally this legitimist view did not go unchallenged. The most serious threat came from the cathedral chapter of Sens, whose picture of the end of the Carolingians, in the so-called *Historia Francorum Senonensis*, written between 1015 and 1030, was distorted by error and conscious lies.[32] Here Charles figures as the brother, not uncle of Louis V, and, though unanointed, is said to have succeeded him (*cui successit Karolus, frater eius*).[33] The *Historia* depicts Hugh in open re-bellion against Charles; having failed militarily, he connives with As-celinus, bishop of Laon, to capture Charles and imprison him and, successful at last, seizes the realm. Because of its brevity and dramatic character, the text of the Sens history was widely distributed and be-came the core of a countervailing tradition to Capetian legitimist claims. In this development Werner sees the origins of the *reditus*: "The necessary prerequisite for the appearance and success of a rein-stitution of the Carolingians into their rights was the widely accepted conviction of the illegitimacy of Hugh Capet's accession to the throne."[34] In Werner's view, without the *Historia Francorum Seno-nensis*, the *reditus* would have been impossible, or at least irrelevant. But just as the Capetians were to succeed, through a variety of insti-tutional devices, in overcoming the political disability of their "usurpatious" election, could they not also have succeeded in over-coming a myth created to discredit the legitimacy of their rule? The answer to this question in large part determines any interpretation of the *reditus*.

The mechanisms employed by the Capetians to convert their elec-tive kingship into a hereditary monarchy are well known. Through association of sons in the regnal office, through repeated coronations of the king and his *rex designatus* at solemn assemblies called *curiae coronatae*, through royal consecration itself, Capetian kings fre-quently reminded their *fideles* of the act that conferred on their dy-nasty perpetuity of power.[35] As Marc Bloch perceptively pointed out, respect for an anointed king "did not prevent revolts, but it prevented usurpation." It exercised such an influence that, when "reenforced by an uninterrupted succession of male births . . . it enabled a com-pletely new form of legitimacy to be built on the ruins of the old."[36] Although the struggle waged between the elective and the hereditary principle under the first Capetians should not be underestimated, most historians agree that by the twelfth century, kingship in France was in fact, if not in law, hereditary.[37]

To be sure, hereditary succession to the throne is not necessarily proof of a dynasty's legitimacy. Questions of legitimacy are as much psychological as constitutional, and indices by which to test it are difficult to determine. One model is the case of a royal son *born* to be king.[38] The expectations surrounding the birth of a male heir capable of succeeding and, conversely, the anxieties professed when one is lacking, combined with the reception accorded the royal infant at birth, indicate that a ruling house has won those sentiments of loyalty and devotion that lie at the heart of any government's legitimacy.

The earliest evidence that the Capetians had achieved such a position in France comes from the reign of Louis VII (1137–80) in the *De Glorioso Rege Ludovico, Ludovici Filio*, whose initial chapters have been attributed to Suger.[39] The first three chapters are devoted to a comparison of English, German, and French history from the point of view of succession. Where England and Germany are racked and devastated by succession quarrels, the former because of the dynastic struggle between Stephen and Matilda, the latter because of its dependence on the electoral principle, France enjoys stability and good government. Alone of all three countries, it possesses a legitimate heir:

> Felice se fore tota existimabat patria, eo quod tante sunt reliquie homini pacifico, nobilissimo patri, que ad robustissimam totius regni defensionem nobilissima proles succederet. . . . Que quidem pericula Francorum solatia existebant, cum illi ex defectu hoc [lack of a male heir] sustinerent, Franci vero tante et tam egregie prolis successione congratularentur et congaudent.[40] (147–49)

> [The whole country can consider itself fortunate, in that so great is the peaceful legacy of the most noble father, to whom the most noble heir succeeds for the strong defense of the whole realm. . . . For the French can take solace in the fact that they are not subject to the dangers endured by others, which are produced by this defect (lack of a male heir). Rather, the French can congratulate themselves and rejoice over the succession of so great and such a distinguished heir.]

Even more telling is the evidence relating to the birth of Philip Augustus in 1165. The *De Glorioso Rege Ludovico* explains Louis VII's marriage to Constance, after the divorce from Eleanor of Aquitaine, as due to the "spem successive prolis que post ipsum regnum regeret"

(164) (hope of an heir to succeed, who would govern the realm after him). Constance failed to provide him with a son, so after her death Louis hastily remarried Adele of Champagne:

> preterea timebat ne regnum Francis ab herede qui de semine sue egrederetur gubernari desisteret. Igitur tam saluti sue quam protectioni reipublice in posternum providens, Alam . . . in matrimonium sibi ascivit. (166)

> [for after this he feared lest the realm of France should be left without an heir who came from his own seed to govern it. Therefore, providing as much for his own welfare as for the protection of the realm in the future . . . he took Adele in matrimony.]

And this was done "with the counsel and admonition of the archbishops, bishops and other barons of his realm." Philip, upon his birth, is referred to as the *tam desiderate prolis* (177), and the phrase emerges not only from the flattering pens of the chroniclers, but in Louis's own charter rewarding the messenger Ogier who brought him the happy news of Philip's birth.[41] Rigord reports that Philip was originally called "Dieudonné" (*a Deo datus*) because "his most blessed father King Louis had had many daughters from his three wives" but had not "been able to have a male heir who would succeed him in the [government of the] realm." Only after Louis and Adele, "cum universo clero et populo totius regni" (with all the clergy and people of the whole realm), had prayed to God, were they answered by the birth of this long-awaited male child.[42]

A further indication that already at the time of Philip's birth the Capetians had consolidated their right to rule and that this right went unchallenged is the neglected fact that Louis VII was the first king to date some of his charters from the time of Philip's birth; for example, the act on behalf of Melun dated "Ann. Dom. Inc. 1166, regni nostri Philippi natalis anno 1."[43] The meaning of this chancery formula is that Philip is considered successor-king simply by virtue of birth and does not require the constitutive act of consecration to figure as associate in the reign. Birth alone guaranteed his royal status and, logically, his eventual succession.

Breaking with Capetian precedent, Louis delayed Philip's consecration and association in the kingship until the last possible moment
when, enfeebled and almost totally paralyzed, he found it necessary
to pass on the functions of government to his willing heir.[44] Some
suspicion exists that it was Louis and not, as generally assumed,
Philip Augustus who was, or would have been if circumstances had
permitted, the first to dare not to associate his heir apparent. For
there are some indications that the consecration of 1179 was tantamount to a royal consecration.[45] Philip fully exercised the royal office
and was, it is worth pointing out, the first Capetian to date his regnal
year from the day of his consecration and not from his father's death.
Stories even circulated that Philip had stolen the royal seal and in effect "usurped" the throne, but the evidence is perhaps too vague to
allow any certain conclusions.[46]

The end of association is often related to the doctrine of the *reditus* on the theory that, having restored the Carolingians to the
throne by means of dynastic alliance, the Capetians no longer needed
to secure their right to rule by such practical devices; as true Carolingians they would naturally participate in the perpetual legitimacy endowed upon that house. But if, as I have tried to show, there is strong
evidence to suggest that Capetians had already won recognition for
themselves and their heirs as legitimate rulers of France before the invention of the *reditus* doctrine, then one link in the chain of reasoning that interprets the *reditus* as a legitimizing fiction is seriously
weakened.[47] It remains to be seen whether or not the other mainstay
of this interpretation—the identification of the Capetians with their
Carolingian forebears—had not also been achieved before the rise of
the *reditus*.

Apart from the chronicles dealing with the *mutatio regni* discussed
above, one of the best sources for the conviction of dynastic continuity in the Capetian period comes from the eschatological literature
that flourished in the late tenth century on the eve of the millennium. Although in no way preoccupied with dynastic succession, it
furnished later writers with the materials from which to construct a
kind of metahistory of the kings of France and their role in world

history. With its emphasis on the "great ruler" who would appear in the last days, and the eventual assimilation of this ruler with the "great Charles," it provided a core of the Charlemagne legend that became of increasing political importance in France, reaching its peak in the Charlemagne ethos that pervaded the court of Philip Augustus.

The political ends that apocalyptic speculation could serve is best exemplified by the case of Adso of Montierender. In his *Libellus de Antechristo* (954), a letter written to Queen Gerberga, widow of Louis IV d'Outremer, Adso glosses Paul's second Epistle to the Thessalonians by prophesying that the last king envisaged by Paul before the coming of Antichrist (2 Thess. 2:3) will be a Frank. He will hold the Roman imperium *ex integro* and will himself be the greatest of all kings, who, after having faithfully governed his realm, at the last will come to Jerusalem and on the Mount of Olives will take off his crown and scepter: "This will be the end and consummation of the Roman and Christian imperiums." However, Adso goes on to state, "as long as there exist kings of the Franks, who ought to possess the Roman imperium, the *dignitas* of the Roman Empire will not totally perish, but will survive in them."[48]

At the time of Adso's writing, the expression *rex Francorum* could apply equally to East or West Frankish sovereigns, both heirs of Charlemagne. But by the twelfth century it had become the exclusive name for the king of the West Franks, that is, of France.[49] Thus, later writers tended to interpret Adso's prophecy in a French vein, and this tendency was reinforced by the confusion of Adso's text with that attributed to the Sybille of Tibur, which prophesied that at the end of the world, universal empire would belong to a Greek king named Constant.[50] Already in 1098, an interpolator of Adso had identified the ultimate emperor with a king *cujus nomen erit* C.[51] And it was but a short step, easily made, before "C" came to stand not for the mythical king Constant but Charlemagne himself. The end result of these literary machinations was to locate the prophetic image of Charlemagne in a firmly French context, ripe for political exploitation by Capetian proponents.

By the mid-twelfth century, Otto of Freising reports a prophecy circulating at the time of Louis VII's departure on Crusade (1147), which promised that Louis would triumph over the entire Orient and foresaw that "your L will be turned into a C." According to Otto, this "document was read repeatedly in these days in many parts of Gaul," a fact that Otto attributes to Gallic credulity.[52]

The political context in which Otto's account occurs points to the period of the first Crusades as the background for the revival of earlier speculations and their reapplication to the conquest of Jerusalem. Typically, Charlemagne was set forth as the prototype of the crusading emperor in the legendary "Journey of Charlemagne to Jerusalem," a creation of the monks of Saint-Denis later included in volume three of the *Grandes Chroniques*.[53] It is hardly accidental that these currents should focus on the person of the French king at a time when the French dominated the crusading movement and the moral prestige accruing to Louis VII as the first Western king to take the cross elevated the heretofore localized authority of the Capetians to international importance.

The monks of Saint-Denis further advanced the process of French monopolization of Charlemagne with a false charter (*Dip. Kar.* 286) fabricated in the mid-twelfth century.[54] This forgery explicitly declared that Charlemagne had donated the realm of France to the monastery of Saint-Denis and that henceforth Charles's successors held the realm from God and the monastery alone, a fiction that was eventually to be transformed into law in Louis IX's famous dictum: "Le roi ne tient de nului fors de Dieu et de lui"[55] (The king holds from no one except God and from the abbey).

The special tie between Charlemagne and France implied in the Dionysian forgery was materially symbolized by the identification of the French royal banner—the Oriflamme—which the king of France had received from the monastery of Saint-Denis as its vassal for the Vexin, with Charlemagne's flag, described in the *Chanson de Roland* as an "orie flambe."[56] The royal flag, first taken into battle by Louis VI in 1124, became a corporate symbol for the whole of France at a time when these inchoate sentiments of nationalism could find no other means of expression.[57]

For our purposes the importance of these Dionysian forgeries and mythical symbols was their effect in attaching the memory of Charlemagne to Saint-Denis and, through Saint-Denis, to France. As Van de Kieft concluded in speaking of the false charter 286: "en effet, en parlant en plusieurs reprises des *Franciae reges* et du *regnum Franciae* il avait fait de Charlemagne le patron de la France proprement dit."[58] And this impression was overwhelmingly confirmed in the popular literature of the period, in the chansons de geste, above all by the *Chanson de Roland*. For here Charlemagne was never represented except as "Emperor of France," and in the *Chanson de Roland* the words *France* and *Franceis* were used 170 times to designate Charlemagne's empire.[59] At the same time the word *France* is equally employed in a much more restricted sense for the lands that had made up the ancient Neustria (less Normandy) and Austrasia—that is, for a France roughly commensurate with that of the eleventh and twelfth centuries. As in the case of the title *rex Francorum*, the terminological difficulties of differentiating between what had once been two Frankias but now were France and Germany redounded to the political benefit of the Capetians. In them, the kings of Roland's "douce France," resided the Carolingian genius.

By all indications, public opinion led by the minstrels followed the king and thought of Charlemagne as a king of France rather than as an emperor.[60] The monks and the minstrels had done their work so well that Folz believes that the canonization of Charlemagne in 1165 by Frederick Barbarossa was an attempt to reappropriate the Carolingian legacy for imperial use to counter the thoroughgoing assimilation of the twelfth-century French to the Franks of Charlemagne's day.[61] It is at this point that the cult of Charlemagne becomes important for kingship itself, establishing the images and claims that were to serve as guides to royal policy for the next century and a half.

This climate of thought helps to explain the extraordinary reaction to Louis VII's marriage to Adele of Champagne, whose illustrious descent from Charlemagne was noted in the *Historia Regum Francorum bis 1214*, written during the reign of Philip Augustus.[62]

Though previous Capetian marriages might have served equally well to establish the desired connection between the two houses, it was only with the full blossoming of the Charlemagne cult during the first decades of the twelfth century that the political significance of the dynastic tie was realized. This alone suggests that the primary importance of blood kinship was not for dynastic legitimation but a much broader program of political action. The quest for a Carolingian tie looked not backward to a presumed usurpation in the past, but forward to a new program to be followed by the Capetians in the thirteenth century, a program designed to regain both the territories and the glory of Charlemagne himself.

Philip Augustus's birth by a Carolingian mother was immediately and widely celebrated. Guillaume le Breton repeatedly referred to Philip as a new "Karolide" in whom the virtue of Charlemagne was revived; Giles of Paris, entitling his poem *Carolinus*, proposed Charlemagne as a *speculum principis* for Philip and his son Louis VIII; at the court of Troyes, Bertrand de Born exalted his Champenois patrons by emphasizing Philip's descent from Charlemagne through their house.[63] Even Innocent III, addressing the French clergy in 1204 in the decretal *Novit Ille*, emphasized Philip's illustrious lineage.[64] Naturally, when Louis VIII was born the son of not one but two parents descended from Charlemagne, the proof of Capetian legitimacy through dynastic relation was all the more firmly established. Nevertheless, it remains true that the essential purpose ascribed to the *reditus* fiction—recognition of the claim of the French king to be descended from Charlemagne—had been fulfilled in official and popular circles on the basis of Adele's descent long before the entrance of the *reditus* into Capetian historiography with Vincent of Beauvais in 1244.[65] Only by the insistence on the necessity of a dual line of descent does Elizabeth of Hainault's genealogy become critical for dynastic legitimation, and the precedent of Carolingian legitimation through a single female relation to the Merovingians proves that medieval people did not make such demands.[66]

Furthermore, given the extensive evidence reviewed above that the Capetians had successfully identified themselves with the Carolingians in a variety of ways, it is at least open to question whether or not a blood tie was required to legitimize the succession. In the Middle Ages the idea of personal legitimacy was weak, and the right to rule was established through a variety of ways, not the least of which was royal consecration, which was antidynastic in principle.[67]

Even if we accept the necessity for a blood-right claim to the throne, there is some doubt whether the *reditus* was a wholly effective response to the taint of illegitimacy or the threat, implicit in the Valerian prophecy, that the end of the dynasty was at hand. Louis IX continued the earlier Capetian practice of seeking marriage alliances with Carolingians by marrying his daughter Margaret to John I, duke of Brabant and Lower Lorraine, who is described in a contemporary genealogy of the dukes of Lorraine as he "who is heir of the kingdom of France by hereditary right, as the oldest of the race of Charlemagne."[68] Louis's deathbed statement to his son Philip, reported by Bernard Saisset, revealed the king's conviction that Capetian rule over France was drawing to a close and would end "in te vel in filio tuo et mutabitur ad aliam generationem" (in you or in your son and will be changed to another generation), though he added that if his successors were faithful to the Church the dynasty might survive to the twelfth generation *et ultra* (and beyond).[69] Such fears about and lingering aspersions on the legitimate status of the Capetian house could not be set to rest by Philip's Carolingian paternity either, but they do suggest that from a purely dynastic point of view, the *reditus* might have been of limited value.

If, then, the fundamental aims attributed to the *reditus* had either been achieved or proven unnecessary, if the practical legitimacy of the Capetian accession dates, at the latest, from the end of the reign of Louis VII, and their dynastic and ideational connection with Charlemagne and his heirs expresses itself with progressively mounting vigor from the beginning of the twelfth century on, what role did the *reditus* play in Capetian history and what explains its central position in the main current of Capetian historiography canalized by the *Grandes Chroniques* of Saint-Denis? The answer lies, half-hidden, in the specific character of the Charlemagne cult that virtually gripped the court of Philip Augustus and in the political aspirations of that prince, who saw in the Carolingian legacy a political program and the possibility of realizing it.

That Philip Augustus was moved, almost to the point of obsession, by the memory of Charlemagne is agreed upon by all historians of this complex and compelling king. He gave one illegitimate child the name Pierre Carlotis and took for himself the title Augustus, in both acts proclaiming his fidelity to the glorious past of the great emperor and, it seems, his dedication to seeking in that past the pattern of the future. For as Petit-Dutaillis noted, the "positive and practical spirit of Philip Augustus was not proof against a mirage-vision of a world-empire."[70] Gerald of Wales relates a probably apocryphal but nevertheless instructive tale of Philip. A group of barons spied Philip dreaming and upon asking his thoughts received the answer, "whether at any time God might grant to me, or another King of France, the glory of restoring to the realm of France the ancient breadth and greatness that it had at the time of Charles."[71] In a not dissimilar vein, the author of the *Historia Regum ab Origine Gentes ad annum 1214*, written during Philip's reign, says Philip "judged one man sufficient for the government of the whole world," while Rigord reveals Philip solicitous *de augmento et amplificatione regni*.[72]

Philip, moreover, seemed consciously to pattern his actions on models drawn from the life of Charlemagne. Philip's speech to the troops before the battle of Bouvines recalled to the knights that they were the descendants of the Trojans and "heirs of the powerful Charles, of Roland and the brave Oliver," and, like Charlemagne at Roncevaux, he blessed his army, assuring them they fought in the service of the faith. Guillaume le Breton celebrated the revival of Charlemagne's "virtue" in Philip and described the battle of Bouvines, fought under the banner of the Oriflamme, as a renewal of Charles's victory over the Saxons.[73]

While these chronicle accounts perhaps should not be given too much weight, the intrusion of such fantasies into official documents signals that the cult of Charlemagne has passed from the level of poetry to that of politics. Philip's third register, redacted in 1220 and known as the *Registrum Guarini* after the bishop of Senlis who was head of Philip's chancery, attempted to compile methodically the documents on which the rights of the crown were founded.[74] At the end of the volume, the chancery clerk Stephen of Gallardon was ordered—at Philip's behest?—to add a Provincial that would list the names of all the popes and the Roman emperors who had reigned since Saint Peter. The Provincial included a catalogue of the kings of France beginning with Pharamond, France's putative first ruler, and ending with Philip himself, whose entry, unlike those preceding, which merely gave the name and the length of reign, contained a long description of the battle of Bouvines. Immediately following the Provincial, at folio 309, comes a document written in Stephen's hand, which contains a text of the Sybilline prophecy that, as we have seen, had circulated in France during the reign of Louis VII. The register's version reads: "in diebus illis Cesari Auguste erit celebre nomen et regnabit in Roma et subiciet terram sibi" (in those days the name of Caesar Augustus will be renowned and he will reign in Rome and subject the world to him) and continues with the assertion, originally part of a later interpolation, that "post hoc surget salicus rex de Francia per K. nomine. . . . Similis autem imperio Romano ante eum rex non fuit nec post eum futuris erit" (after this there will rise up a Salic king of France by the name of K. . . . A comparable king in the Roman Empire there never was before him, nor will there be in the future after him). This text, strangely, is followed by the prophecy of Saint Valery to Hugh Capet revealing the advent of Capetian rule *usque ad septem successiones.*[75] Delaborde explains the insertion of the Valerian prophecy as a reference to the fact that in Louis VIII the crown will return to the Carolingian line. But as we know, the Valerian prophecy itself made no such allusions to a Carolingian restoration, and the doctrine of the *reditus* did not become a part of Capetian mythology until the middle of the thirteenth century with Vincent of Beauvais.[76]

What, then, is the meaning of these two prophecies in an official royal register? Though technically wrong, Delaborde was, I believe, essentially correct in attempting to relate these passages to the tradition of the *reditus*. The Sybilline's reference to a "rex de Frankia per K. nomine" at this time would have been universally interpreted as Charlemagne, and its juxtaposition with the Valerian prophecy implied rather than stated a return to the realm of the great Charles, in one form or another. In this sense, the Register attempted to do, in a clumsy fashion, what was more elegantly and economically performed by the *reditus*. The possibility of seeing this early prefiguration of the doctrine, which would attain its definitive form in the reigns of Philip III and Philip IV, during the reign of Philip Augustus suggests the clue to the meaning and function of the *reditus*. Just as the overriding political concerns of these later Philips was to be with consolidating and building upon the political successes of their namesake, so equally the literary problem of political legitimation would be solved under their aegis by the *reditus* fiction. The context in which the Register employs the prophecies, however obscurely, permits us to explore the probable role assigned the *reditus* in Capetian historiography.

Significantly, the passage relating to Philip in the Register is concerned not with dynastic succession but with territorial conquest, more specifically with Philip's acquisition of the Plantagenets' Continental holdings, especially Normandy, and the final confirmation of this conquest with the triumph over the English and German forces at Bouvines. The identification of Philip with Charlemagne through the use of the prophecies following the account of Bouvines in the Register might, thus, have been intended to legitimize the king's spectacular acquisition of territories from his English vassal—an acquisition vastly expanding the size of the royal domain—and to reaffirm all the rights and privileges which that conquest had brought the crown.

Furthermore, the French at Bouvines not only triumphed over a rebellious vassal but achieved the defeat of an emperor. Just as Louis VI's successful stand in 1124 against both Henry V and Henry I of England had led Suger to see in that moment "the most striking exploit France accomplished in modern or ancient times," so, once again, the simultaneous defeat of an English king and a Roman emperor quickened French national pride and elevated a feudal incident to the level of an international conflict.[77] This treatment of Bouvines, with its implied reference to Charlemagne, thus tended to promote an imperial view of the French king as well as to justify Capetian territorial "imperialism." As a French response to the German myth of the *translatio imperii*, it was an excellent counterpoise to the German canonization of Charlemagne in 1165, itself an answer to the Capetian projection of a French Charlemagne. It gives added significance to the juxtaposition of the Sybilline text and the Valerian prophecy without at the same time losing sight of the more specific reference to Philip's conquests. For the desire to set these conquests within a framework of inherited Carolingian claims is entirely consistent with the imperial aspirations attributed to Philip by the chroniclers, aspirations that encompassed both territorial expansion and the assertion of French sovereignty in the face of the empire's presumed hegemony.

It might be argued that Philip's conquest of Plantagenet lands stood no more in need of legitimation than his possession of the crown. The acquisition of Plantagenet territory was undertaken as a legal penalty for John's failure to appear before the king's court when summoned, and Philip was consistently careful to underline the legal basis of his action. Yet it is hard to believe that Philip's wars were generally understood in this light. Innocent III, in *Novit Ille*, sought to judge Philip *ratione peccati* (by reason of sin) for his continued prosecution of the war against John,[78] and while Innocent eventually accepted the French position, others did not. Stephen Langton, in a commentary on the just war that cannot be dated but which, according to John Baldwin, obviously referred "to the aggression of King Philip Augustus against the Plantagenet holdings in France, or even perhaps to the conquest of Normandy," described a situation in which "rex Francie habet iniustum bellum cum rege Anglie"[79] (the king of France engaged in an unjust war with the king of England). Even on the French side, there was uneasiness over Philip's territorial ambitions for France. Rigord, in *Short Chronicle,* now surviving only in fragments, discusses the two senses in which the word *France* might be understood—narrowly, as those lands between the Rhine, Meuse, and Loire; broadly, as the territory formerly inhabited by the Franks—and concludes that "propter insolentiam regum Francorum, nec tamen terram istam quam Franciam vocant juribus suis integrum habere merentur. Execavit enim illos pestis ambitionis et avaricie et quasi in reprobum sensum traditi non faciunt ea que conveniunt"[80] (because of their insolence the kings of France did not deserve to hold that land which they call France together with all its rights. For they were eaten up by a curse of ambition and avarice as if an evil sense had been passed down and they did not behave as was fitting), and this before the conquest that was nearly to double the size of Capetian holdings. It was Rigord, we might remember, who first gave Philip the title Augustus as that "which it was customary to give to Caesars who augmented the state, from *augere auges*"[81] on the basis of Philip's acquisition of Vermandois alone. Surely there was no precedent for the permanent confiscation of such vast feudal holdings for simple failure to answer a summons to the lord's court. Chroniclers insistently spoke of Philip's confiscations as conquests, and Guillaume le Breton described his return to Paris from Bouvines in terms borrowed from the triumphal entries of Roman emperors.[82] Throughout the Middle Ages the most common surname given Philip Augustus was "the Conqueror."

The need to legitimize the Capetian conquests, thus, is probable, though it cannot be definitely proved. It does help to explain the strange presence of prophetic texts in a Register concerned with royal rights and privileges. But legitimation of past deeds was not the only function that such fictions could perform, for this was a society in which, as Strayer noted, "every deliberate modification of an existing type of activity must be based on a study of individual precedents. Every plan for the future is dependent on a pattern which has been found in the past."[83] Whoever subscribed to the cult of Charlemagne also received a political program for the future. In this sense, the proper political context of the *reditus* is the reigns of Philip III and Philip IV and the program of territorial expansion (in which might even be included the Aragonese Crusade) pursued by those kings and their successors.

The political potential of the Carolingian legacy is apparent already in Guillaume le Breton, who, in the conclusion to his *Philippide*, exhorted Louis VIII to continue his father's work by extending the realm to the Pyrenees, where "Charlemagne had set up his tents," and to

> Dilatare tuos fines huc usque teneris
> Jus patrum et teneas nullo mediante tuorum
> Possideatque nihil in finibus advena nostris.
>> (Bk. 12, v. 8826 sq., p. 380)

> [Extend your borders until you will hold
> your rightful patrimony and you shall hold with nothing
>> between you and yours
> And the stranger shall possess nothing within
>> our boundaries.]

The program of territorial expansion that the Capetians were to pursue under Philip III and Philip IV and the remainder of their rule rested ultimately on the kin-right identification with the Carolingians, in which was included the claim to the empire of Charlemagne. For this purpose, a closer connection with the imperial Charlemagne was required than that afforded by the chansons de geste and related texts of the eleventh and twelfth centuries. Here, precisely, lay the value of the *reditus*. The troubadours had fixed the image of Charlemagne as "the King of France" and in the process had tended to neglect Charlemagne's imperial status. While this perspective continued to be useful in extricating France from the framework of universal empire,[84] it made difficult the assertion of claims over territories that clearly had not been part of the ancient *regnum Francie* in the narrow sense. The principal object of French foreign policy in the last Capetian century—the "recovery" of Lorraine—could not be subsumed among the rights inherited from a merely French Charles. The *reditus* doctrine, by describing a full Carolingian restoration rather than a simple blood tie to the heirs of Charlemagne, emphasized the revival of French imperial status; it signified, in effect, the return of the realm not *ad Karoli Magni Regis Francorum* but *ad Karoli Magni Imperatoris*. It legitimized the Capetian conquest in the most complete fashion and, at the same time, opened up new roles to be played out by these Carolingian *stirps* on a European stage. In a sense, it endowed the Capetians with a new identity—articulated in the title Rex-Imperator—an identity that was subject to shifting interpretation but which was to be a decisive factor in shaping French goals, internal and external, in the centuries to come.

It would be wrong to conclude from this analysis that Philip Augustus and his heirs wished to transform France itself into the former Carolingian imperium. Capetian policy remained firmly directed towards the realization of the possibilities inherent in their status as French kings. Nevertheless, the rights and privileges suggested by the hyphenated identity Rex-Imperator were politically useful in a variety of ways. On the one hand, it made possible an equiparation of France and the empire which enabled Capetian kings to insist on their independent, and ultimately sovereign, status among the rulers of Latin Christendom. Further, it suggested a kind of authority not encompassed by feudal kingship but which, with the aid of revived Roman law, could be elaborated to validate new kinds of royal powers, not the least of which was the right to taxation. Finally, we should not ignore the reality of Capetian imperial aspirations, which were periodically expressed, if always unsuccessfully, in French candidacies for the emperorship, attempts to seize the office that persisted down to Louis XIV.[85] From Philip Augustus on, these strands were increasingly woven into the fabric of French policy and, though temporarily deflected in the reign of Louis IX onto the person of Charles of Anjou,[86] reemerged in the fourteenth century as central concerns of the monarchy.

The important role of the *reditus* in guiding and legitimizing these developments is clarified by its central position, literally and ideologically, in the *Grandes Chroniques* of Saint-Denis. Its position in the history also establishes its meaning. The preamble to the Capetian section immediately follows an account of the *mutatio regni* borrowed without change from the *Historia Francorum Senonensis*, an account which, we have seen, was highly prejudicial to the legitimate status of the Capetian accession. Significantly the preamble, like the narration of Hugh's reign that succeeds it, fails to repeat the Valerian prophecy as a mitigating circumstance, justifying the change in ruling houses as a consequence of Carolingian injustice rather than Capetian aggression. The prophecy and its attendant explanations are deferred until the introduction to Louis VIII's reign, despite the fact that many of the sources employed by the monks of Saint-Denis reported the prophecy as part of the events of Hugh Capet's reign, where, logically, it belonged. This failure suggests, in the strongest possible manner, that the chroniclers were not concerned with glossing Hugh's "usurpation" by means of the *reditus*. The opportunity was twice offered and twice declined. Such an omission permits us to infer that, at least as far as the chroniclers of Saint-Denis were concerned, the *reditus* was not primarily aimed at dynastic legitimation.

The position of the *reditus* in the introduction to the reign of Louis VIII, on the other hand, equally suggests its function in consolidating the new stature achieved by France under Philip Augustus because of his conquests. What better way to glorify this outstanding king than to describe his deeds as a revival of Charlemagne's imperial genius, and what better way to ensure recognition of his newly acquired territories and privileges than by referring them to inherited rights? At Philip's death, France might indeed have seemed to rival its former Carolingian glory. In Louis VIII, by some strange working of fate, the Capetians were to produce a son who could in fact claim dual Carolingian descent and thereby corroborate the already formed conviction that France had returned to its Carolingian heritage.

It is significant that Louis VIII was the first to add the name Charles to those given to royal heirs and that this new Charles was to live with the image of the great Charles always before him, urging him on to new adventures. Louis VIII's brief reign was the link between the struggling early days of the Capetian dynasty and the brilliant reign of Louis IX, in whom the religious and sovereign character of Charlemagne's Teutonic monarchy would find its most perfect expression. The *reditus*, by assigning to Louis VIII the role of transmitter of past greatness, seminally imparted to future generations, expressed the chroniclers' belief that the *troisième race* was fulfilling the destinies that history dictated for it and doing so in the only manner acceptable to the historical mentality of the Middle Ages—by taking its impulse from the past and converting that past into a program for the future. The teleology implicit in this conception of history required the fabrication of fictions like the *reditus* which could bind present to past and future within a fundamentally prophetic framework of analyzing history. That such fictions could at the same time address themselves to the most exacting details of contemporary political life is one aspect of the genius of medieval historiography in general and of the chronicles of Saint-Denis in particular.

The *reditus*, once firmly ensconced in the heart of the *Grandes Chroniques*, became a keystone for a whole structure of Capetian history, legitimizing the dynasty, its activities, and its aspirations by grounding them in a remote past that held unshakable sway over men's minds. Nor should it surprise us that the impulse to the creation of the doctrine derived from the immediate preoccupation of the chroniclers with new patterns of political behavior emerging in France at the turn of the twelfth and thirteenth centuries under the leadership of Philip Augustus.

It would be interesting to speculate what role the *reditus* played in developing the national consciousness of thirteenth- and fourteenth-century France. Certainly, the attempt to make French royal history a "seamless web" must have strengthened tendencies, already present in the chansons de geste, to consider France and Frenchmen as entities distinct from other national groupings. By attaching the Capetians to Charlemagne and his heirs, the *reditus* suggested a new view of the ruling house that inherently denied imperial hegemony and thus furthered the divergent development, centuries in the making, of the two Frankias into France and Germany. And in the emphasis of the *reditus* on the special relation between Charlemagne and those territories which, as Guillaume de Montlauzon was to put it, had made up his "special patrimony, *quod erat regnum Francie,*"[87] would it be too much to see the beginnings of a new territorial conception of the French state, based on the growing territorial acquisitions originating with Philip Augustus and continuing to and beyond the end of Capetian rule?

The answers to these questions do not lie within the scope of this chapter, but any consideration of the meaning and function of the *reditus*, and of the *Grandes Chroniques* as a whole, must ultimately attempt to solve them. What does seem clear from the study of the *reditus* undertaken here is that the interpretation of such fictions must take into account not only the literary traditions that went into their creation, but the specific political context in which they appear and the functional relationship they bear to the ongoing processes of political life. Looked at from this perspective, the *reditus* seems to be directed not so much at dynastic legitimation as at the legitimation of Capetian conquests and the emergence of new modes of political activity associated with the title *Rex-Imperator*. It used the past, with all its mythic qualities, to clarify behavior that was as yet barely discernible in the present and that certainly did not belong to a remote age gone by. In doing so, it redefined the intellectual framework by which events could be understood and evaluated, legitimized and accepted.

8
The Cult of Saint Denis and Capetian Kingship

Bernard Guenée noted recently that the emerging states of western Europe invoked God as their patron less frequently than their own national saints.[1] While God might be seen as favoring certain lands at particular times, He could not be monopolized. The inherent universalism of Christian religious thought potentially militated against the growth of national feeling. To find unfailing support for national causes, the peoples of Europe turned instead to local saints. In Guenée's opinion, the first stirrings of national sentiment among the young states of Europe are expressed, strengthened, and given specific content through the choice of a protective saint whose special responsibility is to oversee the destinies of his people and to preserve the realm from threat. In particular, Guenée called attention to the status of Saint Denis as the principal protector of the French realm under the Capetians. Yet the interaction between the cult of the saint and the development of the Capetian monarchy has never been fully explored.

Throughout its history, the monastery of Saint-Denis sought to establish a tie to the ruling house, to make the abbey indispensable to the crown as the chief and privileged guardian of the royal presence. But beyond that, as the home of the principal apostle of Gaul and the first bishop of Paris, the abbey had a symbolic importance for the whole of France, independent of the monarchy itself. This chapter will attempt to investigate the growth of the cult of Saint Denis, its progressive alliance with the monarchy, and the possible function of the cult within the context of French royal and, ultimately, national history.

Although the material for a full history of the cult is not yet available, what we do know is highly suggestive. If a firm determination of the role of Saint Denis in Capetian history must await the completed study of his cult, an indication of its probable meaning can at least be proposed. While the conclusions drawn at the end of this chapter are for the present hypothetical, they nevertheless seem warranted by the abbey's writings. It is hoped they will have some value for the history of the role of political and national saints in the development of western European states that remains to be written.

The earliest writings relating to Saint Denis date from the end of the fifth century. As far as can be gleaned from the confusion and complexity of the early texts, it appears that the historical Denis was one of seven bishops sent from Rome in the third century to preside over the cities of Gaul. Saint Denis was sent to Paris and became its first bishop. According to Gregory of Tours, he was beheaded during the persecution that occurred under Decius and Gratus, receiving his martyrdom in 251.[2] In conformity to Roman custom, he was executed outside Paris, in all likelihood in the Roman village of Catulacum, now identified as the present village of Saint-Denis.[3] Apart from these salient facts, early histories of the saint supply little authentic information concerning his mission or his martyrdom.

The oldest extant life of Saint Denis, the *Passio sanctorum martyrum Dionysii episcopi, Rustici et Eleutherii*, written at the end of the fifth century at the monastery of Saint-Denis, already sets forth the primary elements out of which the legend of the saint was fashioned. According to the *Passio*, Saint Denis came to France in the first, not the third, century at the instance of Pope Clement I. The *Passio* thus establishes the apostolicity of his mission and, by implication, of Parisian faith. At the same time, the *Passio* provides Denis with two companions, Rusticus and Eleutherius, who share his martyrdom. After their execution, the *Passio* records, a certain pagan woman stole the holy bodies from their Roman persecutors and buried them in a field that she had prepared for sowing. With the passing of the persecution that claimed the saints' lives, a tomb commemorating the martyrs was built, later enhanced by the construction of a basilica.[4] Although the *Passio* does not name this woman, later texts designate her as Catulla, out of evident confusion with the site of the tomb. These additions to the saint's life are already incorporated into the *Vita Genovefae*, composed circa 520, which goes on to describe the church built by Sainte Geneviève in honor of the holy martyrs, and the miracles associated with its construction.[5]

The most important additions to the legend, however, appear in the ninth-century writings of Hilduin and Hincmar, which fix the history of the saint in the form in which it continued to be known for the rest of the Middle Ages. While Hilduin's primary purpose was to confirm the apostolic date of Saint Denis's mission, and hence of the monastery's origin, he also embellished the legend with a series of details that evolved into its most distinctive characteristics and added charm and persuasiveness to his fabrications.

As related by Hilduin,[6] the legend stated that Saint Denis had been born in a suburb of Athens called Areopagus, hence the toponym Areopagite. He was converted to Christianity by Saint Paul, who baptized him and instructed him in Christian doctrine and later appointed him bishop of Athens. Upon learning that Paul had been imprisoned by Nero, Denis hastened to Rome but arrived too late to help his friend or share his fate. Instead, Pope Clement commissioned him as apostle to Gaul. Arriving in Gaul, Denis established a church at Arles and then journeyed north to Paris. Although Hilduin does not explicitly say that Rusticus and Eleutherius accompanied him, they appear later in the account of proselytizing activities in the environs of Paris.[7]

Among Denis's converts was a nobleman, Lisbius, who offered the saint his house and land adjacent to it on which to build a church. There Denis established a community dedicated to propagating the word of God, which served as a center for missionary efforts in the region of Paris. The success of his efforts aroused the envy of the Devil, who directed neighboring pagans against him and, more important, the ire of the Roman authorities. In the general persecution ordered by Domitian, Saint Denis and his companions were made the object of a special attack led by the provost Sisinnius as agent for Domitian. Arrested by Sisinnius, Denis was commanded to abjure his faith; when he refused he was tortured and cast into prison. Dionysian writings portray the saint's steadfastness in the face of innumerable tortures, which were commemorated in the twelfth century by the chapel of Saint-Denis-du-Pas, located just behind the chevet of the cathedral Notre-Dame de Paris.[8]

The night before the execution, Christ appeared outside the cell window and administered mass to the martyr and his holy companions. The next morning they were led to the top of Montmartre and executed. It is Hilduin who first mentions Montmartre as the site of the decapitation, explaining that it formerly had been called Mons Mercurii but now takes the name of Mons Martyrum from the popular memory of their passion.[9] There then occurred the famous miracle with which Saint Denis is so particularly associated. No sooner had the severed head dropped to the ground than Saint Denis reached down, picked it up, and, accompanied by a host of angels and singing God's praises, walked five miles to his chosen burial place, the site of the present church dedicated to him.[10] Like so many other elements, the introduction of this miracle is the work of Hilduin and rests, as Levillain has shown,[11] on a misreading of a passage in the *Passio*.[12] Despite this, it became the most dramatic and best-known episode in the saint's life.

An important debate arose several centuries later concerning whether the head of Saint Denis had been cut off whole at the neck or had received an additional blow, severing the top of the cranium. In the twelfth century, Rigord reports that the canons of Notre-Dame claimed to possess this partial relic as a gift from Philip Augustus.[13] The monks, for their part, insisted that they retained the head intact, and the matter so threatened the abbey that it decided to exhibit the head separately for a year in refutation of the Parisian rumors.[14] In addition to describing this event, Rigord offered the supporting testimony of Haimo, whose *Detectio corporum marcharii Areopagitae Dionysii* had been written in 1053 on the occasion of an opening of the saint's tomb.[15] At that time, the monks were defending their possession of Denis's relics against the pretensions of the monks of Regensburg, who claimed to have discovered the saint's body under their church. The invention of Saint Denis similarly uncovered the saint's relics intact.[16] Debate over the fate of this capital relic persisted well into the fifteenth century. In 1410 the case appeared before the Parlement of Paris. The proceedings of the trial have survived but do not reveal the outcome.[17] Popular legends of the fifteenth century indicate, however, that many sided with the canons, believing the relic to be in the possession of Notre-Dame.[18] Even then, the monks felt it necessary to oppose such notions.

To Hilduin, too, is due the identification of Saint Denis as Dionysius the Areopagite. In seeking to strengthen the theory of Saint Denis's apostolicity, he found it highly convenient to confuse him with the author of the famous writings attributed to the Areopagite, a Greek manuscript of which had, in fact, just been sent to Louis the Pious in 827 by the Byzantine emperor Michael the Stammerer. When, in 835, Louis commissioned Hilduin to write a life of Denis, he requested him to base his account on all available Greek and Latin sources.[19] Included among them were the Areopagite's writings, and Hilduin devoted several chapters of his work to summarizing their contents. The identification of Saint Denis as their author became, like the miracle of the decapitation, a primary and characteristic part of the legend henceforth, contributing greatly to the fame and prestige of the abbey.

The historical sleight of hand involved in this identification was discovered by none other than Abelard, during his stay at the abbey after his mutilation. For as he tells us in the *Historia calamitatum*, he "happened one day across a statement of Bede's in his *Commentaries* on the Acts of the Apostles in which he said that Dionysius the Areopagite was bishop of Corinth, not of Athens." True to form,

Abelard did not tactfully refrain from pointing out this contradiction to the monastery's claim that its Dionysius was the Areopagite. In response, the monks threatened to turn him over to the king, who, they believed, Abelard says, "would wreak vengeance upon me as one who would take from him the glory and crown of his kingdom."[20] Rather than face such consequences, Abelard fled in the middle of the night to the neighboring county of Champagne, placing himself under the protection of Count Thibaut.

That the doubts raised by Abelard did not disappear can be seen from a letter of Innocent III in 1216. While ostensibly declining to determine whether the body of the blessed Dionysius resting at the monastery was that of the Areopagite, "qui mortuus fuit in Graecia," or another's, Innocent nevertheless promised to send "true relics" of the Areopagite's body so that, in having both, the monastery would necessarily have the authentic one.[21] Despite these lingering suspicions, only Abelard seems to have questioned seriously Hilduin's theory of Areopagitism, and even Abelard later retracted in a letter to Abbot Adam.

But such troublous questions arose only later. In the meantime, a local cult of the saint soon flourished. The *Passio* already speaks rather vaguely of a church elevated by the faithful gathered around the primitive tomb of the saint shortly after his martyrdom, suggesting that a shrine for Saint Denis existed possibly as early as the fourth century.[22] The first clear evidence of a church constructed to serve the needs of a religious community comes from the *Vita Genevofae*, which records the foundation of a basilica by Sainte Geneviève some time around 475. The earliest miracles appear in connection with the building of Geneviève's church, and they refer to the cult of Saint Denis as an established fact.[23] In the sixth century, Gregory of Tours speaks of *custodes*, or guardians of the cult, who are attached to a basilica, that is, a church containing relics, as distinct from an *ecclesia*, or place of liturgical assembly. The cult, while still local, was steadily gaining prominence, and Gregory recounts two miracles relating to the saint's capacity for protecting his tomb from attack.[24] At this time the objects of veneration were the relics of Saint Denis alone; the relics of his companions Rusticus and Eleutherius were added only in the seventh century, when a special chapel to house them was built.[25] The fame of the saints and the growth of their cult was sufficient by the seventh century to attract larger and larger numbers of pilgrims to an annual celebration of Denis's feast on October 9. The grant of the Fair of Saint Denis by Dagobert in 630 or 636, the first royal concession of its kind, testifies to the growth of the cult in Merovingian France and the increasing homage paid to the saint.

The greatest infusion to the treasury of Dionysian miracles resulted from the ninth-century work of Hincmar. In his *Gesta Dagoberti I regis Francorum*, Hincmar not only recorded with almost obsessive concern the marks of favor conferred upon the monastery by this magnanimous prince, he also elaborated a series of miracles involving saint and monarch that added a significantly new dimension to the legend of Saint Denis. In addition, it was Hincmar who compiled the *Miracula sancti Dionysii*, which detailed in one convenient place the saint's miraculous acts beyond those already set forth in the history of Dagobert's reign.[26] The miracles described by Hincmar in the *Gesta Dagoberti* serve to explain Dagobert's extraordinary devotion to the monastery of Saint-Denis, which subsequently expressed itself in the series of privileges and donations given to the abbey recounted at the end of the *Gesta*. At the same time, they establish the saint's protective capacity over all those who seek his aid in times of stress. In this, Hincmar struck a theme that was to resound throughout the rest of Dionysian literature.

Two miracles reported by Hincmar exemplify this point. In chapters 2–4, Hincmar relates how the young prince Dagobert chased a serf who, in seeking to escape the pursuing dogs, took refuge in the little household sheltering the relics of the holy martyrs, which Hincmar describes as that constructed by Catulla. The dogs, having followed the serf to the spot, were unable to enter the shrine, as if restrained by a supernatural force, although the door was open. When the news of this miracle reached Dagobert, he greatly wondered at it, and according to Hincmar, this incident marks the beginning of Dagobert's special love and devotion for the holy martyrs.[27]

A short time afterwards, as Hincmar explains in chapters 6–11, Dagobert himself had occasion to seek the saint's protection. In order to avenge an affront that the governor Sadrigesilus, duke of Aquitaine, had inflicted upon him, Dagobert had the duke whipped by his servants and shaved his beard. Clothar, informed of this attack, ordered his son's arrest, and Dagobert, to escape his father's vengeance, took refuge in the house sheltering the martyrs' bodies. Although Clothar dispatched his sergeants to pursue the fugitive, they, too, like the dogs, were prevented from entering the shrine. In the meantime Dagobert fell asleep and saw in a marvelous dream a vision of the three saints whose abode he had entered. One, clearly Saint Denis himself, stepped forward and promised their support in all circumstances, if Dagobert in return promised to honor their memory by refurbishing their tombs.[28] Once king, Dagobert kept his promise, exhumed the bodies and founded nearby another church which he adorned with great beauty.[29] After describing the translation of the saints' relics to their new church, Hincmar continues with an account of the miracles performed by Saint Denis as evidence of his unfailing efficacy and concern towards those devoted to him.[30]

The two miracles clearly aim at providing a fabulous background to explain and make plausible the history of the translation and the new foundation of the abbey church that Hincmar actually invented. Despite this pragmatic purpose, they also constituted a dramatic episode in the saint's legend and signaled his protective alliance with a Frankish monarch. In this, Hincmar brought to the fore a theme that had only been briefly suggested before and gave it a central place in subsequent Dionysian tradition. More immediately, he promoted the cult of the saint by showing his concern for the lowliest as well as most exalted among his followers. By means of Hincmar's works, Saint Denis's fame grew steadily and the monastery increasingly became a center of pilgrimage in northern France.[31]

In all this, there is nothing particularly to differentiate the cult of Saint Denis from a number of others in France. Every saint exercised miraculous powers on behalf of his devotees, and by the ninth century most had well-developed local traditions that recounted their beneficent actions and exalted their religious utility. Even the story of the "cephalorie"—the saint's decapitation and miraculous journey—which we associate especially with Saint Denis, is attributed to at least four other local saints of France and probably stems from the early custom of representing a beheaded martyr holding his head in his hands.[32] What does distinguish the cult of Saint Denis is the saint's subsequent elevation as a national saint of France and, more specifically, the patron saint of the monarchy.

To a certain extent Saint Denis's position as the first bishop of Paris and the principal apostle to Gaul logically entailed a special degree of veneration. Nevertheless, it remains true that Saint Denis's position as the patron saint of the monarchy was not a foregone or necessary conclusion. In every age, under each successive dynasty, the monks of the abbey consciously sought to present its saint as the special guardian of French kings, in whose hands lay the fate of the nation.

There were, roughly speaking, two types of documents and two stages in which the monks of Saint-Denis promoted their special relationship to the throne. One was by means of false charters, common until the twelfth century, which were designed to support legal claims to territories, restore lost or precariously held economic privileges, and authenticate relics. Saint-Denis was not alone in this practice, although the extent of the monks' efforts and the enormity of their claims do set it apart somewhat. In such charters, assertions concerning a special bond between the abbey and the king were set forth in a sense incidentally, as cause for the confirmation of territorial, legal, or religious privileges. The other, more broadly based type of document relied instead on the persuasion of historical propaganda. The thrust of the entire magnificent historiographical tradition of the monastery of Saint-Denis was to establish the interpenetration of the history of the monarchy and the history of the abbey, each conducted under the aegis of the blessed martyr. While this type of document dates from as early as the ninth century, its chief works begin in the twelfth.

Taking the latter first, I think it clear, in terms of the historiographical traditions of the monastery, that the monks sought, from the twelfth century on, to present Saint Denis as the supreme patron of the royal house by consistently underlining his protective role in all circumstances when Capetain kings found themselves in danger. The theme is so pervasive that it functions almost as an organizing principle of the monastery's vast historical works, both Latin chronicles and the vernacular *Grandes Chroniques*. But in addition to these texts dealing with the history of the monarchy as such, the monks also recorded the life of the saint. And in these smaller works, the tie between the monastery and the king, their bond under the saint's patronage, and the numerous occasions on which his miraculous intervention had been exercised for their mutual benefit was made clearer still.

There are three distinct groups of works emanating from Saint-Denis which deal with the saint's life. The first, and least important from our perspective, consists of mere hagiographical collections, or legendaries, in which the life of Saint Denis is treated among many others. Although these collections retain the distinctive features of the saint's legend, they contribute only incidentally to the historical theme of his actions in support of the monarchy. They are important only peripherally as a source for other works, supplying details in the saint's history. A second group is composed of illuminated manuscripts, intended as picture books, which tell the story of Saint Denis by word and image equally. Of these, the mid-thirteenth-century manuscript B.N. n.a. fr. 1098 is an outstanding example. While these works incorporate the "historical" contributions of Hilduin and Hincmar, their primary focus remains the legend of Saint Denis, to which the illuminations are directed. A final group consists of true historical works, chronicles in their own right. In them, the life of Saint Denis, while only a part, is nevertheless the principal part.[33] Their distinguishing characteristic is the fusion of the life of the saint and his monastery with the history of France. The first work in this tradition is the *Vita et actus beati Dionysii*, written in 1223.

The *Vita et actus* is important for the history of the cult of Saint Denis because it is the first work to utilize both Hilduin and Hincmar and to project, in its totality, the new version of the Saint Denis legend that had been in the process of fabrication since the ninth century. At the same time, the life of the saint is inserted into the history of France, and throughout, the underlying intention of the work is to set forth the history of the protection extended by Saint Denis to the kings of France from the time of Dagobert to 1223. The royalist character of the work intrudes even into such unexpected passages as those dealing with the abbey's relics, whose translation to Saint-Denis is usually recorded as an act of royal devotion to the monastery in recognition of the saint's special relation to the kings of France.[34] These stories were original to the *Vita et actus* and emphasized royal involvement in all aspects of the cult objects worshiped at the monastery.

Shortly after the *Vita et actus*, a French version of the saint's life appeared, *Vie de Saint Denis*, including thirty miniatures representing his legend and the origins of the monastery dedicated to him as narrated in the text. This manuscript (B.N. n.a. fr. 1098) dates from around 1250 and is divided into three parts. A first, consecrated to the life of Saint Denis and a history of the abbey's origins, is based on Hilduin and Hincmar and incorporates elements of the text of the *Vita et actus*. The second part is made up of thirty miniatures depicting scenes from the preceding text, described in Latin verses below the illuminations. A final section deals principally with liturgical pieces and includes parts of the history of relics taken from the *Vita et actus*. The brevity of the *Vie de Saint Denis* and its utilization of the vernacular suggests that it was written for the instruction of visitors to the monastery who wished to learn, in an abridged form, the principal circumstances of the saint's life and the acts of protection that he had performed for the king and realm of France.[35] As such, it testifies to the growth of the cult in the thirteenth century and its increasingly popular character.

The *Vie de Saint Denis* in turn became the model for what is probably the most important of this series of works, the *Vita et passio sancti Dionysii* of Ivo of Saint-Denis, written at the request of Philip IV the Fair and presented in 1317 by Gilles of Pontoise, the abbot of

Saint-Denis, to Philip V the Long, at which time a French translation of the original Latin text was added.[36] Like its forerunners, Ivo's
work was not simply a life of the saint but a true historical collection
comparable, in smaller proportions, to the *Grandes Chroniques* in its
desire to collect into one place the material concerning the history of
the monarchy in relation to the cult of Saint Denis.

Ivo's text is divided into three parts. It is more of a chronicle than
the earlier works and possesses a certain logical superiority over the
Vita et actus in its strict adherence to chronological order in the treatment of the diverse miracles and relic histories that had become a
standard part of Dionysian tradition by the fourteenth century. The
first part contains a history of Saint Denis from his birth until the period of Saint Paul's preaching at Athens; the second, an account of
the acts of Saint Denis from the time of his conversion until his
death; and the final historical section serves as a summary of French
history from the Trojan origins of the Franks to the death of Philip
the Fair, viewed principally in relation to the cult of Saint Denis.[37]

In the introduction to the third, historical section, Ivo emphasizes
that he will treat specifically those instances in which Saint Denis,
through his protection, had brought victory to French kings who
fought under his banner.[38] For he concludes, "Verum sanctus ipse
Dyonisius regni regumque Francorum patronus praecipuus" (B.N.
lat. 5286, fol. 117r) (In truth this Saint Denis was the special patron of
the kings and realm of the French). Throughout, Ivo's overriding preoccupation is to supply evidence to support his claim that Saint Denis is indeed the patron saint of French kings and that Frenchmen
everywhere owe a large measure of their prosperity to his miraculous
protection. In effect, what all these works have in common is their
desire to develop and spread the cult of Saint Denis while at the same
time, as Delisle remarked, "imposing upon it a national and patriotic
character."[39] By furnishing concrete, specific examples of the saint's
intercession on behalf of the monarchy and the people of France,
they sought to persuade the reader that the history of the saint and
that of the kingdom were inextricably linked.

Although the texts just discussed are the most pointed in their effort to interweave the cult of Saint Denis with royal history, they are not alone. The same motif is discernible in almost all Dionysian texts, and the chronicles, Latin and vernacular, supply significant testimony which, because of the more restricted scope of the *vitae*, could not have been included in them. The chronicles offer two general types of acts performed by Saint Denis in service to the crown. The first, and less numerous, are miraculous cures or acts of deliverance of the royal person himself. The importance of this genre is that it reiterated and expanded upon Hincmar's theme of Saint Denis's direct concern for the kings of France. It also implicitly bespoke the king's inherent worthiness to be the recipient of such grace and thus contributed to the image of French kings as devout and holy men.

An interesting example of the abbey's jealous solicitude in relating Saint Denis's curative powers is Rigord's account of the recovery of Philip Augustus after an illness incurred during a hunting expedition in 1179. As Rigord explains, Philip had become separated from the main hunting party; fearing for his safety he prayed to God, the Virgin Mary, and Saint Denis, *regum Francorum patrono et defensori*,[40] inscribing the sign of the cross upon his forehead and commending himself to their care. Finally discovered by a serf and returned home, Philip fell ill from the experience. According to Rigord, Philip was then cured by the incessant prayers of his father, Louis VII, and miraculously restored to health. What Rigord fails to mention is the pilgrimage that King Louis made to the tomb of Thomas Becket at Canterbury to obtain his son's recovery, the first voyage of a French king to English soil and one universally reported by English chroniclers.[41] Indeed, in recognition of the English saint's response to his prayers, Louis placed gold on the altar of Canterbury and granted the monks a rent of one hundred muids of wine from the lands of Poissy, a grant that Philip confirmed the following year.[42] Clearly, to Rigord, the intervention of Thomas Becket was an incursion on the privilege of Saint Denis, as the official patron and protector of French kings, to cure the king, a status Rigord had carefully mentioned in his description of the hunting incident.[43]

If the hunting incident afforded Rigord only an ambiguous opportunity to report Saint Denis's curative powers, a better occasion presented itself in 1191, when the young prince Louis fell seriously ill while Philip was away on Crusade. When all the physicians despaired of the child's life, the queen, Adele, taking council with the prelates and barons of the court, decided that relics should be brought from Saint-Denis and a procession held in the streets of Paris to pray for divine aid. Rigord contends that this was the first time the saint's relics had been taken outside the village of Saint-Denis. Moreover, while Rigord states only that the queen and her counselors decided upon this course of action, the *Grandes Chroniques* interpolate the text by adding that "il fu accordé de common conseil que on eust recors et refuge à celui qui est garde et defense du roiaume: c'est li glorious martyrs Saint Denis"[44] (it was agreed by common counsel that one should have recourse to and take refuge in him who is the guardian and defense of the realm: that is, the glorious martyr Saint Denis). Both, of course, attribute the ultimate cure to the power of the exhibited relics.

Similar instances of Saint Denis's compassion for kings in sickness are reported by Guillaume de Nangis in 1244, and by the second continuation of his *Chronicon* in 1321. In the case of Louis IX's illness in 1244, even invocations to God throughout all the churches of the realm were unable to ameliorate the king's condition. Louis lay periously close to death when Queen Blanche ordered Eudes Clement, abbot of Saint-Denis, to take the bodies of the holy martyrs out of their tombs and exhibit them at the abbey. This was done, Guillaume explains, because "Rex siquidem post Dominum et sacratissimam Virginem matrem ejus, in ipsis (sc. Denis, Rusticus and Eleutherius) utpote in suis et regni sui advocatis et protectoribus, confidentius sperabat" (The king, indeed, after God and the most sacred Virgin his mother, confidently placed his hope in these [Denis, Rusticus, and Eleutherius] inasmuch as they were advocates and protectors of his and of his realm). Guillaume further emphasized the particularity of the tie between saint and monarch by explaining that the opening of Denis's tomb was never done "solummodo pro salute regis Franciae, vel regni sui periculo"[45] (except for the safety of the king of

France, or in cases of danger to his realm). The saint's efficacy proved itself again, and within a few days Louis was cured.[46]

In Philip V's case, the relics actually were brought to his bedside for him to see and touch. In this instance, Saint Denis provided only temporary relief, for the king died shortly afterwards. Nevertheless, the chronicler reports that Philip's last words confirmed Denis's powers, for in dying Philip proclaimed: "scio me meritis et precibus beati Dionysii curatum fuisse, et malo meo regimine iterum in eamdem aegritudinem incidisse"[47] (I know that I was cured by the merits and prayers of the blessed Denis, and that I have fallen ill a second time on account of my evil regimen). Even Saint Denis, it seems, could not prevail against royal unworthiness.

While these few cases are not in themselves of great importance, they do reveal a basic conviction on the part of the monks and, if the evidence of the chronicles is to be trusted, of kings and queen mothers who requested the saint's intervention, that Saint Denis was peculiarly the patron of the monarchy, who could be counted upon to give his support in times of great need. The intimate, almost familial, relation between the monarchy and the abbey is perfectly expressed by Rigord, who speaks of Philip Augustus as entering Saint-Denis "as if descending into his chambers."[48] And it is instructive that the *Couronnement de Louis,* a chanson de geste composed between 1131 and 1137,[49] already speaks of the king of France as "li reis de Saint Denis."[50] Similarly, the Anglo-Norman chronicler Jordan of Fantosme, writing in 1174, addresses Louis VII as "gentil rei de Saint Denis."[51] Of all the saints invoked by the chansons de geste, Saint Denis is mentioned most often; by the twelfth century the position of Saint Denis as the special benefactor of French kings is already part of popular legend.

The second and more interesting type of miraculous act reported in the chronicles of Saint-Denis deals with the saint's general protective role over the realm as a whole. The significant aspect of this genre is the relationship that the chronicles project between the saint and all the peoples of France. The tradition of calling upon Saint Denis to protect the realm from danger goes back as far as Merovingian times. It was in keeping with the general practice of this religious age, for as the *Vita et actus* reminds us, it was customary to turn to the saints in times of urgent necessity, of death, pestilence, and war.[52] Under the Capetians, this general practice was in the case of war focused on a ritual assumption of the banner of Saint Denis, accompanied by prayers for his support before the opening of military engagements. The most significant moments when French kings beseeched their patron's support and recognized his endeavors on behalf of the realm are, therefore, involved with the removal and return of the monastery's standard in times of national emergency.

The practice of depositing a royal flag at the monastery of Saint-Denis begins with Hugh Capet. This flag was not the abbey's own, but one that had belonged to Charlemagne. Legend, history, and poetry described it as a gift from Pope Leo to Charlemagne in recognition of his imperial status as emperor of the Roman people, for which reason it was sometimes called "Romane."[53] The *Chanson de Roland* describes it as an "Orie flambe" and gives Montjoie as its preferred name. Throughout Carolingian times, until at least the end of the eleventh century, the banner retained something of the religious overtones of its origins while taking on more and more of a national character.[54]

The standard of Saint-Denis, however, was that of the Vexin. It had devolved to the king when the Vexin was added to the royal domain in the reign of Philip I, the county being held by the kings of France in fee from the monastery. The standard was, thus, in origin feudal and seigneurial, without previous royal associations. In the hands of the king, however, it soon acquired royal dimensions. Its fame and importance as a royal standard were sealed when, in 1124, Louis VI, threatened by the invasion of Henry V of Germany, approached the altar of Saint Denis and pronounced him the special patron and, after God, special protector of the realm. Taking the standard from the saint's altar, he "invited all France to follow him." Suger's account of these events vigorously asserted the saint's privileged position as protector of the realm; he emphasized that Frenchmen considered it their prerogative that "if the subjects of any other realm dare to invade theirs, the relics of this Saint, this admirable defender, be, with those of his companions, placed upon his altar to defend it."[55] Although Suger is the first to report this practice, Odo of Deuil, describing Louis VII's departure on Crusade in 1148, already speaks of it as customary.[56]

In his account of Philip Augustus's war with Flanders in 1184, Gervais of Tilsbury designates the flag carried by Philip as the *signum Karoli Magni*.[57] It was but a short step to the identification of the banner of Saint-Denis with Charlemagne's Oriflamme. Both Rigord and Guillaume le Breton describe the banner of Saint-Denis in this way, and from their time on, the confusion of the two flags is complete, as is clearly reflected in the dual battle cry of the French: Montjoie Saint Denis.[58]

The significance of the Oriflamme was twofold. As the flag of Charlemagne, it recalled the tie between the Capetians and this illustrious ancestor and was a physical embodiment of the imperial pretensions which French kings inherited from their Carolingian predecessors.[59] Further, like any flag, the Oriflamme had the quality of a corporate image. In handing it over to Louis VI, Suger gave the monarchy a symbol of collective unity hitherto lacking, but one which retained its distinctive association with the cult of Saint Denis. As the special ensign of Saint Denis, the Oriflamme represented his spiritual leadership, as Suger declared, over "all France" (*tota Francia*) which followed it in battle.

Time and again, the chronicles record the victories won under the saint's banner as a consequence of his intercession. During Louis IX's attack on the port of Damietta, the Oriflamme preceded even the holy cross carried by the papal legate.[60] On leaving for his second Crusade, Louis took up the Oriflamme and devoutly recommended the French realm to the "garde et en la protection du martyr Saint Denis."[61] Philip III, forming his battle lines against the king of Tunis, aligned them behind the saint's standard "donec divina potentia concessisset eis ex hostibus victrici dextera triumphari" (until divine power shall grant them the ability to triumph over their enemies). Again, when seeking to avenge the rights of Blanche, daughter of

Louis IX and wife of Ferdinand of Spain, whose children were disinherited by the king of Castile, Philip went to Saint-Denis to receive the banner and to seek assurances of victory against his proud enemies.[62] Philip the Fair, as well, attributed the success of his armies against the Flemish in 1304 to Saint Denis, under whose banner they had fought. He gratefully recognized the saint as "Franciae specialis patronuus, quorum patrociniis confitebatur praecipue se protectum"[63] (the special patron of France, whose patronage he acknowledged to have specially protected him). Lest he seem neglectful of the grace extended to him by the saint, he presented the abbey with £100 of rent from the royal treasury.[64] The accumulated force of these reports was to fix the image of Saint Denis above all others as, in Guillaume de Nangis's words, "regni Franciae et populi Gallici defensoris."[65] Beyond his curative and protective functions for kings and the ruling dynasties, Saint Denis played a critical defensive role in the history of the French realm and in the life of its people.

Perhaps more telling even than the historical writings of the abbey were the works of outright forgery, got up by the monks to authenticate relics and vindicate claims to lands and privileges. Freed from the restraint of historical truth and endowed with more than sufficient historical imagination, the monks advanced propositions concerning the relation between the monastery and the throne that sometimes reached outrageous proportions. While the fabulous background with which these charters were supplied was in a sense ancillary to the original intention of the documents, they set in motion traditions that came to have a life of their own.

Of these forgeries, one is of particular relevance for this inquiry—namely, the false charter of Charlemagne, published in the *Monumenta Germaniae Historica* as *Diplomata Karolinorum*, no. 286, and known as the "Donation."[66] According to this charter, Charlemagne called a council at Saint-Denis, wishing to recognize the saint's aid in protecting the realm from danger against its enemies. He therefore decreed that all kings, archbishops, and bishops should venerate the monastery as the "caput omnium ecclesiarum regni" (head of all the churches of the realm) and its abbot as Primate of France, whose consent was to be sought in the election of bishops and abbots. Further, he declared that he himself held France in fief from God and the holy martyr—"quod a Deo solo et a te regnum Franicae teneo." In acknowledgment of this dependency, he placed four gold besants upon the altar of Saint-Denis and directed that his successors should do so also, bound not by human but divine servitude. Henceforth the kings of France should be crowned at Saint-Denis and leave the insignia of their office at the abbey.[67]

By this single act the monks asserted a territorial right to France, a right to the consecration of French kings as against that of Reims, a position as treasurer of the royal insignia (ultimately achieved), and a commanding status of primacy over the French church. The leading idea of the "Donation," that the king of France was in essence the vassal of the saint, can be seen translated into stone in the iconography of the monastery's Porte des Valois, dated shortly after 1175, which depicts thirty-six voussoir figures paying homage to Saint Denis.[68]

The language of the charter is feudal in tone and closely resembles Suger's account of Louis VI's assumption of the Oriflamme in 1124, at which time Louis had also declared himself a vassal of the saint, calling the abbey the *caput regni nostri.*[69] But, in effect, the claims of the Charlemagne charter are larger still. For in relating that Charlemagne placed four gold besants upon the altar of Saint-Denis, the charter framed not an act of devotion, nor even an act of vassalage, but a virtual act of serfdom. Four pieces of money, usually four deniers, ordinarily constituted the *chevage*, the *capiti proprii*, paid by serfs to their seigneur, and these were, as a consequence, often called *homines quatour nummorum*[70] (men of four coins). Where Suger carefully explained that Louis would have done homage for the Vexin *"si non rex esset"* (if he were not king), lest it derogate from his royal majesty, the charter did not shrink from inscribing the king of France on its lists of spriritual serfs. The author of the *Grandes Chroniques* was so taken aback by the implications of the charter that he hastened to add that the practice should be considered not a token of servitude but a command of freedom. To support this interpretation, he recalled that Alexander the Great, when he conquered the East, relieved those who rendered him four deniers from all other exactions. When French kings placed gold on the altar, it signified only their recognition that they held the realm from Saint Denis, "qui il ne feissent en nule maniere, se ce fust en nom de servage"[71] (which they would never do, if it was in the name of serfdom). Despite this demurral, the meaning of the charter remained clear, and it was incorporated, without interpolation, into later Dionysian works.

Surprisingly, Louis IX was to reenact literally the conditions of the Charlemagne forgery. The anonymous *Gesta Sancti Ludovici*, written by a monk of Saint-Denis, informs us that Louis annually visited the monastery on the saint's feast day and, kneeling with his son before the Great Altar, head bared, offered four gold besants to the holy martyr as token of the dependence that he wished to recognize with regard to the saint as protector of his person and his realm.[72] Further, the fact he brought his son along suggests that he felt the ceremony was creating or recognizing a hereditary bond.[73] The same story is related by the chronicler known as the Confessor of the Queen Margaret, who adds that when Louis returned from Crusade in 1254, he made a collective offering of twenty-eight besants, four for each of the seven years he had been absent.[74] The Confessor's chronicle invites belief as a faithful summary of the inquiry, now mostly lost, conducted for the purpose of Louis's canonization.[75] If the monks of Saint-Denis had invented the story, other churches surely would have challenged such extraordinary testimony.

That Louis IX was capable of a servile act of devotion towards a revered saint of the realm no one doubts. If evidence of this obeisance were confined to him alone, it would be possible to question its importance among the ritual practices of Capetian kings. But new evidence, discovered in the Vatican Library by John Baldwin, reveals that Louis was only following a custom that can be traced back to the reign of his grandfather, Philip Augustus. The section of an accounting of royal jewels in Philip's Register A contains a final entry which reads: "Dominus rex quando ivit ad sanctam dyonisium iiii bizantios"[76] (The lord king [paid] four besants when he went to Saint-

Denis). From paleographical evidence, Baldwin believes that the entry was inserted into Register A between 1204 and 1211. At the time of Louis's return from Crusade in 1254, then, the practice was already of half a century's standing. Not only had the monks of Saint-Denis persuaded the kings of France to accept their banner as the national standard; they had convinced them to perform an act of servitude to the saint. No clearer evidence of the status of Saint Denis as the patron saint of the monarchy can be imagined.

It is easy to ascertain the motives that lay behind the monks' efforts. From a purely economic point of view, a tie with the royal house was a lucrative and important business connection. It led to such obvious economic privileges as the Fair of Lendit, granted to the monastery by a grateful Louis VI in 1124, continuous donations of lands, rents, and the like. Even less directly remunerative marks of favor, such as the fact that Saint-Denis became the normal burial place of Capetian kings, could be turned to profit. And one should not, of course, underestimate the importance to men of this age of purely honorific signs of prestige and status.

But it is perhaps less clear why kings both as practical and protective of the royal dignity as Philip Augustus and Louis IX cooperated in this enterprise. Literary and documentary evidence overwhelmingly confirms that the Capetians consciously promoted the cult of the saint, identified the abbey's interests with their own, and accepted the saint as their benefactor. What did they hope to gain by acknowledging their debt to Saint Denis, by symbolically placing themselves in the position of his vassal and servitor, and by addressing him as their patron and protector? Why, in the simplest terms, did Philip Augustus and Louis IX make royal policy out of the fantasies of the false Charlemagne charter?

Bossuat has suggested that the history of Saint Denis as written at the monastery, with its emphasis on the special concern of the martyr for the king, furnished French kings a defensive arm in times when the legitimacy of their power was contested, and this explains their interest in advancing the cult.[77] Certainly, in a period when royal power was only newly won, the patronage of France's leading national saint buttressed the sense of royal legitimacy and contributed to the creation of a mystique of kingship with enormous potential for the future of the monarchy. Similarly, the Polish historian Karol Gorski has proposed that the notion of a "Roi-Saint," a holy king, be used as a comparative measure of royal power. In lands where kings successfully portrayed themselves as devout (and devotion to a saint was one means of doing so), we can expect the emergence of strong state organizations, reinforced by the devotion and loyalty of subjects, who share the religious ideals embodied in the figure of the holy king.[78] Strayer's article, "France: The Holy Land, the Chosen People and the Most Christian King," functions almost as a case study of this principle. Strayer argues convincingly that the position of the French king as the "most Christian" in Europe, combined with the union of the ideas of the "sacred king" and the "holy country," accelerated the emergence of the French state at the end of the thirteenth century.[79] At the same time, it enabled Frenchmen to identify the king, and through him the kingdom, as a worthy object of loyalty, even love, and thereby immeasurably strengthened the ability of the state to confront the crises of the coming centuries. As Schramm once remarked, belief in the state and the people means in the High Middle Ages belief in the king.[80] And it might be added that this is especially true in France, which lacked the territorial cohesion of England or the ideological legitimacy of the empire.

To be sure, royal sanctity functioned as a step in the building of national loyalties. But a problem still exists in understanding how the king, in this case the French king, came to acquire a national identity through which the sentiments of his subjects could be channeled. As Strayer himself pointed out, the thirteenth-century Capetians "had to invent the France which they claimed to rule . . . they had to expand the idea of France to make it match the expansion of their own power."[81] France in the thirteenth century was no longer the feudal monarchy of Louis VI, nor yet the absolute monarchy of the Ancien Régime, but something in between, "still medieval and already modern."[82] It was, essentially, a developed bureaucratic state with claims to national loyalty, and the question still remains: how was this transition effected? How did the king shed his more limited identity as feudal overlord and become a national leader?

It is worth at least the status of a hypothesis to suggest that one of the things French kings sought in allying themselves with the cult of Saint Denis was the enlargement of the royal personality. As the monks progressively stamped a national character on the cult, they constructed a bridge by means of which the kings of France could reach out and tap a significant reservoir of national feeling. By identifying themselves with a revered national saint, Capetian kings could hope to win a comparable status in the affections of their subjects by transferring to themselves a position already credited to the saint.

The whole tenor of Dionysian writings suggests that the cult of Saint Denis served not only French kings but, as Guillaume de Nangis had said, all the *regnum et populi Franciae*. The language of the chronicles is filled with references to *France* and *li Franceis* that reveal a new consciousness of the nation as a historical personality, bound together in devotion to a national saint. Precisely because of his position as both national saint and patron of the monarchy, the cult of Saint Denis could bind together king and people. Where other national saints might become the focus of opposition to the monarchy, in France saint and monarchy cooperated to endow the realm with a religious character, following the tendency so brilliantly traced by Kantorowicz of the spiritualization and sanctification of the secular state in the twelfth and thirteenth centuries.[83] While the cult of Saint Denis is not solely responsible for this development, it made its contribution.

Further, the cult had a specific importance for the monarchy as such, and for the transition from feudal forms of rulership to a more expansive concept of the state. For if one considers the claims of the false charter seriously for a moment, Saint Denis ruled all France. It is possible that rulers as different in character as Philip Augustus and Louis IX saw in this claim an ideological justification for shared aspirations. By adhering strictly to the terms of the false charter, they framed the conviction, or at least the pious hope, that they too ruled all France and, as the charter stated, recognized no superior except for

God and Saint Denis. The putative Charlemagne origin of the charter added historical legitimacy to its precepts, and the implicit contention that France was not included in the Carolingian imperial legacy fueled Capetian efforts to assert their national independence from imperial hegemony.

From Louis VI on, the kings of France carried the banner of Saint Denis into war with them and exhorted their followers to battle with the cry "Montjoie Saint Denis." In taking the saint's symbols as their own, were they not seeking to demonstrate that they, like him, bore the responsibility for the preservation and protection of the entire realm? The image of the king as the defender of the realm was a critical component in royalist theory, in the early and High Middle Ages alike. By allying themselves on the side of a saint whose principal function was the defense and protection of the French realm, Capetians emphasized the national scope as well as religious character of their mission.

The utilization of the cult of Saint Denis by Capetian kings for the creation of a national identity parallels the development of France as a legal personality, a process marked by increasing references to the crown, the *corona regni*, as a juristic entity throughout the twelfth and thirteenth centuries. Yet it can be argued that the cult's significance results from the relatively weak juristic notion of the crown in France, compared at least to England. Precisely because France failed to achieve a national legal community comparable to its English neighbor's, it was necessary to look to other sources of cohesion.

The absence of a legal, political, or constitutional community of the realm, as Langmuir argued, radically tipped the balance of power in favor of the monarchy, which "emerged as the sole symbol of unity in the kingdom, far above the many communities it ruled."[84] In France, personal kingship dominates the crown as the principle of French unity. There was no tension between dynastic patriotism and popular nationalism, and the cult of kingship, of the king as *Pater patrie*, evolved naturally and without strain into a patriotic cult of the kingdom of France.[85] As a Venetian ambassador remarked at the beginning of the sixteenth century: "there are states more fertile and richer than France, such as Hungary and Italy. There are greater and more powerful ones, such as Germany and Spain: but none is so thoroughly unified."[86]

The history of this evolution is not the concern of this chapter. But it can be said that the achievement of a national identity by the Capetian monarchy marked its beginning. And in this process the cult of Saint Denis played a part. The success of French kings in representing themselves as national leaders, responsible for the defense and direction of the whole realm, owed something to those small acts of devotion and obedience that they performed at the altar of the saint. By them, Capetian kings claimed not only the saint's exalted position as national patron and protector but also a community of feeling with all Frenchmen who similarly recognized the role of Saint Denis in their well-being.

By the end of the thirteenth century, the king of France had become the object of intense devotion on the part of his subjects. With Louis IX's canonization in 1297, France produced the perfect type of the sacred king. His relics, lying in state at the Abbey of Saint-Denis, became the focus of a cult of kingship, an appropriate culmination to the monastery's efforts to fuse its history with that of the monarchy. Here Frenchmen worshiped a national saint and the nation's sainted king: royal sanctity, national loyalty, religious personality, and historical identity all drew easily together to collaborate in the construction of a French state whose distinctive feature was the commanding position of the king in the life of the nation. If the monks promoted the kings of France for their own economic benefit, perhaps the return to the king on his investment in the monastery was in the end, though different, no less profitable.

9

History as Enlightenment

Suger and the *Mos Anagogicus*

In any list of twelfth-century monastic writers of history, Abbot Suger of Saint-Denis would surely rank among the select few whose works have achieved an enduring significance, both for their intrinsic excellence and for what they teach us about the nature of life and modes of thought during this crucial and innovative period of the Middle Ages. Suger's *Life of Louis VI* and the beginning of his work on the life of Louis VII, interrupted by death, were the first in a series of royal biographies written at Saint-Denis to record—and, in recording, to celebrate—the deeds of France's monarchs. As abbot of Saint-Denis when the first collection of chronicles was compiled in the opening decades of the twelfth century, Suger probably supervised, or at least stimulated, the inception of royal historiography at the abbey.[1] From small beginnings during his abbacy would flow a veritable stream of historical works, making the chronicles of Saint-Denis, like the abbey itself, a symbol of the unity of France and the greatness of its kings.

Yet a curious fact of Sugerian scholarship is that, to date, no thorough study of his historiographical activity has appeared.[2] In particular, after 850 years, we still lack a comprehensive investigation of the *Vita Ludovici Grossi* that explores its historiographic aims, structure, and craft, a prerequisite for any serious interpretation of the work. This is not to say that the importance of the text has gone unnoticed. It was repeatedly copied from the twelfth century on, both within the Abbey of Saint-Denis, beginning with the *Gesta Gentis Francorum*, to which it was appended circa 1160,[3] and without, notably at the nearby Abbey of Saint-Germain-des-Prés, where work on the *Continuation of Aimoin* was then in progress.[4] At the end of the twelfth century it was incorporated into the Dionysian handbook represented by Paris, Bibliothèque Nationale, MS Lat. 12710,[5] and was copied again in the middle of the thirteenth century as part of the major compilation of Dionysian Latin histories contained in Paris, Bibliothèque Nationale, MS Lat. 5925, from which it was translated into French by Primat in 1274 as part of the initial installment of the *Grandes Chroniques de France*.[6] At present, Suger's *Life of Louis VI* is available in ten manuscripts and six printed editions—two possessing French translations—which testify to its continuing popularity throughout the Middle Ages and thereafter.[7]

The relative scholarly neglect of Suger as historiographer is all the more surprising given that he was almost alone among his contemporaries in his marked preference for historical rather than theological inquiry. Indeed, among monastic authors of his time, Suger is probably the only one who did not compose a single theological treatise. His Dionysian biographer, the monk Guillaume, copiously documented Suger's passion for history: his practice of recounting the deeds of past kings named to him at random; his long discourses on French history continued far into the night; and, in characteristic Sugerian fashion, his frequent accounts "of his own actions, as much as those of other men."[8] But his historical interests have not encouraged our interest in his historiography.

The reasons for this neglect appear to fall into two basic categories. The first, and doubtless most significant, has been the tendency for scholars to read the *Vita Ludovici* simply as a source of information for the political history of Louis's reign. Such an approach to the text is ultimately allied to a view of Suger himself as, to borrow the title of a seventeenth-century biography written by Jean Baudouin, "le ministre fidèle."[9] A product of "the faithful minister," Suger's account of the reign of Louis VI has attained a privileged status for its presumed fidelity to factual accuracy, with certain notable but easily recognizable lapses. To read the *Vita Ludovici* in this way legitimately calls for no more than the factual correction of the text, and in large part this is the reading it has received. That the positivist assumptions governing the historian's utilization of the work might prove untenable in light of its literary character and goals is a question that has never been raised, although, upon reflection, such assumptions may seem naive.

The second reason for the neglect of Suger's historiographic art stems from the complexity of the *Vita Ludovici* itself as a piece of historical writing. As almost every editor of the text has recognized, the work defies easy classification. More panegyric than history, say some; a work of edification and practical instruction, say others; marred, all agree, by a literary style that strains for rhetorical elegance but achieves only affectation at best, prolixity, confusion, and obscurity at worst.[10] Although entitled *Vita*, the work fails to conform to the normal standards of biography—even those of the Middle Ages—as it persistently loses the expected focus on its subject in favor of long digressions, disproportionate attention to events whose pertinence to Louis seems insignificant, and an apparently haphazard criterion of historical selection that makes it difficult to identify the principles guiding Suger's choice of material. Even less can the work be treated under the rubric of autobiography, a recent, if regrettable, trend among historians concerned with the "discovery of the individual" in the twelfth century.[11]

Clearly, the simplest solution is to call it a regnal history, one concerned not so much with the "life" of the king as with the deeds done during his reign, *res gestae*, whose importance is judged by their contribution to the furtherance of monarchical power and prestige.[12] Even this, however, is less than satisfactory, for the *Vita Ludovici* lacks the distinguishing features of chronicles of this kind—namely, a commitment to chronological progression through the reign; clear thematic development, usually governed by ethical precepts defining "good" and "bad" kingship; and at least an avowed, if perfunctory, concern for historical completeness. One need only compare the *Vita Ludovici* to Rigord's *Gesta Philippi Augusti* to perceive the gulf that separates Suger's work from other Dionysian regnal histories, a genre at which, in fact, the Abbey of Saint-Denis excelled.

How, then, should the *Vita Ludovici* be characterized? How can its confused chronology and seemingly capricious handling of events be explained in terms of an encompassing historiographic intention that, one assumes, a writer of Suger's experience and purposefulness possessed? If not biography or royal *gesta*, what is the *Vita Ludovici*? In the following pages I should like to propose one possible interpretation of the *Vita Ludovici* based on an analysis of its underlying narrative structure, for it is my contention that this narrative structure provides a clue to the intended meaning of the work.

The Prologue aside, a close examination of the *Vita Ludovici* reveals that each chapter contains the narration of a single "event-unit" that may, but does not necessarily, delimit a comparable unit of historical time, hence the chronological imprecision all commentators on the text have found so puzzling. Study of these narrative units, moreover, discloses a virtually identical internal structure in which historical action is inaugurated by a disturbance to an existing situation, followed by the king's attempt to deal with the consequences of that disturbance, and concludes with the restoration of "correct" order, viewed either as a return to the previously existing situation or as the institution of a new and ethically more just arrangement. Lest this narrative structure be seen only as another example of a pattern common to all clerical chroniclers, as William J. Brandt has argued,[13] it should be pointed out that in the *Vita Ludovici* the initial disturbance that sets the narrative action in motion is specifically treated as a disruption of the proper hierarchical ordering of society, and it is towards the restoration of this order that the remaining historical action is directed. The internal structure of Suger's narrative "event," then, is basically triadic, consisting of an initial deformation of historical order, corrective action taken by the king, and the final resolution, more often than not presented as a form of restoration.

A sampling of the opening chapters of the *Vita Ludovici* serves easily to illustrate this narrative pattern. Chapter 1, which treats Louis VI's early struggles against King William Rufus of England, attributes the cause of war to William's aggressive aspiration to possess the French throne—in Suger's view, a violation of the legal subordination of the English king to his French overlord.[14] But, "because it is neither proper nor natural for the French to be subject to the English (but rather for the English to be subject to the French),"[15] Louis valiantly withstood the onslaught in a series of military engagements, until William was killed in a hunting accident, an unforeseen outcome that Suger nonetheless advances as a resolution of the conflict, achieved through administering to William the very wrongs that he had attempted to impose on others: for, "he who had unreasonably disquieted others was himself much more heavily disquieted, and he who had coveted all was himself despoiled of all."[16]

Chapter 2 describes Louis's attacks on Bouchard, lord of Montmorency, who had despoiled the lands of Saint-Denis. For this act of violence, Bouchard was judged in King Philip I's court. When he refused to accept the royal judgment, Louis—acting as his father's agent—humbled him "to his will and pleasure" and made Bouchard experience "just what inconvenience and misfortune are deserved by the insubordination of those subject to the royal majesty" (16). Bouchard's insubordination calls forth the corrective response of the prince, who, by humbling him, promotes the cause of order and justice. Similarly, in chapter 3, Suger reports how Matthew, count of Beaumont, unfairly seized the castle of Luzarches from Hugh de Clermont, who then appealed to Louis for aid. Louis, "giving Hugh his hand in friendly fashion," ordered Matthew to "restore in full the man he had despoiled without proper form." When the count refused, Louis "avenged the refusal," took the castle by force, and "restored it to Hugh" (20).

If we skip ahead, chapter 18 recounts Louis's appropriation of the castles of Mantes and Montlhéry from his half brother, Philip, who, "pluming himself on his noble birth, had the impertinence to be recalcitrant" (122), and schemed even to capture the throne for himself.

The king, tired of his brother's "depredations of the poor, the wrongs done to churches, and the disorder he had brought to the whole countryside" (124), found himself forced to raise an army, for which he "drew to himself all the better men of the land in the hope of receiving the benefit of his known generosity and proven mercy" (126). Meanwhile, Philip had conferred the honor of Montlhéry on Hugh de Crécy, from whom Louis now reclaimed it by force of arms, expelling Hugh, whose "shameful expulsion taught him to reflect on what it meant to enter into alliance against his lord with his lord's enemies" (128). Once again, the forces of insubordinate pride trigger those willful acts of wrongdoing that it is the king's duty to correct and avenge in order to maintain the stability and peace of the realm.

Perhaps the most interesting example of Suger's narrative scheme is afforded by his handling of the continuing conflict between Louis VI and Henry I of England, which will serve here as a last, and highly telling, illustration of the lengths to which Suger was willing to go to preserve the underlying triadic structure of his narrative units. The action, recounted in chapter 26, opens characteristically with a disturbance to right order stemming from the refusal of the English king to recognize his hierarchical subordination to royal majesty, which Suger presents in his most rhetorically insistent voice, inaugurating the chapter with the kind of aphoristic assertion he reserved for particularly compelling occasions, in this case that "arrogant ambition is worse than pride, because pride admits no superior, while ambition admits no equal" (182). Having thus set the moral tone for the ensuing discussion, he proceeds to explain:

> King Louis of the French was perpetually raised in majesty above Henry, king of the English and duke of the Normans, by the fact that Henry was his feudatory. The king of the English was made impatient of his inferiority both by the nobility of his kingship and the marvelous abundance of his wealth. He labored to derogate from Louis's lordship, to upset his kingdom and disturb Louis at the request of his nephew, Count Theobald, and of many who envied the kingdom. (184)

War naturally followed. Since not even Suger could pretend that Louis was the instrument of Henry's correction (if one could call it that), it was left to the wheel of Fortune to play the role of royal avenger: "Thus it was that the king of England, after such long and marvelous successes of a most peacefully enjoyed prosperity, as if falling from the highest point of the wheel, was harassed by the changeable and unlucky ways things turn out . . . and reached the depths of misfortune" (188). To be sure, God rescued Henry and raised him once again in time for his crushing defeat of Louis's army at Brémule (in 1119), in which 140 French knights were taken prisoner. At Brémule, Louis personally lost his horse and battle standard, which Henry subsequently purchased from the soldier who had captured them. Henry returned the French king's charger, saddle, and bridle, but retained the standard as a souvenir of victory (facts known to us not from Suger, who supresses them, but through the account of Ordericus Vitalis).[17] Undeterred by this turn of events, Suger boldly resolves the narrative unit with the patently false conclusion that Louis and his men returned home "not ceasing to repay their momentary misfortune with a long, continuous, and very heavy revenge."[18]

While examples such as these could be enumerated from almost any chapter of the *Vita Ludovici*, those already reviewed should suffice to demonstrate the general point that Suger's narrative units are triadic in structure and are intended to promote a larger thematic purpose—namely, to show how, in Suger's words, "if anything which offended the king's majesty occurred anywhere in the kingdom, he would not put up with it in any way, nor leave it unavenged" (271). The offense to royal majesty represents a deformation of hierarchical order and unleashes Louis's vengeance against the pillaging, despoiling, overweening, ravening disturbers of the peace of the kingdom so familiar to all readers of the *Vita Ludovici*. To sustain this theme, Suger willfully violates chronological order, conflating events or deferring the conclusion of a chapter until he can properly narrate the resolution of the disturbance and the restoration of order, always carefully marked by the repetition of lexical formulae of "recovery," "return," "restoration," and the like. The chronological looseness of the *Vita Ludovici*, therefore, is the result not of confusion but of narrative intention—for the sake of which, it might be added, Suger avoids mentioning any dates at all.

The total narrative structure of the *Vita Ludovici* consists not so much in the progressive unfolding of an overarching theme (a familiar enough pattern in monastic chronicles) as in the assembling of detached histories—what I have called "event-units." Chapters are strung out in a paratactically juxtaposed sequence, whose movement is reiterative rather than strictly linear. Within each chapter appear recurrent themes of reciprocity: of friendship and enmity, vengeance and gracious aid, pollution and purification, treachery and loyalty, tyranny and justice. For the expression of these themes, Suger employs a rhetoric of reciprocity that greatly contributes to the inflated literary style of the text. To cite a few examples: "Plunderers were plundered and torturers were tortured as vigorously, if not more so, than they had tortured" (26); Philip I is "ravished by lust for his ravished wife" (82) (whom of course he had ravished in the first place); Louis's troops "repelled those who had repelled them" (72); Henry I "worked for the profit of all, so also all served him" (102); Haimo of Bourbon is reduced by Louis "to a state and depth of humility . . . equal to his previous height of pride" (182); the king's goodness and friendship "draw" the better men to him in affection, while his vengeance repels wrongdoers. Ever in flux, Suger's world is one of perennial challenges to order that must be set right, a world in which the bonds of friendship and enmity determine the lines of force, the ebb and flow of human striving for justice and peace. It is a hierarchically ordered world constantly undergoing deformation and thus continually in need of reformation and restoration.

If one inquires into the sources of such a view of human history, it seems reasonable to conclude, as Georges Duby has suggested in another context,[19] "that Suger translated into human events and actions the principles governing the celestial and ecclesiastical hierarchies of Pseudo-Dionysius the Areopagite, the anonymous fifth-century theologian whom the monks of Saint-Denis mistakenly identified with their own patron saint."[20] For both Suger and Pseudo-Dionysius, the concept of hierarchy is the keystone of the divine regulation of all good order, which requires, as Pseudo-Dionysius had written, that every being "pursue just things justly . . . not contrary to one's rank and place."[21] Hierarchy is an *ordo sacer* that arrays all created things in a vertical chain of being reaching from the lowest to God, from the material reality of the sense-perceptible world to the invisible being of the intelligible world. Such a concept of hierarchy presupposes, as Dom Chenu demonstrated in his brilliant discussion of the Platonisms of the twelfth century, that "classic Platonic thesis of two worlds, of intellect and of sense; but it alters this thesis profoundly by taking the sense-perceptible world as a field in which symbols were in play."[22] The Pseudo-Dionysian theology to which Suger was heir through the medium of John Scotus Eriugena was built on the principle, enunciated in John's *De divisione naturae*, that "there is nothing among the visible and corporeal things that fails to signify something incorporeal and intelligible."[23] The world's *visibilia*, its corporeal realities, are true ontological symbols (not merely epistemological signs)[24] of the *invisibilia*, the hierarchically ordered realms of being, towards which they point. While there is hierarchy, there is no dichotomy;[25] communication with, or more nearly participation in, the divine truths of the intelligible begins with the apprehension of material symbols, the cruder the better, since according to Pseudo-Dionysian theology the crudest symbols are those most capable of signifying mystery, a principle giving rise to what Chenu has called the "object-centered culture" of Pseudo-Dionysian symbolism.[26]

Within each ordered rank of being, the subordinate strive to ascend, as far as lies within their power, to be united with God, a process achieved, according to Pseudo-Dionysius, by "continuous and persistent struggles toward the One, and by the entire destruction and annihilation of things contrary."[27] In this process, inferior beings pursue the path of anagogy, the "upward-leading" movement of the mind from (and through) material symbols to an understanding of the invisible being of the intelligible. To achieve this ascent, inferior beings are aided by the exemplary attraction of those above them, which acts by means of the exchange of affection with the good, just as it "justly reproves anyone who rouses hatred against good men."[28] Within the duly ordered ranks of the Pseudo-Dionysian cosmos, then, is found the eternal, cyclical movement produced by the strivings of beings towards higher beings and towards the first principle of their being.[29]

In the *Vita Ludovici*, only one figure stands outside the reiterative flux and reflux of human striving, and that is the king himself. For, Suger proclaims, the king "is the vicar of God, whose image he bears." At his coronation Louis "put off the sword of secular knighthood" and "was girded with the sword of the church for the punishment of evildoers," in order to perform the "office of the king, who does not bear the sword in vain" (Romans 15:4).[30] Through royal consecration and anointment, the king is elevated to an ontological level far above those over whom he has been appointed by God to rule.[31] To attack the king is to oppose God, to go against, as Suger says of Hugh du Puiset, "the king of the Franks and the King of Kings."[32] The human hierarchy mirrors the heavenly hierarchy and the king, like God, surmounts an ordered pyramid and is charged with protecting the lives and tranquillity of all, while ceaselessly suppressing evil and tyranny.

At the very center of the *Vita Ludovici*, Suger provides a carefully articulated image of this perfectly ordered society in the famous account of the battle plans drawn up at Reims to meet the invasion threatened by the imperial forces of Henry V in 1124. Here, for once, the whole kingdom was gathered in a properly arrayed series of ranks around the king, forming "a large army of men devoted to the crown" (222). The royal summons dissolved all hostilities—Thibaut of Champagne and others at war with the king nonetheless answered the royal appeal—and joined all in a common unity of purpose. While the army assembled at Reims, Suger reports, "many devout people and religious women" frequented the altar of Saint-Denis, where the relics of the holy martyrs remained in place for the duration of the crisis, and where the brethren sang the office "day and night" (228). Linked by the sympathetic bonds of a shared enterprise, secure in the justice of their ultimate victory, king, army, Church, and people compose an ordered unity. "Never," boasts Suger, "in modern times or ancient, had France accomplished a more striking exploit than when, uniting the strength of her members . . . she triumphed over the Roman emperor. After this, the pride of enemies was stifled . . . and, in every direction she could reach, her enemies, returning to her favor, stretched forth their hands in friendship" (230). Suger thus terminates the account with a characteristically Dionysian resolution of conflict and restoration of order in which enmity is reciprocally exchanged for friendship, war for peace, the whole accomplished by the process of human striving so central to the natural dynamism of Pseudo-Dionysius's cosmos.

If at the center of the *Vita Ludovici* there stands an ideal image of human society, one symbolizing the order and justice of the invisible, divine hierarchy, so also is the work as a whole framed by a movement best understood in terms of the Pseudo-Dionysian notion of anagogical ascent. In the *Vita Ludovici*, this anagogical ascent is symbolized by the passage of Louis's life. As Suger presents it, Louis's life moves from the external, corporeal beauty of youth to the spiritual majesty of death. Louis, when first introduced to the reader at the age of tweve or thirteen, is a "handsome youth in the first flower of his age, admirable for his development of moral character and for the growth of a well-made body" (4). Yet at the end, when sensing the approach of death, "in the sight of all, clerks and laymen, he put off his kingship, laid down his kingdom . . . and invested his son Louis with his ring. There and then, for the love of God, he distributed to the churches, the poor, and the needy his gold and silver, his valuable vases and goblets, his clothes and cloaks; nor did he neglect to give his garments or his royal robes [down] to his very shirt." Making his communion, Louis "returned to his chamber and, having rejected all pomp of worldly pride, he lay down with only a single sheet" (274–76). Moreover, these acts were performed in the context of Louis's desire to make his profession as a monk of Saint-Denis, to exchange,

Suger says, "his royal insignia and imperial ornaments for the humble habit of Saint Benedict" (272). Although Louis's wish to become a monk was thwarted by the increasing pains of the illness that finally overtook him, "what he could not do in fact he did in heart and soul" (284), and the series of distributions listed in the text stands as testimony to the sincerity of his intentions.

In disrobing and unburdening himself of the royal insignia, Louis in effect becomes invisible, through a material process that parallels exactly the Pseudo-Dionysian idea of death as "becoming invisible to human ken." The act of disrobing has, as well, a precise spiritual significance that Pseudo-Dionysius explains in his discussion of monastic ordination in the *Ecclesiastical Hierarchy* and that, given the context of Louis's act, acquires a particular relevance. In Pseudo-Dionysian symbolism, "the casting aside of a different habit [in the ceremony of monastic ordination] is intended to show the transition from a middle religious life to the more perfect . . . just as in baptism the exchange of clothing denotes the elevation of a thoroughly purified life to a contemplative and enlightened condition."[33] To become invisible is also to ascend, to recover, and to be restored to that state of contemplative enlightenment for which it is the life-task of every being to strive. The history of Louis's life enacts this passage from the material state of external beauty to the invisible state of enlightenment, and it remains only for Louis to be wholly hidden from human ken by burial, where, Suger asserts in closing, "he waits to partake in the future resurrection."[34]

The *Vita Ludovici*, it is now possible to suggest, is Suger's offering of yet another material symbol through which the mind of the beholder can ascend to an understanding of the intelligible, a symbol comparable in purpose, if not in scale, to the abbey church. Just as the observer who enters the church is anagogically elevated by the contemplation of its beauty to an understanding of the divine, so the reader, in contemplating the life of Louis VI, shares in the experience of enlightenment that his life reflects. In this context, the figure of Louis VI functions not as a moral exemplar but as a material symbol bearing the full ontological significance conferred on such symbols by Pseudo-Dionysian theology. As such, the *Vita Ludovici*, I would like to propose, is intended as a work of edification in the root sense of the word, that is, as a formal construction—which is to say, the construction of forms—whose purpose is to effect the spiritual reconstruction of the reader.[35] And it is precisely the narrative structure of the text that reveals this historiographic intention by repeatedly providing models (forms) of human restoration pointing the reader towards an understanding of a future spiritual restoration, in keeping with the ontological bias of Pseudo-Dionysian theology that permitted access to the transcendent through the mystical absorption of the concrete, achieved by following the *mos anagogicus*, the anagogical way.

"Praeteritorum recordatio futurorum est exhibito," Suger wrote in *Liber de administratione*; the recollection of the past is the promise of the future.[36] History, no less than gold and gems, buildings and ornaments, becomes in Suger's hands an appropriate object of anagogical contemplation, a form of theological enlightenment, aiding the reader in his upward ascent and helping him to anticipate the spiritual rewards of the future. It is, as Suger says in the Prologue to the *Vita Ludovici*, a "monument more durable than bronze," by which he pays back the gifts of "charity and gratitude"[37] shown him by his friend and ruler, and through which he passes down to posterity the image of a model life.

The preceding interpretation of Suger's aims in writing the *Vita Ludovici*, if granted, raises several questions. To begin with, the normal question one asks of any historical text: Does it work on its own terms? Can history—that is to say, the study of past deeds, of *res gestae*—bear the weight of such Pseudo-Dionysian symbolism, particularly in light of that symbolism's underlying Platonic disinterest in contingent events?[38] This is only another way of inquiring whether *gesta* (or gold and buildings, for that matter) are really appropriate objects of anagogical contemplation. Just as generations of art history students have found in Suger's architectural writings little more than a thinly disguised aesthetic indulgence, a formalized, theological justification for what they, not so naively, perceive as the expression of an unabashed entrepreneurship of *objets de luxe*, so, too, Suger can perhaps be accused of an unseemly level of political enthusiasm, an enthusiasm encouraged to a certain extent by the importance of material symbols in Pseudo-Dionysian thought, but more specifically discouraged by Pseudo-Dionysius's tendency to relegate any reference to history to a place of secondary consideration. Inevitably, the invisible order of the divine hierarchy remains only implicit in the *Vita Ludovici* while its narration fills page after page with busy human activity. One may reasonably ask whether Suger's own enjoyment of and commitment to the dignity and majesty of the secular world do not impede the reader's ascent from the contemplation of material forms to the comprehension of the invisible and unchanging.

A related problem stems from the necessarily linear nature of historical narration, which does violence to the architectonic structure of Suger's Pseudo-Dionysian model and thus sabotages, in ways that it would have been difficult for Suger to avoid, the hierarchical ordering of the material world in relation to the immaterial forces of which it is but a symbol. The clarity of vertical hierarchies, so brilliantly expressed in Suger's abbey church, was bound to be lost when laid out along the narrative grid of a chronologically ordered historical sequence. Although it can be argued that the absence of dates or a fixed chronology in the *Vita Ludovici* represents Suger's attempt to overcome this problem, the very nature of written history worked in this case against the historiographical goals of the text. To the extent that Suger failed, understandably, to solve this difficulty, the *Vita Ludovici* retains some characteristics of a genuine biography, at least insofar as it follows an apparent biographical sequence. To view the *Vita Ludovici* simply as royal biography is to miss its true intent, but the external form of the narration may well be cause for confusion.

However one resolves these questions, it seems clear that no discussion of the *Vita Ludovici* can afford to ignore them. Traditional positivist approaches to the text, which seek to extract from it the data upon which to build an understanding of the growth of the feudal state or Capetian kingship in the twelfth century, must proceed with caution. For, if correct, the foregoing analysis suggests that

Suger was more concerned with providing a cultural image of kingship and its role within a cosmologically defined hierarchy of being than with reporting the operations or administrative achievements of the monarchy in the political universe of twelfth-century France. This does not mean that Suger's *Vita Ludovici* has nothing to tell us about the increase of royal power, or even about the practical doings of the king, only that the communication of factual information is not the goal of the *Vita Ludovici*, and to read the text as if it were is seriously to misunderstand it and to risk misjudging the nature of the information it conveys.

For too long, the study of medieval historiography has been subjected to the demands of positivist research, which, not surprisingly, has left scholars with a deep-rooted suspicion that what is being reported in chronicles, *gesta*, biographies, and the like, is not always or wholly credible. The instrumental and "scientific" aims of scholarship have required the use of such texts for the construction of historical narratives, and so, for better or worse, medieval narration has had to serve those ends. In the case of the *Vita Ludovici*, the very abundance of such information, recorded by a man universally deemed worthy of belief, has inhibited the study of the text in terms of its own expressive purposes and modes of elaboration. Although the *Vita Ludovici* may finally be considered unsuccessful in realizing its historiographical intentions, to make this judgment is to say something very different from declaring that it has failed to live up to our standards of historical reliability. That history, in the end, proved a difficult vehicle for the encouragement of mystical contemplation does not mean that Suger did not wish it to be used in this fashion, and it behooves us to pay close attention to the ways in which his intentions shaped and gave meaning to the work. To Suger, the recollection of the past was not only a memory; it was also, and perhaps more important, the promise of the future.

10

Social Change and Literary Language

The Textualization of the Past in Thirteenth-Century Old French Historiography

The opening decades of the thirteenth century were a crucial moment in the social and political history of medieval France. Long-term transformations in the economic character of medieval society, originating as much as a century and a half earlier, culminated in these years to produce profound changes in the social and political structures which for centuries had served to order French society. On one hand, new wealth generated by the rising commercial sectors of medieval society created novel economic cleavages within the heart of France's traditional social hierarchy that undermined the dominance, based on the possession of vast amounts of land, enjoyed for so long by the aristocracy. Threatened from below by the villein upstart who benefited from the increased prosperity of the age to raise himself to a position of economic equality with the knight, and threatened from within by their own growing indebtedness which forced them to sell lands and homages, French nobles by the early part of the thirteenth century experienced a period of progressive impoverishment, making them particularly vulnerable to the shifting gravity of political power, itself a product, at least in part, of the revived prosperity of the twelfth and thirteenth centuries.

Joining with, and reciprocally acting upon, the threat to aristocratic status from below was a new and powerful challenge to the political autonomy of the French nobility, posed by the centralizing policies of Philip Augustus. Between 1180 and 1223, the French monarch relentlessly prosecuted his claims to overlordship of the French realm, repeatedly demanding, in numerous acts both large and small, that due service and obedience whose performance the French aristocracy had successfully evaded for centuries. By the beginning of the thirteenth century, the revival of a money economy and the growth of royal centralization had collaborated to undermine the sources of aristocratic strength and to delimit spheres of aristocratic activity, creating a highly destabilized political environment which worked to the advantage of the king. With the triumph of monarchy at the battle of Bouvines in 1214, an era of aristocratic domination over medieval French society came to a close. After the battle of Bouvines, reported an anonymous chronicler from Béthune, "there was no longer anyone who dared to make war against the king."[1] Henceforth, an ascendant monarchy gradually impressed its own style of rulership and dictated its own conception of social value upon the realm.[2]

It is neither insignificant nor accidental that these same decades witnessed a striking transformation in the historiographical praxis of the French aristocracy. For it was precisely during the reign of Philip Augustus that the earliest chronicles in French prose made their appearance, marking a decisive evolution in the historical tastes and concerns of the French-speaking lay world of the early thirteenth century.[3] Until that time, lay taste for history had been satisfied by rhymed chronicles or epic chansons de geste, chanted history with a large component of legend and fiction. But about 1200, a new popular demand for historical works in prose began to make itself felt. Little by little, vernacular prose, until then confined to translations of biblical or homiletic texts, became the preferred form of history.

The earliest products of the movement towards vernacular historiography were the translations of the *Pseudo-Turpin Chronicle*, the largely legendary account of Charlemagne's expedition to Spain. Near the year 1202, Nicolas of Senlis translated the *Pseudo-Turpin*

Chronicle for Countess Yolande of Saint-Pol.[4] At the same time, a certain "Master Johannes" made a separate translation which was copied, in the year 1206, for Renaud of Dammartin, and in the following year for Michel of Harnes.[5] Subsequent translations appear in a Francien version; in a recension from the area around Hainaut, Flanders, and Artois; in Anglo-Norman; and in Burgundian.[6] These *Pseudo-Turpin* translations constitute the first stage in the adoption of prose for historical writing.

Within a decade, original histories in French by Villehardouin (*Conquête de Constantinople*, between 1207 and 1213), Henri de Valenciennes (*Histoire de l'Empereur*, 1209), and Robert de Clari (*Conquête de Constantinople*, 1216) were composed, crusading chronicles which perfectly suited the tastes and interests of the lay aristocracy.[7] A translation of William of Tyre's *Historia rerum transmarinarum*, known as *Eracles*, dates from the same period (1190–1200) as does the Crusade history of Ernoul, known to us now only in the adaptation of it made by Bernard de Corbie (1232) and others in France and the East.[8] These crusading texts represent a new phenomenon in medieval historiography—the lay participant as chronicler, a genre of historical writing that was to come to full flower in the later work of Joinville and Froissart.

Indicative of the wider interest in the past are the contemporary French histories of antiquity, principally of Rome. Between 1208 and 1213, Roger of Lille commissioned a *Histoire Ancienne jusqu'à César*[9] while, simultaneously, Jean de Thuin recast the *Roumanz de Jules César* into prose in his *Hystore de Jules César*, on which he worked some time between 1215 and 1235.[10] In Champagne, the cleric Calendre wrote a history of the Roman emperors (1213–20),[11] and in the Ile-de-France, the most successful of these texts, *Li Faits des Romains*, was composed by an anonymous author in the years close to 1213–14.[12] Trojan history also attracted attention and was treated in the *Histoire Ancienne* and in the prose version of the *Roman de Troie*.[13]

By the end of the reign of Philip Augustus, vernacular history was adapted to contemporary chronicles as well. Beginning with the recently discovered *Chronique des Rois de France*, which survives in two rather different versions, one at the Vatican (Reg. Lat. 624) and a more complete recension found at Chantilly (Musée Condé, MS 689), the work of an anonymous author/translator whom for the sake of convenience I shall call the Anonymous of Chantilly, the focus of vernacular historiography shifts to royal history.[14] A contemporary work by the Anonymous of Béthune, also entitled *Chronique des Rois de France*, based largely for its early history of France on the *Historia Regum Francorum usque ad annum 1214*, recounted the deeds of French kings for an audience of purely French-speaking laity, answering the widening demand for authenticity of content and clarity of style in vernacular historiography.[15] A similar work was commissioned by Giles of Flagi, a Burgundian lord who charged an anonymous author to compose in French a history of Philip Augustus, no doubt based on the Latin chronicles of Rigord of Saint-Denis and of Philip's chaplain and chronicler, Guillaume le Breton. Although the work sponsored by Flagi is lost, the prologue, which survives, shares the growing aversion to poetic history, announcing the author's intention to write a prose life because "il est difficile de rimer une histoire sans y ajouter des mensonges pour faire la rime"[16] (it is difficult to rhyme a history without adding lies to make the rhyme). Fragments of a verse translation of the *Gesta Philippi Augusti* by Guillaume le Breton, possibly written by John of Prunai, have survived,[17] as have fragments for the years 1214–16 of another prose chronicle of this monarch, sometimes attributed to Michel of Harnes or to a member of his household.[18] Thirty years after the Anonymous of Béthune composed his work, the Ménestrel d'Alphonse de Poitiers freely translated the *Historia Regum Francorum* once again, defending his plain, unembellished style on the grounds that it was more conducive to truth and more appropriate to his audience of "*bones et vaillanz gens.*"[19]

These early-thirteenth-century translations and chronicles formed a critical stage in the development of vernacular historiography and served as important intermediaries between the Latin historiography of the twelfth century and the full-scale vernacular historiography of France signaled by the appearance of the multivoume *Grandes*

Chroniques de France, the first installment of which was completed by Primat in 1274.[20] By meeting the demand for a vernacular prose history that was both truthful and based on authoritative Latin sources, they helped to win respectability for French historiography. By the last third of the thirteenth century, one can confidently say that historiography in Old French was successfully established in the France of the Capetian dynasty.

In the main, scholars concerned with Old French historiography have tended to view it as a late, and not altogether welcome, addition to a centuries-old and already sophisticated tradition of Latin historical writing, in relation to which vernacular history, at least in its initial phases, receives rather low marks. This view of vernacular historiography seemed to be justified by the fact that the earliest texts consisted of translations of Latin works and thus, in the nature of things, invited comparison with their Latin sources. Although it is true that early vernacular chronicles translated Latin texts, they did so in a way that clearly demonstrates their ties to an already existing vernacular literary culture, distinct in its origins and modes of operation from Latin literature. Indeed, it is a striking, although as yet unexplored, fact that the evolution of vernacular historical genres—from *Pseudo-Turpin* translations, to ancient histories, to Crusade and contemporary chronicles—recapitulates the evolution of romance literary genres from epic, to *romans d'antiquité,* to courtly romances, while recasting them in prose.

The curious parallel between the generic evolution of romance literature and vernacular historiography suggests that vernacular culture itself was the generator of Old French historiography and that Old French historical writing is perhaps best viewed as one among a variety of vernacular literary genres through which the French aristocracy sought to resolve the tensions created by its changing social status. Additionally, there is the possibility that the emergence of a specifically prose historiography is, as well, functionally related to the transformations occurring within aristocratic society during the period under examination, although the specific ways in which this might be true remain to be discovered.

As a starting point for such an inquiry, it is useful to note that modern sociolinguistics has demonstrated that social groups most affected by changes in status tend to be the most conscious of alternative modes of discursive behavior, that they are, in other words, most sensitive to the power of language to register social transformations.[21] Language games, Lévi-Strauss insists, are essentially power games, and it follows that disputes over language domains and usage are contests of power. The profound shift in language use from poetry to prose among the French aristocracy of the thirteenth century appears, therefore, to point to a perception of dislocations in the social order by the aristocracy, a perception registered in a revision of its customary discursive behavior. Whereas earlier romance genres sought to explore the newly problematic aspects of aristocratic life, to forge a literary language by which, to quote R. Howard Bloch, "to articulate the crisis of its own changing status,"[22] I would like to suggest that the adoption of prose as the language of vernacular history represented, rather, an effort on the part of the aristocratic patrons of Old French chronicles to "deproblematize" aristocratic culture in an age of anxiety whose social ground was the radical challenge to aristocratic autonomy and prestige posed by the revival of monarchical authority during the very period that witnessed the birth of vernacular prose history. Moreover, I would argue, such a "deproblematizing" posture was inscribed in the nature of vernacular history's evolving narrative structures and forms of discourse. And to illustrate this latter point, I would like to begin by locating vernacular historiography within the framework of that commemorative culture which, in a broad sense, characterized the literature of the High Middle Ages, and then to trace the ways in which it progressively distanced itself from both the goals and techniques that it had shared with other vernacular genres.

That medieval culture was in some sense a culture of commemoration would, I think, be agreed to by everyone engaged in its study. Commemoration may be taken to mean, in the words of Eugene Vance, "all gesture, ritualized or not, destined to recapitulate in the name of the collectivity an event, whether earlier or outside of time, in order to render fruitful, vibrant, and significant the *hic* et *nunc* of the lived past."[23] Understood in this way, the rubric of commemoration can include an enormous range of behavior and literary production. Not only were the central rites of Christianity based on such commemorative practices, inscribed, for example, in the liturgy of the Eucharist (bestowed by Christ upon the faithful *in meam commemorationem*), but a commemorative model underlies a variety of customary legal practices, the genealogical concern with ancestors, the political theory of *translatio imperii* (and its derivative, the cultural model of *translatio studii*), as well as the exemplary nature of history itself.[24]

There is a more specific sense, however, in which medieval literary practice was grounded in rituals of commemoration, in that the defining mode of literature was, until the rise of silent reading, that of oral recitation.[25] The performed text, which we associate with epic but which was a far more comprehensive phenomenon throughout the High Middle Ages, represented a periodic, ritual reenactment of the basic values of lay culture by means of a shared, public recitation of traditional stories. All texts, to the degree that they formed part of the oral culture of lay society or entered into it by being read aloud, enjoyed a public, collective status as vehicles through which the community reaffirmed its sense of historical identity. The nature of oral culture is such that human action is best understood by comparison with the legacy of stories about the past,[26] and the fundamental goal of oral recitation is, precisely, to revivify the past and make it live in the present, to fuse past and present, singer and hearer, author and public, into a single collective entity. In an oral performance, the past exists only by means of the poet's voice; "hero and poet are born together"[27] and are sustained in relation to an audience, which itself existentially participates in the reactualization of a bygone age. The written literary text, when it represents a transcription of a once-live recital, commemorates both the past which is sung about and the performance itself.

Even if we restrict ourselves, as inevitably we must, to the evidence of purely written accounts of history, it is useful to remember that writing, too, is in part commemorative in nature, for as Vance has already recognized, societies in which commemoration plays a central role invariably incline towards a metaphysic of the sign, since past events, being necessarily absent, are transmitted to the present only by means of verbal signs which, thus, constitute the "reality" of history. This does not mean that there is no difference between oral and written culture. On the contrary, as the critics of the god Thoth, the inventor of writing, already remarked in Plato's *Phaedrus,* the ability to record in writing may promote forgetfulness as much as remembrance and serves to a high degree to keep the past in the past, instead of continuously recreating it in the present (as in oral performance).[28] Indeed, Thoth's critics feared that the diffusion of his art would weaken the function of memory in society and, with it, the mythopoetic basis of social community. But it is helpful, in a consideration of the place of vernacular historiography in medieval culture, to see that it emerged within the framework of literature's commemorative rituals and, like Old French literature, embodied the collective values of the group, rather than the ideology of the individual. In that sense, vernacular history's closest literary kin in the Middle Ages was epic. The earliest vernacular histories are, in fact, prose translations of the *Pseudo-Turpin Chronicle* and retain a close textual relation to the legendary form of the Charlemagne cycle as it had originated in the French epic. And as with epic, the principal means of communication for the vernacular chronicle was the performed text, for it is absolutely clear that early vernacular histories were intended to be read aloud in accordance with the standard practices of oral performance.[29]

Confirmation of the fundamental affinity between the Old French epic and history emerges from an analysis of the vernacular chronicle's narrative structure, from the way it emplots the matter of history.[30] As all students of medieval vernacular historiography have recognized, the narrative structure of historical literature in the Middle Ages was shaped by the conventions of fictional narrative. In the earliest works of vernacular history, the chroniclers' method of narration appears to be based on the uncodified but consciously practiced techniques of epic composition.[31] Epic narrative, generally, consists of a series of episodes or tableaux serially ordered in paratactic juxtaposition along a temporal axis, not of fixed dates (i.e., chronology) but of sequences. Because the connection between these juxtaposed scenes is serial rather than causal, the overall effect of such narrative organization is to produce a nondevelopmental, episodic narrative informed by a theme that is continually reexpressed in separate events, lending to epic narrative its sense of existing in an eternal present, of constituting a series of "nows" placed side by side, which move forward in discrete, seemingly unrelated steps. In pure epic, the interrupted quality of the narrative line—a consequence of its unremitting parataxis—is reinforced by the inclusion of *laisses similaires*, subepisodic fragments in which a just-completed narrative element is repeated, further suspending the forward movement of the story. The structural pattern of epic literature is, therefore, basically repetitive and sequential, and it seems logical to conclude that it was a form of narration well suited to the ritual, commemorative aims of the performed text and expressed, on the level of narrativity, epic's desire to revive the past and make it live again in the present.

Early vernacular histories such as the translations of the *Pseudo-Turpin Chronicle*, *Li Faits des Romains*, the *Chronique des Rois de France* of the Anonymous of Chantilly, and the Crusade history of Villehardouin share this underlying narrative pattern, even in cases, like that of *Li Faits des Romains* and the *Chronique des Rois de France*, where it is not a characteristic of the Latin sources that are being translated to create the history. Vernacular history differed from Latin historiography (hence from its own Latin sources) in its division of the narrative into a series of episodic units, aimed at presenting sharply defined, visualized scenes and exemplary heroes in an action-oriented narrative. Identifiable epic techniques such as the doubling of verbs, the use of oral interjections like *oyez* (hear) and *voyez* (see), to invoke audience participation, and the rendering of historical situations in vividly realized, dramatic form were part of the vernacular chronicler's technical repertoire and were extensively used to recreate the past in ways similar to fictional narrative.

The purely serial arrangement of episodes characteristic of epic has its counterpart in the chronicle in the chronologically strung-out but causally unrelated sequence of events which, as in epic, develops along a more or less clearly defined temporal axis. Nor is the Old French chronicle immune to those interruptions of plot commonly found in contemporary fictional literature. While such interruptions obviously do not take the form of *laisses similaires*, the frequent discursive and episodic digressions to which the early Old French chronicle is prone produce comparable results in terms of the disruption of narrative continuity and movement. All these practices appear to locate vernacular history in the same commemorative, if not actually ritual, context of the performed text occupied by medieval French literature in general.

Yet it can be argued that the very rise of Old French historiography is evidence of a growing dissatisfaction with epic form as a vehicle of historical thought and points to a certain discrediting of epic as history. Although, initially, the vernacular chronicle may have functioned as a complementary historical genre, ultimately it competed with and came to displace epic as the bearer of lay society's historical traditions. And it is striking that the success of vernacular history was accompanied by transformations in the character of its narrativity, transformations that served to remove it from the realm of performance and place it closer to the pole of textuality.

While it is not possible to demonstrate here the full range of changes that the Old French chronicle underwent in the course of its development, a few points can be briefly noted. To begin with, there occurs a gradual withdrawal of the poet's voice, a diminution in the frequency of those narrative interjections by which the chronicler had established his presence in the text and impressed his personality on it through apostrophes to the reader, the enunciation of proverbial wisdom, the framing of moral judgments on the events recounted, or the simple admission of incapacity for the task at hand, due to lack of literary skill or ignorance. Instead, the vernacular chronicler re-treats behind an increasingly reflective discourse, in the dual sense that he assumes that his narrative will transparently reflect an objec-tive "reality" and that he strives to produce a more systematic, reflec-tive treatment of his subject matter, as distinct from the evocative, emotive treatment characteristic of earlier Old French literature. To be sure, individual points of view and ideological biases remain, but they are integrated into the narration of fact, behind which the his-torian holds secret his moral personality.[32]

The best illustration of this evolution is found by comparing the *Chronique des Rois de France*, by the Anonymous of Chantilly (be-tween 1210 and 1230), and the quasi-official *Grandes Chroniques de France*, produced fifty years later (in 1274 at the royal Abbey of Saint-Denis). These works translate exactly the same body of Latin sources, and it can even be shown that Primat, author/translator of the Dionysian version, used the earlier work when he encountered diffi-culties in rendering the Latin that he could not solve on his own.[33] Yet the difference between the two texts is remarkable. In the *Chron-ique*, the Anonymous repeatedly intervenes to engage his audience's attention, to formulate moral judgments, to offer wonderfully irrele-vant commentary, or simply to express his fatigue with the whole en-terprise, which he knows full well will never be adequately remuner-ated. In contrast, Primat cloaks his authorial persona in a steady stream of factual narration that buries its messages in an imper-sonal—that is, deproblematized—narrative mode of pure referen-tiality. The disappearance of the narrator announces a desire to cre-ate the illusion of objectivity, an ideological gesture not unrelated to the broader ideological purposes of royal historiography. At the same time, it signals the movement of history out of the collective, public community created by oral performance and into the arena of private reading and textual debate.

A comparable movement from authorial presence to textual ob-jectification can be traced in the very manuscript tradition of the *Histoire Ancienne jusqu'à César*. This text, the earliest universal chron-icle in Old French prose, was written some time between 1208 and

1213 at the behest of Roger IV, châtelain of Lille. According to the verse prologue, the author planned to cover the history of the world from the creation down to the Norman Conquest and the peopling of Flanders.[34] In fact, for reasons that remain unknown, the chronicle abruptly terminates with an account of Caesar's conquest of Gaul, after the defeat of the Belgae in 57 B.C.[35] The work as a whole is divided into seven sections beginning with Genesis (I), and progressing through the history of Assyria and Greece (II), of Thebes (III), via a somewhat confused section that treats the history of the Minotaur, the Amazons, and Hercules (IV), and continues with an account of Troy (V), and Aeneas (VI), closing with the history of Rome (VII), which contains an oddly placed and extremely lengthy interpolation devoted primarily to the history of Alexander the Great.[36] Although the author shares the general aversion to romance characteristic of early vernacular chroniclers, it is striking that the best-realized portions of his history are those that cover the terrain of earlier romances—the accounts of Thebes, Troy, Aeneas, and Alexander—works that he clearly knew and used, all the while fiercely maintaining his textual independence of such "fables" and his strict reliance on Latin sources "que de verité iert creüe"[37] (whose truth is to be believed).

There are forty-seven extant manuscripts of the first recension of the *Histoire Ancienne*, of which eight date from the thirteenth century.[38] Of these, only two preserve a series of twenty-one verse moralizations in which the anonymous clerical author engages in a personal appeal to his listeners to hearken to the moral lessons that history proffers, lessons ranging from the necessity to do good, fear death, and avoid envy and greed, to the benefits of loyal servitors, humility, virtue, and the political advantages of largesse as exemplified by Romulus.[39] The verse moralizations are scattered throughout the text at fairly regular intervals, but are notably absent from the sections that deal with Theban and Trojan history and that recount the deeds of Aeneas and Alexander, that is, from precisely those parts of the work most indebted to romance verse narrative. The absence of verse moralizations in those sections suggests a conscious strategy to avoid contamination of his own verses by a too-close association with the *matière* of the *romans d'antiquité*, whose mendacious treatment of history is routinely criticized.[40]

On four occasions, the moralizations are clearly marked in the text as establishing the author's personal voice, being introduced with well-rubricated titles announcing that "ci parole cil qui le livre fait" (here speaks he who writes the book) or "ci parole le maistres qui traite l'estorie"[41] (here speaks the master who treats the history). Elsewhere, the author initiates his moral commentary with a direct address to his audience of "seignors et dames," a live voice calling to a live and listening public, whose participation in the recitation of the great deeds of the past he hopes will bring them moral profit.

Later manuscripts of the *Histoire Ancienne* progressively suppress both the verse moralizations and the interpellations to the audience. First to disappear is the extensive prologue, in which the author had located his enterprise in a personal context of patron and purpose, doubtless deemed overly specific by later copyists operating in other milieux and for new patrons. Manuscripts such as the thirteenth-century B.N. fr. 9682 not only suppress the prologue but transcribe the verse moralizations in prose format, without, however, bothering to rewrite the verses, so that they remain embedded in what appears, visually, to be a uniform prose text. The effect of this method of transcription is textually to efface authorial presence without actually silencing the author's voice, for when the passages are read aloud, that voice instantly reemerges in the octosyllabic couplets that still make up the moralizations, despite the fact that they are no longer perceivable in the written text as such. This masking of authorial presence is the first step in a steady process by which the verse portions of the *Histoire Ancienne* are little by little abridged, prosed, or dropped altogether (as is the direct address to the audience)[42] in favor of a textually coherent prose narration which has lost all traces of the author's original moral preoccupations. The burden of the moral lessons that ancient history conveys is, in the end, carried by an "objective" historical narration, unassisted by authorial commentary, which refuses engagement in a direct dialogue with its public.

Completing this transformation from live performance into objectified text was the vernacular historian's abandonment of parataxis in favor of a hypotactic construction of the narrative, in which individual scenes (the old building blocks of episodic narration) were gradually subordinated to a theme whose component elements were united not, as before, by syntactic devices, but by logical, causal relations. As Northrop Frye has shown, causality in narrative develops with second phase, or metonymic, writing,[43] which replaces the metaphoric language of myth and presents itself as a verbal imitation of a reality outside itself, thus strengthening the referential, "objective" status of historical discourse. The appearance of a synthetic, causal narrative in the vernacular chronicle represents, therefore, a literary preference for metonymic as against metaphoric discourse, for an ideological as against an imaginative performance of history. In lieu of its once frankly acknowledged desire to divert, the Old French chronicle increasingly claims to function as a conveyor of information, to be a written monument to the actions, beliefs, and ideals of the past which, in theory, it transparently reflected. The so-called realism of vernacular historiography is nothing more than the visible symptom of this ideological turn, and the growth of "realism" can be associated with vernacular history's most significant achievement, the adoption of prose as the form deemed most appropriate for the communication of those truths about human experience that it was the task of history to recount. The distinguishing feature of the early vernacular chronicle lies in its militant insistence on prose as the necessary language of history and its critique of the mendacious tendencies of verse historiography.[44]

As vernacular prose matured, it not only propagated a variety of literary genres, of which historiography was the most novel, it also displaced poetry as a narrative vehicle, a process accompanied by a wholesale attack on the veracity of poetic discourse and, with it, on the encompassing social context in which the performed, poetic text had functioned. As the first translator of a *Pseudo-Turpin Chronicle*, Nicolas of Senlis, asserted, "Many peoples had heard sung and recited the deeds of Charlemagne in Spain, but never were there so many lies as those spoken and chanted by the minstrel and jongleur," for, he maintained, "no rhymed tale is true; all that it speaks is lies, for it knows nothing except hearsay."[45] This is so, as the prologue to Michel's *Turpin* explains, because "in order to fit the rhyme, it borrows words outside of history."[46] Boldly rejecting any history which, as one manuscript proclaimed, when "treated in rhyme is a lie,"[47] these translations insist on the veracity of their tales, the truth of which is guaranteed by being faithfully transmitted in the lucid medium of prose.

Thus Johannes, in the prologue to his translation, affirmed the authority of his version against those that had preceded it on the basis of his faithful reproduction, in French, of the Latin prose of his exemplar: "although others have taken away from or added to [this history] , here you can hear the truth of Spain [*la verité d'Espaigne*] according to the Latin of the history which Count Renaud of Boulogne had with great effort caused to be sought out in books at the abbey of Saint-Denis."[48] The latter was invoked—falsely, we know— as an additional guarantee of the text's historical authenticity. This vernacular history makes a privileged claim to authority on the basis of its utilization of an authentic Latin text found at Saint-Denis which is accurately reconstituted in French by means of a literal prose translation. The proclaimed "truth" of the chronicle separates it from fictional genres such as epic and romance. This "truth" is reinforced by the listing of acknowledged guarantors of veracity—author, patron, and manuscript owner—the aim of which is to surround the translation with an aura of credibility lent by the discussion of the circumstances of the work's composition, the historian's awareness of the difficulty of his task, and his avowed commitment to remain faithful to historical truth where others before him had failed.[49] The emergence of prose in place of verse (and history in place of fiction) represents the displacement of linguistic mediation towards a low mimetic (or "realistic") literary mode as a means of enhancing the credibility of aristocratic ideology by grounding it in a language of apparent facticity, in contradistinction to the overt use of fantasy in epic and romance.

In that sense, the new prominence of prose signals the rise of textuality as a privileged instrument of aristocratic culture. Since the earliest works of vernacular historiography, although employing prose, remained nonetheless within the domain of the performed text, it seems difficult to ascribe this change in aristocratic language use merely to the growth of literacy and a widening process of textualization, presumably occurring everywhere in medieval society in the twelfth and thirteenth centuries. The vacillation of vernacular history between the poles of performance and textuality, together with its ability to sustain a variety of narrative structures, offers further evidence that, in any case, the traditional distinction between oral and literate culture has been too sharply drawn (a conclusion already forcefully stated by Stock and others)[50] and that both the performed and the written text might be more helpfully situated in the broader framework of medieval society's commemorative practices. In a commemorative culture, it may be supposed, history can be equally well served by reading or by recitation, and the choice of one over the other has less to do with strictly technical issues like literacy, and more with social issues involving status and social cohesion within the community addressed by the history, especially if that community was confronted with new forms of institutional power threatening its traditional position in society.

The substitution of prose for verse, of the written for the performed text, seems to be the product of an ideological initiative on the part of the French aristocracy, whose social dominance in French society was being contested by the rise of monarchical authority during precisely the period that witnessed the birth of vernacular prose history. By appropriating the inherent authority of Latin texts and by adapting prose for the historicization of literary language, vernacular historiography emerges as a literature of fact, integrating on a literary level the historical experience and the expressive language proper to the aristocracy.[51] No longer the expression of a shared, collective image of the community's social past, vernacular prose history becomes instead a partisan record intended to serve the interests of a particular social group and inscribes, in the very nature of its linguistic code, a partisan and ideologically motivated assertion of the aristocracy's place and prestige in medieval society.

That this shift in aristocratic language use and historiographical praxis is rooted in new forms of historical understanding on the part of the aristocracy is perhaps confirmed by the contemporary recasting of Arthurian romance into prose in the so-called Vulgate cycle. For there, too, as many scholars have noted, we see the abandonment of the experimental and overtly fictional world of twelfth-century romance in favor of a newly historicized and, in the case of the *Mort Artu*, deeply pessimistic vision of the chivalric world of the aristocracy, a pessimism that increasingly extends, as Lee Patterson has suggested in his discussion of the later Alliterative *Morte Arthure*,[52] even to the significance and possibility of historical action itself. Looked at in this perspective, the collapse of a unified, public community receptive to the oral recitation of performed texts, and the rise of written, ideologically oriented historical narratives might be seen as registering, within the domain of literature itself, the revised conditions of aristocratic life in the early thirteenth century. And it is here, at the intersection of literary practice and social life, that the study of vernacular historiography finds its most compelling vantage point for understanding the role of the past in medieval France.

11

Medieval Canon Formation and the Rise of Royal Historiography in Old French Prose

In a given country's history of historical writing, there are relatively few periods that witness the foundation of a new structure of historical memory, a vision of the past sufficiently strong and durable that it establishes a veritable canon of historical thought and writing, taking *canon* to refer to a structure of thought, a frame of reference, or a disciplinary boundary rather than a list of works whose attribution of aesthetic excellence has won them a permanent place in a hierarchy of literary value. Such a canon, once achieved, shapes for centuries a nation's consciousness of its development and essential character. France, in the opinion of Pierre Nora, has witnessed only three such historiographical transformations during the entire span of its history. The first of these occurred with the redaction of the *Grandes Chroniques de France* at the Abbey of Saint-Denis, the initial installment of which was completed in 1274 by the monk Primat on the basis of his translation of a corpus of Latin texts collected and preserved at the abbey.[1] The *Grandes Chroniques* condensed the genealogical and dynastic memory of France into a simple edifice that inaugurated a new understanding of French history as the history of the *trois races* of kings—Merovingians, Carolingians, and Capetians. The appearance of the initial installment of the *Grandes Chroniques* in

1274, therefore, represents a significant moment not only in the history of medieval France but in the unfolding of French historical consciousness.

Already present in the *Grandes Chroniques* is the basic articulation of French medieval history as a dynastic chronicle narrating the succession of kings from Pharamond forward, with critical nodal points of meaning clustered around a few hallmark figures: Clovis, Charlemagne, Philip Augustus, Saint Louis, Philip the Fair, and so forth. As Tyvaert has demonstrated, both the structure and sense of critical conjuncture around these figures continued unchanged until the seventeenth century.[2] In many ways, a comparable structure and rhythm of French history can still be found in Robert Fawtier's *Les Rois Capétiens*, first published in 1960 and reissued in both French and English several times after that date. A durable canon, indeed!

Virtually all scholarship on the chronicles of Saint-Denis assumes that the creation of the historiographical canon of French medieval history was a slow but continuous process of building up factual content and narrative strategies to express a deeply rooted understanding of the nature of French history which, both in its making and in its continued viability within French historical thinking down to the twentieth century, was essentially uncontested. It also assumes an unproblematic relationship between the vernacular *Grandes Chroniques* and the Latin sources therein translated, from which the Old French text appears directly to flow. Unfortunately, this proves to be wrong.

The error lies not so much in the claims made for the impact of the *Grandes Chroniques* on subsequent interpretations of French history as in a mistaken conception of the processes by which that canon, if indeed that is what was achieved, came into being, and more particularly in the contention that the creation of this "canonical" structure of history was uncontested and possessed unproblematic relations both to the Latin sources employed and to other vernacular versions of those sources. It is, in fact, on the basis of new research on alternative versions of vernacular prose translations of the same body of Latin sources that I have come completely to revise my view of the impulses and procedures that went into the composition of the *Grandes Chroniques*. This chapter seeks to provide, in brief and summary form, the results of that research and the implications that it possesses for our understanding of the production of medieval history and, more generally perhaps, of medieval canon formation, at least with respect to vernacular prose historiography.

Prior to the composition of the *Grandes Chroniques de France*, there were three prose vernacular histories that sought to erect a structure of French history apparently focused on the kings of France, of which I will discuss two here: the *Chroniques des Rois de France* by the Anonymous of Béthune, written between 1220 and 1223, and the newly discovered *Chronique des Rois de France*, preserved in manuscript 869 of the Musée Condé at Chantilly, of which a second, truncated version exists in Vatican Reg. Lat. 624.[3] These texts share with the *Grandes Chroniques* a community of Latin sources, a concern with royal history, and the emplotment of history as a series of accounts of French kings, in which French medieval history is constituted as the narration of *gestes* performed by successive kings whose personal characteristics and deeds, extensively chronicled in essentially biographical modes, bespeak the enduring meaning of history as the collective action of royal lineages in relation to those values to which their *gestes* gave life. At least this is what most present-day historians have claimed. But the story is both more complex and more interesting, one that sheds novel light on the essentially contested character of historical production in the Middle Ages and the dialectical tensions that underlie its formation. I would like to discuss each text in turn and then offer some observations on the relations between them, concluding with some suggestions about how so-called canons might be read in the Middle Ages, suggestions that are prompted by my belief that it is the pervasive presence of medieval intertextuality that has led present-day historians to misread the play of interests and ideological stakes at issue in the production of medieval vernacular historiography.

The *Chronique des Rois de France* by the Anonymous of Béthune figures as one of the earliest works of contemporary history in thirteenth-century France,[4] following by a decade or so the first texts of vernacular prose historiography represented by translations of the *Pseudo-Turpin Chronicle* and compilations of classical historians such as Caesar, Sallust, Suetonius, and Lucan (to name only a few) in the *Faits des Romains, Hystore de Jules César,* and *Histoire Ancienne.* Although his name is lost to us, the extant evidence suggests that the Anonymous was a literate ménestrel attached to the household of Robert VII of Béthune, for whom he also wrote the *Histoire des ducs de Normandie et des rois d'Angleterre,* a text that—quite remarkably—in the sections devoted to contemporary history recounts precisely the events covered by the *Chronique des Rois de France,* but from the perspective of an English partisan. What ties the two chronicles together most powerfully, in fact, is the intermediary and mediating role played in each by the Flemish, whose incessant crossings of the Channel bind together the histories of the royal powers contending for their allegiance.

The Anonymous's patron, Robert VII of Béthune, was the second son of Guillaume II, lord of Béthune, advocate of Arras, and, by marriage, lord of Dendermonde.[5] Robert belonged to a small group of Franco-Flemish lords circulating in the orbit of the count of Flanders in the opening decades of the thirteenth century which, by its patronage, was responsible for the rise of vernacular prose historiography. These lords formed a tightly knit circle of Flemish aristocrats who lived in close proximity to one another, often intermarried, and, in the crucial years of the early thirteenth century, were caught up in an era of political turmoil unmatched in Flemish medieval history. All but one joined the English (anti-Capetian) coalition in the wars between King John of England and King Philip Augustus of France, and all were forced to submit to royal authority in the years after the battle of Bouvines (1214) and the collapse of the French expedition to conquer England in 1216, in which Robert of Béthune had enlisted as a constable in the English army.

For reasons it would take too long to discuss here, Flemish patronage of contemporary chronicles can be seen as a form of political action, an attempt to control the subject matter of history and the voices on the past as an instrument of domination over the collective memory of feudal society. The political goals that promoted the patronage of contemporary history in thirteenth-century France, therefore, signal the beginning of an overt contest over the past that would scarcely have been conceivable in an earlier period, when history represented the trace of God's operation in human affairs. The secularization and laicization of historical writing in the thirteenth century, by removing from view God's active participation in human affairs, brought history squarely into the realm of human contest and historiographical contestation.

Noble patronage of contemporary history similarly effected a change in the scope of historical investigation. In contrast to epic and romance, which treated the theme of individual heroic action in past times, the vernacular chronicle tended, instead, to provide a history of larger social collectivities. For the narration of the deeds of individual heroes, the Old French chronicle substituted an account of aristocratic lineages, which were usually inserted within the narrative frame of royal history, even though this use of royal history as an organizational device in some cases paradoxically contradicted the ideological import of the chronicles themselves, at least to the degree that such chronicles sought to validate principles of aristocratic autonomy. But the absence in medieval Europe of a clear governmental entity like the Roman Republic meant that there was no natural political unit on which to focus historical narration.

The titles employed by a contemporary chronicler such as the Anonymous of Béthune, whose dual histories seemingly highlight the kings of France and England as the interpretive foci of his accounts, have traditionally led historians and literary scholars to classify them as works of royal history.[6] Because he wrote a history called the *Chronique des Rois de France*, the Anonymous of Béthune is often thought to represent a proto-nationalist tendency in Old French historiography, a tendency only fully realized fifty years later with the production of the *Grandes Chroniques de France*. But does the use of royal history as title and narrative frame necessarily betoken ideological assent to monarchical hegemony? On the other hand, if such assent is absent, why privilege the king by writing under the titular aegis of the royal name?

An approach, if not a definitive answer, to these questions lies in seeing the thirteenth-century contemporary chronicle as a site for the negotiation of competing interests, opening up the historical text as a locus for contestation over the past. Precisely because it treated the events and dilemmas of the present, the contemporary chronicle created a textual space for the presentation of a variety of voices on the past. In moving from the distanced, absolute past of the Carolingian epic and classical antiquity, contemporary history changed not only the temporal model of the world but the moral significance of history itself. History presented not an icon of an idealized and stable world, but an image of an inconclusive present, whose full meaning could not be disengaged from a mere account of events in their unfolding, since those events were incomplete and harbored as yet unknown consequences. The shift in temporal perspective, in this sense, produced a radical relativizing of all historical knowledge, both in terms of the perspectives brought to bear upon it and in terms of the impossibility of interpretive closure on events that continued beyond the temporal scope of the historical work itself. Historical writing in the form of the contemporary chronicle thus became both dialogic (to use Bakhtin's terminology) and dialectical, producing an image of past and present as composed of a variety of vying voices on and diversity of participants in present happenings.

Furthermore, not only were events themselves incomplete, but the political environment in which the vernacular chronicle was generated—*by* which it was generated—enforced a sense of relative values and competing loyalties. In the work of the Anonymous of Béthune, the rivalry between the Capetian and Plantagenet monarchies for the loyalties of northern French lords discloses a society riven by internal schisms and contested allegiances, in which the progress of royal warfare eventually pits blood relations against one another and spells the destruction of those principles of lineage and solidarity that had once formed the basis of the nobility's social cohesion and strength. In that sense, the Anonymous's *Histoire des ducs de Normandie et des rois d'Angleterre* and *Chronique des Rois de France*, by rewriting exactly the same segment of contemporary history alternatively from the point of view of the two main forces vying for political influence over contemporary Franco-Flemish society, embody the new conditions under which his own patron's house of Béthune was compelled to operate, in a world in which competition for loyalty, authority, and political power had radically changed the social and political rules of the game. Just as Flanders was trapped politically between the rivalries of England and France—and, within Flanders, no family more so than the Béthunes—so the Anonymous's vision of history is fractured into competing versions, disclosing the incoherence of the nobility's position and the impossibility of negotiating a secure ground for the conduct of aristocratic life.

The Anonymous of Béthune also integrates the contemporary history of Capetian France into its ancient (Trojan), Merovingian, and Carolingian pasts. It is here that the Anonymous's use of Latin sources similar to those later employed by the *Chronique des Rois de France* of Vatican-Chantilly and the *Grandes Chroniques de France* has proven so misleading in the interpretation of his work, suggesting to scholars a community not only of sources but of historical goals and ideological interests. But, unlike the royal histories in Latin on which he draws for his material, and unlike the later vernacular uses of these same Latin texts, the Anonymous's work does not offer an exclusively monarchical past. The Anonymous of Béthune turns to the dynastic past of France not to validate the monarchy's right to govern, but as an essential political framework for considering the relations of a crisis-beset aristocracy to the monarchy. In so doing, he converted the historiographical text into a site for a contest over the past that is the textual analogue of the political contest for power and authority in contemporary society. At the same time, the writing of history served an expressive function, giving voice to aristocratic ambivalence about and resentment towards newly powerful kings. The Anonymous of Béthune's *Chronique des Rois de France* provides a striking illustration of the nobility's complex attitudes about the ways in which the rise of a centralized monarchy had fundamentally changed the status and spheres of operation of the French aristocracy. His *Chronique des Rois de France* is the first work of vernacular historiography in medieval France to confront these changed conditions and to incorporate them as the very structure of a new kind of history capable of addressing the inherent instability and contested nature of the past.

If, as I have argued elsewhere, vernacular historiography initially represented—in its adoption of prose with the translations of the *Pseudo-Turpin Chronicle* from Latin into Old French—an attempt to deproblematize aristocratic culture in an age of anxiety whose social ground was the challenge to aristocratic autonomy posed by a resurgent monarchy, what the contemporary chronicle indicates is the impossibility of sustaining this deproblematized posture towards a past seen as a unitary source of authority, for that past spoke with more than one voice. The very complexity of contemporary history served to redefine and reinterpret both past and present as inherently complex structures of meaning over which it was difficult, if not impossible, to establish control.

If the rise of a newly powerful monarchy placed in question the ethical underpinnings of the feudal world of the aristocracy, what has been too little appreciated is that this was a process that affected the moral predicates of royal ideology as well. Yet to the extent that the chivalric values that made up noble culture were shared by the French monarchy, it could be expected that the king would participate in the refiguration of those aspects of moral and historical thought which until then had provided a common basis of action for royalty and nobility alike. Insofar as new conditions of political action demanded new forms of moral imagination in the thirteenth century, this demand weighed equally upon the monarchy, for the terms of its modes of operation had changed no less significantly than those of the aristocracy.

Fortunately, it is now possible to begin to trace the royal response to the emerging world that royal power itself had done so much to create. For we now have in a hand a new text, only recently discovered at the Musée Condé in Chantilly, which represents the earliest example of royal historiography in Old French known at present and which was composed between 1217 and 1237, that is, around the same time as the Anonymous of Béthune's *Chronique* and at exactly that moment when the long thrust towards the recovery of royal power was brought to brilliant fruition by Philip Augustus.[7]

The text of Chantilly 869 is entitled *Chronique des Rois de France* and includes a history of the kings of France from the Trojan origins of the Franks to Philip Augustus inclusively. It is written in the language of the Ile-de-France and draws its materials from texts lodged in the Parisian Abbey of Saint-Germain des-Prés and at the nearby Abbey of Saint-Denis. The production of royal historiography in Francien prose has until now been thought to begin only fifty years later with the compilation of the *Grandes Chroniques*. Strikingly, the anonymous author/translator of this *Chronique*—whom I shall call the Anonymous of Chantilly—used as a Latin base for his history a corpus of Latin historical texts virtually identical to that exploited by Primat, and it can be shown that Primat frequently incorporated readings from the *Chronique des Rois de France* when he encountered difficulties in translating his Latin sources. Like his later Dionysian emulator, the Anonymous writes to celebrate and justify Capetian kingship. In this, he can lay fair claim to being the first royalist historian of Capetian France to work in Old French, initiating a tradition of vernacular royal historiography that would ultimately dominate historical writing in medieval France and beyond. He can, therefore, be seen as a critical figure in the formation of a canonical structure of French medieval history.

Among the extraordinary features of this altogether extraordinary *Chronique* is the fact that the Anonymous concludes his work with a translation of Guillaume le Breton's *Philippide*, a Latin verse panegyric of more than nine thousand lines, originally written by Guillaume, chaplain to Philip Augustus, to commemorate Philip's victory at Bouvines in 1214. The Anonymous of Chantilly attempts to provide a faithful, although not wholly literal, translation of the *Philippide*. The task he faced was formidable on several levels. Not only was he required to derhyme and cast into the new language of Old

French prose Guillaume's often complex and obscure Latin verses, but the very act of translation into French indicates that he was aiming at a public very different from the clerical and court circles to which Guillaume's learned and classicizing work was addressed. Whereas Guillaume elaborated his narrative on the model of Walter of Châtillon's *Alexandreis* and ornamented his text with classical allusions and Virgilian topoi, the Anonymous of Chantilly reshaped his source to suit the tastes and expectations of a lay audience accustomed to romance conventions. The translation of Guillaume le Breton's Latin into Old French placed the text within a lexical and discursive register that connected it to the body of romance literature and transformed it into something resembling a prose romance work, locating the *Chronique des Rois de France* in an entirely new corpus of implicit intertextual references and allusions. The resulting effect is not merely a change in the tone of the work, but an ideological displacement which, in the employment of the language of chivalric romance, generates a novel set of textual problematics.

The opening sections of the *Philippide* are concerned with the king's struggles against the great barons of France and in particular against Philip of Alsace, count of Flanders, with whom the king was engaged in a drawn-out dispute over the Vermandois succession. The basis of Philip of Flanders's tenure of Vermandois and its allied counties was a grant by Louis VII in 1179, confirmed by Philip Augustus himself in 1180, but which the king now sought to revoke, demanding that the counties be returned. Against this assertion of royal will, Philip of Flanders takes his stand on the grounds of fidelity to feudal law and the maintenance of the traditional legal order.[8] But the king wholly rejects this appeal to the traditional customs and usages of the kingdom, responding that brief tenure is no guarantee of possession[9] and willfully demanding that his wishes be obeyed. In the war that ensues, the contrast between the count's adherence to the governing principle and values of the feudal world of the aristocracy and the goals that shape the exercise of royal power is sharpened. Whereas Philip of Flanders remains faithful to the virtues of prowess, bravery, and the pursuit of glory that make up the chivalric conspectus of value, the counselors of the king advance the values of calculation, restraint, and planning in a language that emphasizes a lexicon of order and reason.[10] They excoriate the young king, calling him a *vil chevalier*, ready to place his troops in danger for the sake of a misguided notion of honor, and they counsel him against *aventure*—a word redolent of chivalric pursuits—in favor of management, preservation of resources, and strategy. *Proesce*, in their mouths, loses its chivalric significance of individual prowess and acquires the connotation of calculation of advantage, consideration of the needs of the state against those of personal honor.

The antinomies expressed in this opening section of the *Chronique*—between feudal tradition, prowess, boldness, chivalry on one hand, and royal power, calculation, and the management of resources on the other—are repeated throughout the *Chronique* in a series of escalating conflicts between the king and his barons which lead to the final conflict at Bouvines. Yet with each reprise, the consequences of allegiance to the values that constitute chivalric ideology become more severe, so that the progress of the chronicle entails a deepening critique of the ethical underpinning of chivalric society. Repeatedly, assent to the dictates of *proesce* proves to be the way of disaster, for it blinds men to the true needs of society and diverts them from the recognition of their proper interests. The moral vision of the battlefield as an arena of personal glory and honor, in this text, has become a darkened realm of self-deceit and failure, incapable of sustaining the meaningful pursuit of chivalric action within the terms set forth by traditional chivalric morality.

Seen *seriatim*, the episodes that make up the repeated encounters between king and nobility give voice to a profound critique of the ethical structure of chivalric ideology which, by the reign of Philip Augustus, had come to prize above all else courage and what Duby has called the "arabesques of boldness."[11] As such, they are also a powerful critique of the cultic world of the feudal aristocracy based on chivalric morality and on a chivalric model of socially derived value, in which personal honor and family pride demand the performance of consummate acts of valor, however dangerous the undertaking or tragic the consequences. This is a world, the *Chronique* seems to argue, in which fidelity to ancestral traditions of honor and obedience to feudal custom and usage no longer guarantee protection against the forfeiture of rights and possessions or success in the prosecution of one's causes. Blinded to its true purposes, the feudal aristocracy has dethroned prudence, wisdom, and justice in a specious glorification of honor and has become, therefore, the agent of its own imminent defeat at the battle of Bouvines (1214).

Against this image of an aristocratic world ensnared within a web of false consciousness and internal contradictions, the *Chronique* poses that of the king and his court, the world of rising monarchical power in constant strife with the feudal aristocracy. It is only by learning to disengage and distance himself from the values of aristocratic society that the king is able to triumph over his adversaries. Thus, the progress of the *Chronique* entails not only a devaluation of chivalric morality, but a complementary valorization of a new set of royal virtues, one that places the claims of state above those of personal honor, that demands loyalty, obedience, and subordination, and that seeks to "mectre soubz soy le coul des orguellieux"[12] (place beneath him the neck of the proud). Here action is guided not by the promptings of inherited status or the demands of honor, but by counsel. Not the old Frankish and feudal *concilium*, given and received according to custom, with its legal and potentially constitutional edge, its ritual function in open, public assemblies, but the counsel taken from creatures of the king, of a private, domestic, even familial order, furnished by an incipient service aristocracy which, already by the time of Philip Augustus, had succeeded in supplanting the barons and prelates in the royal court and in the court of the king's mind.[13] It is they who at the battle of Bouvines see to it that the royal forces before the opening of combat are "arrayed and ordered each one in his battle line, knights inspired by boldness [but now disciplined by royal supervision], who maintained their lines closely pressed together [i.e., collectively], and held themselves at the ready to run and fight the enemy whenever the trumpets would sound the call to battle."[14]

By Bouvines, Philip Augustus had learned his lesson well; his triumph is the triumph of management and planning over *proesce* and *hardiesce*; of the collectivity over the feudal aristocracy. Philip's lesson is also the lesson of the *Chronique des Rois de France*. The defeat of the aristocracy at Bouvines is a defeat for those codes of conduct and ethical aspirations that had for so long served to define the aristocracy's sense of itself and its role in feudal society, but which now stand revealed as dysfunctional in a new era of monarchical consolidation and authority. The contradiction between the high ideals of courtly ideology and the realities of royal power can no longer be masked, and the futility of persevering in the defense of chivalric values is all too patent. Even the king must abandon his allegiance to chivalric notions of honor and glory; neither he nor his barons can maintain the pretense that he is a *primus inter pares*, a *chevalier* among *chevaliers*, for he now has his foot too firmly set upon "the neck of the proud."

What is involved here is an extended metaphor for the shift from feudal to administrative kingship that characterized the governmental innovations of the reign of Philip Augustus.[15] The *Chronique des Rois de France* represents a first step by royal propagandists to present to aristocratic audiences a new image of Capetian government in order to reconcile the baronial classes most affected by royal centralization to the "new order of things," to proclaim not only the power of monarchy but its inhering righteousness as well.

Fifty years later, the *Grandes Chroniques de France* would complete this process. But if we ask ourselves why the monks of Saint-Denis, after compiling an extensive series of Latin chronicles, should have undertaken to translate that corpus into the vernacular, that decision must now, I believe, be seen in dialectical relation to the prior development of vernacular historiography and the contest over the past for which it served as a vehicle. In effect, Primat's history, although structured around the genealogy of the three "races" of French kingship, is as much a saga of the French nation as it is a chronicle of the kings of France.[16] To the extent that French history was understood to begin with the Trojans, the origins of France went back to a period that antedated the institution of kingship. In the beginning was the nation, not the monarchy. Only later did the princes and the people determine to set a king over them as lord and ruler "in order to be like other peoples."[17] The legendary origin of the French monarchy with the election of Pharamond postdates the legendary origin of the French people with the exile of the Trojans after the fall of Troy, their wanderings in Sicambria and eventual migration to the Seine Valley.

To be sure, Primat's historiographical goals in compiling the *Grandes Chroniques* were thoroughly royalist in inspiration, and his *roman des roys*, as the medieval manuscripts most often termed it,[18] was precisely that, a vernacular history of the kings of France, whose rulership over the French realm owed more to the grace of God than to election by the people. The monarchy was hedged with the aura of sacred kingship and exercised a dynastic right to the throne of France, and the notion of its popular election disappears from the *Grandes Chroniques* almost as soon as it is mentioned.[19] If the participation of the "people" in the election or, more nearly, acclamation of French kings is occasionally still mentioned, the "people" so designated represent a small elite of princes and barons, who alone play a role alongside the king as actors in the medieval drama of French history recorded in the *Grandes Chroniques*. Nonetheless, as Guenée has recently stressed, "ce rôle, à côté du roi et parfois même avant le roi, est primordial. . . . Tout au long de l'histoire de France, les 'barons' pèsent d'un poids décisif. L'oeuvre de Primat c'est le roman des rois, l'histoire du royaume, mais aussi l'épopée des barons du royaume."[20]

It is difficult not to see in Primat's intense concern to integrate the French nobility into the chronicle of royal history a reflection of that impulse towards reconciliation which, I would argue, figures as a primary factor in the rise of royally sponsored vernacular historiography in thirteenth-century France. In recounting the history of the kings of France in Old French prose, the *Grandes Chroniques* and its literary heirs adopted a language and literary form first devised for the elaboration of a historiography of resistance to royal authority. Historical writing in Old French prose had begun as the historiography of a lost cause, offering a threatened elite a vehicle through which it sought to recuperate a sense of social worth and political legitimacy. The French aristocracy's romancing of the past, in that sense, had entailed both the *mise en roman*—the recasting of historical writing into Old French—and the quest for a lost world of chivalric power, ethical value, and aristocratic autonomy, all of which had been severely undermined by the growth of royal government in the thirteenth century. Viewed from this perspective, the patronage and consumption of vernacular history represented a search for ethical and ideological legitimacy that was displaced to the realm of culture, taking the form of a recreated past that could correct the deficiencies of the present. This recreated past asserted the perduring validity of the aristocracy's once potent political presence, potentially recoverable precisely because it was historically "true."

With the emergence of the contemporary chronicle, vernacular historiography consolidated its generic identity while at the same time bringing the contested nature of past and present to the fore as the focus of historical narration. This contested history, as set forth in a chronicler such as the Anonymous of Béthune, challenged royal legitimacy by offering an account of both past and present history that was no longer exclusively monarchical. Royal historians answered this contested past by creating a historiographical corpus that both responded to the rise of aristocratic vernacular historiography and the challenges implicit in it, and at the same time provided the basis for a reconciliation of the now defeated aristocracy with an increasingly powerful monarchy by integrating its history into the framework of royal history. Like the work of the Anonymous of Béthune and the *Chronique des Rois de France*, the *Grandes Chroniques* spoke to the aristocracy in the language of its class and on the subject from which it drew its own sense of identity.

Somewhat paradoxically, French kings and their propagandists, victors in the contest for power and authority that had set aristocracy and monarchy against one another for nearly a century, adopted the language and literary forms of the defeated aristocracy as the means both to conciliate the losers and to proclaim their own, newly won, hegemony over the French realm. With the creation of Old French royal historiography, the winners in this struggle for political authority absorb and revalorize the terms and language of the losers for their own purposes, creating a vast corpus of historical writing to establish the legitimacy of their rule over their former antagonists. The French aristocracy, no longer able to impose its needs and concerns in the governance of the realm, contributed to the dominant ideology its own defeated discourse, achieving on a literary level the success that eluded it on the political. From this perspective, it is hardly surprising that Primat accorded such a large place in his historical text to the nobility, for the first and most crucial audience for his *roman des roys* was the French aristocracy. It is, perhaps, one of the finer ironies in the history of medieval historiography that the original quest involved in the French aristocracy's romancing of the past should issue, ultimately, not in an idyll of a lost age but in a new vision of the French nation.

What is specifically telling for an understanding of the formation of a medieval historiographical canon is that all three texts discussed here employ essentially the same body of Latin sources. And it is this intertextual commonality that has led scholars to misinterpret radically the purposes to which these texts were put and to argue that all three should be seen as lineal descendants in a single corpus of royal historiography. Despite the community of sources, however, the texts pursue completely different ideological goals. The power of the representation of history in these works derives in large part from their respective social contexts and their relation to the social and political networks in which they are elaborated. Each text achieves a particular meaning and authority within the social space from which it is articulated, a meaning completely different from what it had possessed in the hands of its original Latin authors, and from what it would come to signify when finally incorporated into royal history. That meaning, therefore, is relational, not stable or inherent within the text itself; it emerges only when the text is situated within a local environment of social and political networks that it seeks to shape and that are being organized around it. The earlier, discarded meanings of the chronicle, moreover, are never wholly lost, but linger on beneath the defeated discourses and suppressed resonances, potentially recoverable given the right circumstances, a never entirely lost legacy from the past.

From this perspective, the contested nature of the past is crucial not only to the formation of a historiographical canon, which itself represents merely one move in the struggle for control over the voices on the past, but remains a permanent aspect of all historiographical structures of meaning, in which suppressed meanings and voices always threaten to break through, to reopen the contest and overcome the silences that history inevitably imposes. One is even tempted to conclude that the very rigidity of historiographical canons is a symptom of the vulnerability of all historical discourse to precisely this fracturing of meaning and reappropriation of lost terms on the part of new groups, whose changing social conditions and needs endlessly generate the demand for new kinds of history and for access to earlier structures of significance. Against the canon, social reality always stands as a certain pressure, a destabilizing force in cultural production. In that sense, any canon of history contains within it an already contested past and potential and is, by its very nature, the product of a continuing negotiation among competing interests, values, and ideological aspirations.

In tracing the emergence of a canonical structure of historical thought, then, we should bear in mind Raymond Williams's dictum that "social orders and cultural orders must be seen as being actively made; actively and continuously, or they may quite quickly break down."[21] It is here that ideological assertion comes into play, arguing for the continuing relevance of the values that the past enshrines; for the inherent rightness of the social order that had governed political life; for the importance of restoring to their former authority the old rules of the social game. Ideology seeks to revive lost dreams of glory, to vindicate motives, and to mantle the discomfort that the contemplation of unwanted or adverse change germinates. Because success and failure are rooted in historical transformations, the past becomes the repository of those dreams and desires, both because it can offer up a consoling image of what once was and is no longer, and because it contains the elements by which to reopen the contest, to offer an alternative vision to a now unpalatable present. Historical writing is a powerful vehicle for the expression of ideological assertion, for it is able to address the historical issues crucially at stake and to lend to ideology the authority and prestige of the past, all the while dissimulating its status *as* ideology under the guise of a mere accounting of "what was." The prescriptive authority of the past makes it a privileged locus for working through the ideological implications of social changes in the present and the repository of contemporary concerns and desires. As a locus of value, a revised past holds out for contemporaries the promise of a perfectible present. At the heart of all historiographical contests lies a competition not merely for control over the voices on the past but, more important, for value, which is to say, for control over the meaning of human history itself.

▌ Notes

Chapter One: History, Historicism, and the Social Logic of the Text

The author would like to thank Carroll Smith-Rosenberg, Phyllis Rackin, Lynn Hunt, Stephen Nichols, David Cohen, Judith Walkowitz, Jeanne Rutenberg, Arthur Eckstein, James Henretta, J. S. Cockburn, Samuel Kinser, and members of the Mellon Seminar on the Structures of Power and Diversity of Languages at the University of Pennsylvania and the Atlantic Seminar at the Johns Hopkins University for their careful readings and acute criticisms of this chapter. In particular, the University of Pennsylvania Mellon seminar, under the direction of Carroll Smith-Rosenberg, has long provided me with a congenial set of companions and a probing forum in which to explore the issues raised here. I am especially grateful to be able to participate in its meetings, from which I have taken away far more than I contribute. I would also like to thank the John Simon Guggenheim Foundation for a fellowship which supported the research and writing of this article, as well as the Rockefeller Residency Fellowship program in Atlantic History and Culture, which gave me a study and a home during the tenure of my Guggenheim fellowship. The chapter has enormously benefited from, but does not necessarily reflect, the opinion of the scholars listed above.

1. See Martin Jay, "Should Intellectual History Take a Linguistic Turn? Reflections on the Habermas-Gadamer Debate," in Dominick LaCapra and Steven L. Kaplan, eds., *Modern European Intellectual History: Reappraisals and New Perspectives* (Ithaca, N.Y., 1982): 86–110; and John E. Toews, "Intellectual History after the Linguistic Turn: The Autonomy of Meaning and the Irreducibility of Experience," *American Historical Review* 92 (1987): 879–907.

2. See Nancy Partner, "Making Up Lost Time: Writing on the Writing of History," *Speculum* 61 (1986): 95.

3. Catherine Belsey, *Critical Practice* (London, 1980), 4.

4. To take an example cited by Belsey (p. 39), the meaning of *river* and *stream* in English do not correspond to *rivière* and *fleuve* in French. In English, what distinguishes a river from a stream is their respective size. In French, on the other hand, a *fleuve* is a body of water that flows into a sea, while a *rivière* flows into another *rivière* or a *fleuve*. The referents of these terms change as one passes from one language to another, and what determines the referent within each language is its place within the linguistic code or rules that govern the production of meaning.

5. Williams, *Marxism and Literature* (Oxford, 1977), 167.

6. Toews, "Intellectual History," 882.

7. Thus, in classic demonstrations of semiotic analysis, Barthes in *S/Z* shatters a Balzac novella into a random operation of multiple codes, and Hayden White analyzes *The Education of Henry Adams* in terms of the patterns of code shifting by which ideological implications are substituted for the straightforward representation of a social life that the text "pretends" to be. See Hayden White, "Method and Ideology in Intellectual History: The Case of Henry Adams," in LaCapra and Kaplan, *Modern European Intellectual History*, 280–310.

8. The term that Jacques Derrida uses to designate this endless multiplication and diffusion of meaning within all writing, which continually threatens to outrun the sense that the categories of the text's structure try to limit it to, is *dissemination*. See his *Dissemination*, trans. and ed. Barbara Johnson (Chicago, 1981). For Derrida, all language displays this "surplus" of meaning, not merely literary language, although it is most evident in literature. See also Terry Eagleton, *Literary Theory: An Introduction* (Minneapolis, 1983), 134. It is precisely this mobility of meaning, the discontinuous, fractured, and indeterminate nature of writing, that makes it impossible for us to establish a fixed point outside of discourse which guarantees its objective reality. Thus the text is radically decentered, since there is no referent outside the play of linguistic signifiers, no ground outside language that controls its interpretive range. The interpretation of any signifying chain (or of any text) produces only another chain of signs, and we enter, as Northrop Frye foresaw, "an endless labyrinth without an outlet" (*The Anatomy of Criticism* [New York, 1969], 118), which is essentially what Derrida means by a decentered structure. For an excellent discussion of Frye and Derrida, see Frank Lentricchia, *After the New Criticism* (Chicago, 1980).

9. Jay, "Intellectual History," 89.

10. Jacques Derrida, *Of Grammatology*, trans. Gayatri Chakravorty Spivak (Baltimore, 1974), 157. See also Lee Patterson, *Negotiating the Past: The Historical Understanding of Medieval Literature* (Madison, 1987), 58.

11. Derrida, *Of Grammatology*, 158.

12. See the critique by Toews, "Intellectual History," 882.

13. Patterson, *Negotiating the Past*, 59.

14. No one has been more forceful in articulating the implications of post-Saussurean linguistics for the practice of history than Hayden White, who has assessed the challenge of semiotics for historical research by recognizing that once the relationship of the classical literary text to its social environment is problematized, so too is that of putatively "transparent" texts or documents. There are no epistemological grounds, once one has accepted a post-Saussurean view of language, to bracket documentary uses of language as somehow standing apart from the self-referential play of language generally, however necessary such attempts to protect historical "evidence" might appear for the continued practice of history. See especially White's collected essays, *The Content of the Form: Narrative Discourse and Historical Representation* (Baltimore, 1987).

15. Geertz, "Thick Description: Toward an Interpretive Theory of Culture," in *The Interpretation of Cultures* (New York, 1973), 14.

16. Geertz, "Deep Play: Notes on the Balinese Cockfight," in *The Interpretation of Cultures*, 448, 449.

17. Geertz, "Introduction," in his *Local Knowledge: Further Essays in Interpretive Anthropology* (New York, 1983), 4.

18. Geertz, "Blurred Genres: The Refiguration of Social Thought," in *Local Knowledge*, 21.

19. Ibid., 22–23.

20. Geertz insists on distinguishing his own interpretive procedures from Claude Lévi-Strauss's structuralism, on the grounds that Lévi-Strauss takes myths, rites, and so on, as ciphers to solve, but does not seek to understand symbolic forms in terms of how they function in concrete situations to organize perceptions, meanings, emotions, concepts, and attitudes. Unlike interpretive anthropology, Lévi-Strauss's structuralism, Geertz claims, is concerned only with the internal structure of myths and rituals, independent of all context. "The Way We Think Now: Toward an Ethnography of Modern Thought," in *Local Knowledge*, 147–63.

21. For an excellent discussion of this tendency in Geertz's work, see

Lynn Hunt, "History beyond Social Theory," unpublished paper. I would like to thank Professor Hunt for permission to read and cite from her paper. That this aesthetic approach to social and cultural behavior is largely an act of interpretive violence wreaked upon the ethnographic communities that come within the anthropologist's purview is a point made by the anthropologist Vincent Crapanzano, who, in a critique of Geertz's "Deep Play," notes that "cockfights are surely cockfights for the Balinese—and not images, fictions, models, and metaphors. They are not marked as such, though they may be read as such by a foreigner for whom images, fictions, models, and metaphors have interpretive value." "The Hermes Dilemma: The Masking of Subversion in Ethnographic Description," in James Clifford and George E. Marcus, eds., *Writing Culture: The Poetics and Politics of Ethnography* (Berkeley, 1986), 73.

22. Geertz, "Blurred Genres," 34.

23. Nicole Polier and William Roseberry, "Tristes Tropes," unpublished paper, 10.

24. For an excellent review of these developments, see Lynn Hunt, "History, Culture and Text," introduction to *The New Cultural History*, ed. Lynn Hunt (Berkeley, 1989), 1–22. I would like to thank Professor Hunt for sending a copy of the introduction before the book's publication.

25. Culler, "Literary History, Allegory and Semiology," *New Literary History* 7 (1976): 260.

26. Geertz, *Negara: The Theatre State in Nineteenth-Century Bali* (Princeton, 1980), 136.

27. Roger Chartier, "Intellectual History or Sociocultural History? The French Trajectories," in LaCapra and Kaplan, *Modern European Intellectual History*, 41. Since writing this essay, Chartier has considerably revised his views, and would now grant far greater autonomy to the social and its reciprocal implication in social construction. See, for example, the essays in *Cultural History Between Practices and Representations*, trans. Lydia G. Cochrane (Ithaca, N.Y., 1988), especially intro. and pt. 1.

28. Chartier, "Intellectual History or Sociocultural History?" 40. Since Chartier has now moved away from this position, it is perhaps not fair to cite from his former writings. I do so only because he, indeed, held to such notions at one time and because they constitute a particularly acute statement of a widely shared view among many cultural historians.

29. See the critique by Toews, "Intellectual History," 886.

30. The specific formulation is that of Hunt, "History, Culture and Text," 10.

31. Thus Hayden White can claim that "the best grounds for choosing one perspective on history rather than another are ultimately aesthetic and moral rather than epistemological" and that "the demand for the scientization of history represents only the statement of a preference for a specific modality of historical conceptualization, the grounds of which are either moral or aesthetic." See *Metahistory: The Historical Imagination in Nineteenth-Century Europe* (Baltimore, 1973), xii.

32. Krieger, "The Literary, the Textual, the Social," introduction to *The Aims of Representation: Subject/Text/History*, ed. Murray Krieger (New York, 1987), 18.

33. Jay, "Intellectual History," 105–6.

34. As David Carroll insists: "Formalism in some form or other just won't go away no matter how often and how forcefully history and politics are evoked to chase it away or at least put it in its place. Another version of formalism always seems ready to rise out of the ash can of history to take the place of previously discarded versions." "Narrative, Heterogeneity, and the Questions of the Political: Bakhtin and Lyotard," in Krieger, *The Aims of Representation*, 69–70.

35. Montrose, "Renaissance Studies and the Subject of History," *English Literary Renaissance* 16 (1986): 6.

36. Ibid., 8; and Stephen Greenblatt, "Capitalist Culture and the Circulatory System," in Krieger, *The Aims of Representation*, 257.

37. Compare the critique of New Historicism by Myra Jehlen in "Patrolling the Borders: Feminist Historiography and the New Historicism," *Radical History Review* 43 (1989): 23.

38. Montrose, "Renaissance Studies," 8.

39. Hence Jean Howard, in an article that both advocates and criticizes the practice of New Historicism, suggests that a requirement of the New Historicist position is to accord literature real power: "Rather than passively reflecting an external reality, literature is an agent in constructing a culture's sense of reality. It is part of a much larger symbolic order through which the world at a particular moment is conceptualized and through which a culture imagines its relationship to the actual conditions of its existence. Instead of a hierarchical relationship in which literature figures as a parasitic reflector of historical facts, one imagines a complex, textualized universe in which literature participates in historical processes and in the political management of reality." "The New His-

toricism in Literary Study," *English Literary Renaissance* 16 (1986): 25. One can admire and share Howard's desire to reject a mimetic view of literary discourse, but the question of precisely how literature politically manages reality goes largely unexplained. Until New Historicism, and cultural history more generally, is able to explain the supposed links between literary and social praxis in concrete and persuasive terms that can be generalized in the form of a social theory, the interpretive moves, however dazzling, of which it is capable will remain unconvincing. It is also clear that the totalizing view of culture New Historicists tend to project will sit uneasily with historians trained to an awareness of the discontinuous stages of social change, in which certain sectors of a society appear to hold quite distinct views and beliefs—to belong, in current terminology, to a distinctive discursive regime—not necessarily shared or compatible with those held by other sectors of society. While New Historicism has used deconstruction to argue for the contradictory and fragmentary nature of textuality, it has not extended this perspective to history itself. On this, see below.

40. Williams, *Marxism and Literature*, 99, 165, 37.

41. Said, *The World, the Text and the Critic* (Cambridge, Mass., 1983), 4.

42. A point well made by Williams, *Marxism and Literature*, 169.

43. Fredric Jameson, to cite one example, forthrightly proclaims that, for him, "interpretation is . . . construed as an essentially allegorical act, which consists in rewriting a given text in terms of a particular interpretive master code." *The Political Unconscious: Narrative as a Socially Symbolic Act* (Ithaca, N.Y., 1981), 10. And for Jameson, the privileged master code is history (understood in Marxist categories), since his own rewriting of the literary text is predicated on the idea that the literary text "itself may be seen as the rewriting or restructuration of a prior historical or ideological subtext, it being understood that such a 'subtext' is not immediately present as such" (81). If the literary text is, in this sense, already an allegory of history, then historical criticism is devoted to recuperating the original meaning of that allegory through its reallegorization. In viewing history as the "absent subtext" of the literary work, Jameson comes close to Macherey's notion of history as the text's "unconscious," in the latter's adaptation of Freudian theory for literary criticism. Freudian psychoanalysis offers another privileged master code by which literary works can be allegorized as enactments of the hidden work of the unconscious. See Pierre Macherey, *A Theory of Literary Production*, trans. Geoffrey Wall (London, 1985).

44. Wellek and Warren, *The Theory of Literature* (New York, 1977), 73–74.

45. Darnton, *The Great Cat Massacre* (New York, 1984), 3–5. As Lynn Hunt shows, the shift from inferring causal explanation to deciphering meaning that results from the adoption of a discursive model "throws into doubt all the conventional language of historical investigation by denying historians the essence of their enterprise, which traditionally has been the explanation of change over time." See "History beyond Social Theory," 12.

46. Toews, "Intellectual History," 906.

47. To quote Hayden White's cogent formulation in "The Problem of Change in Literary History," *New Literary History* 7 (1975): 99. White has moved away somewhat from this position and would now claim that the text-context problem is "resolvable from the semiological perspective to the extent that what conventional historians call the context is already in the text in the specific modalities of code shifting by which discourse produces its meaning." See "The Context in the Text: Method and Ideology in Intellectual History," in *The Content of the Form*, 212. But to say this is to resolve the problem by collapsing text and context into a single textualized unit in the examination of which essentially formalist procedures (to trace the patterns of code shifting) are called for. It is difficult to see how such an analysis will answer the set of descriptive and causal questions that White posed in 1975, how the interpretation of a single text can, in the end, address the problem of change in literary history, which he then identified as crucial to the historical investigation of literature.

48. Partner, "Making Up Lost Time," 95.

49. In the insightful phrase of Toews, "Intellectual History," 906.

50. I owe this particular formulation to Dominick LaCapra, "Rethinking Intellectual History and Reading Texts," in LaCapra and Kaplan, *Modern European Intellectual History*, 44. LaCapra, however, draws from it the conclusion that such a view of textuality implies that the context or "real world" is itself textualized in a variety of ways, and thus we must admit that one "is 'always already' implicated in problems of language use as one attempts to gain perspective on these problems . . . ; for the historian, the very reconstruction of a context or a 'reality' takes place on the basis of 'textualized' remainders of the past" (50). LaCapra thus joins the semiotic camp, at least in his conception of the inaccessibility of a past reality in any other than a mediated, textualized form,

although LaCapra does recognize that "the most distinctive issue in historiography is that of the relationship between documentary reconstruction of and dialogue with the past," and the collection of essays cited above powerfully presents the current state of this question in historical, philosophical, and literary studies.

51. Bakhtin, *The Dialogic Imagination*, ed. Michael Holquist, trans. Caryl Emerson and Michael Holquist (Austin, Tex., 1981), 259.

52. Walkowitz, "Patrolling the Borders," *Radical History Review* 43 (1989): 31.

53. Smith-Rosenberg, *Disorderly Conduct: Visions of Gender in Victorian America* (Oxford, 1985), 43–44.

54. Carroll Smith-Rosenberg, "The Body Politic," in Elizabeth Weed, ed., *Coming to Terms: Feminism, Theory, Politics* (New York, 1989), 101.

55. Macherey, *A Theory of Literary Production*, 80.

Chapter Two: Orations of the Dead / Silences of the Living

1. Kellner, "Triangular Anxieties: The Present State of European Intellectual History," in Domnick LaCapra and Steven L. Kaplan, eds., *Modern European Intellectual History: Reappraisals and New Perspectives* (Ithaca, N.Y., 1982), 112.

2. Hassan, *The Postmodern Turn: Essays in Postmodern Theory and Culture* (Columbus, Ohio, 1987), xvi.

3. Jacques Derrida, "Shibboleth," in Geoffrey H. Hartman and Sanford Budick, eds., *Midrash and Literature* (New Haven, 1986), 323.

4. A "narrative" of the main elements of Derrida's *curriculum vitae* is given on pp. 325–36 in the odd collaborative work by Derrida and Geoffrey Bennington called simply *Jacques Derrida* (trans. Geoffrey Bennington [Chicago, 1993]), one part of which (above the line) consists in Bennington's *Derridabase*, while below the line Derrida himself provides a running commentary entitled *Circumfession Fifty-nine periods and periphrases*.

5. Derrida, "Plato's Pharmacy," in *Dissemination*, trans. and ed. Barbara Johnson (Chicago, 1981), 101. In *Positions*, Derrida claims that he wants to "put into question the major determination of the meaning of Being as presence, the determination in which Heidegger recognized the destiny of Philosophy." *Positions*, trans. Alan Bass (Chicago, 1981), 7.

6. Derrida praises Saussure for "desubstantializing both the signified content and the 'expressive substance' of the sign," thereby contributing

to "turning against the metaphysical tradition the concept of the sign that he borrowed from it." At the same time he criticizes him for "leaving open the possibility of a concept signified in and of itself," in doing which, Derrida believes, Saussure "accedes to the classical exigency of the 'transcendental signified': which in and of itself, in its essence, could refer to no signifier." *Positions*, 18, 19. For Derrida, every signified is also in the position of a signifier, making the distinction between signified and signifier problematical at its root. Ibid., 20. For a fuller critique of Saussure and semiotics on Derrida's part, see also the chapter "Linguistics and Grammatology" in *Of Grammatology*, trans. Gayatri Chakravorty Spivak (Baltimore, 1974), 27–73.

7. See, for example, the statement in "Structure, Sign and Play in the Discourse of the Human Sciences" that "center can also indifferently be called the origin (or end, *arche* or *telos*); repetitions, substitutions, transformations, and permutations are always taken from a history of meaning [*sens*]—that is, in a word, a history—whose origin may always be reawakened or whose end may always be anticipated in the form of presence. This is why one could say that the movement of any archeology, like that of any eschatology, is an accomplice of this reduction of the structurality of structure and always attempts to conceive of the structure on the basis of a full presence which is beyond play." *Writing and Difference*, trans. Alan Bass (Chicago, 1978), 279.

8. Ibid., 280.

9. Another consequence of the concept of infinite play, Derrida asserts, is the exclusion of totalization, because the nature of the linguistic field as a field of play, of infinite substitutions, renders such totalization impossible since there is no center that arrests and grounds the play of substitutions. Thus, "the movement of play, permitted by the lack or absence of a center or origin, is the movement of *supplementarity*. One cannot determine the center and exhaust totalization because the sign which replaces the center, which supplements it, taking the center's place in its absence—this sign is added, occurs as a surplus, as a supplement. The movement of signification adds something, which results in the fact that there is always more, but this addition is a floating one because it comes to perform a *vicarious function*, to supplement a lack on the part of the signified. The overabundance of the signifier, its supplementary character, is the result of a finitude, that is to say, the result of a lack which must be supplemented." "Structure, Sign and Play," 289–90.

10. Derrida, "Plato's Pharmacy," 152.

11. Derrida, *Of Grammatology*, lxxiii.

12. Ibid., xvi, xxxix.

13. Martin Jay, "Should Intellectual History Take a Linguistic Turn? Reflections on the Habermas-Gadamer Debate," in LaCapra and Kaplan, *Modern European Intellectual History*, 89.

14. It is interesting that Derrida himself speaks of the appearance of a new structure (in which, presumably, one could include the idea of a structureless, or decentered, structure) as a rupture, on the model of a "catastrophe." See "Structure, Sign and Play," 292. This association of deconstruction with rupture and catastrophe is a point to which I will return.

15. Pierre Macherey, *A Theory of Literary Production*, trans. Geoffrey Wall (London, 1985), 80.

16. See chap. 5, "After the Apocalypse: Paul de Man and the Fall to Silence," in Shoshana Felman and Dori Laub, *Testimony: Crises of Witnessing in Literature, Psychoanalysis and History* (New York, 1992).

17. Ibid., xx. Specifically, Felman argues that de Man's theories inscribe "the testimony of the muted witness and . . . address the lesson of historical events, not (as some would have it) as a cover-up or dissimulation of the past, but as an ongoing, active *transformation* of the very act of bearing witness. History as Holocaust is mutely omnipresent in the theoretical endeavor of de Man's mature work. The war's disastrous historical and political effects are what is implicitly at stake in the text's insistent focus on, and tracking of, an ever-lurking *blindness* it underscores as the primary human condition. De Man's entire writing effort is a silent trace of the reality of an event whose very historicity, borne out by the author's own catastrophic experience, has occurred precisely as the event of the preclusion—the event of the impossibility—of its own witnessing" (140).

Moreover, she argues, de Man's very notion of language is invaded by the mute understanding of history. In de Man's mature work, what he calls language "is not simply language as it is commonly understood to be: an alleged isolated verbal entity framed by a bracketing of history and politics. . . . [Rather] 'language' should be understood dynamically and differentially, only in its interaction with the term 'history.' Language is, in matter, what resists, it is, in history, what differentiates it from itself, what designates the fact that history is never present to itself and cannot be guided; the fact is that, as de Man puts it, 'history is not human,' that any attempt at a human guidance of history invariably turns out to be either deceptive or illusory. . . . History is, at the same time, what designates the fact that language is, in turn, not present to itself. History, therefore, is not, as it is commonly understood to be, a model of continuity that defines itself in opposition to the mode of fiction, but a mode of interruption in which the unpredictability and uncontrollability of fiction, acting itself out into reality, 'becomes the disruption of the narrative referential illusion,' in much the same way as the historical reality of the war has in effect been the historical disruption of the pseudo-referential narrative of the journalistic witnessing of history" (147–48).

Whether or not one accepts Felman's attempt to see de Man's immersion in his own version of deconstruction as a meditation on and acting out of his wartime mistakes in a nonconfessional, nonapologetic mode, the tie that she seeks to establish between the history of the Holocaust and the elaboration of deconstruction is, to me, entirely persuasive. In Derrida, the specific relations between the two are quite different (as is his brand of deconstruction different from that of de Man), and no more openly articulated than in de Man himself. Yet it is interesting, as Dominick LaCapra points out, that since de Man's death Derrida has tended to proclaim the basic similarity and/or convergence between his and de Man's thought. See LaCapra, *Representing the Holocaust: History, Theory, Trauma* (Ithaca, N.Y., 1994), 133. For the revised version of Derrida's defense of Paul de Man in the wake of the revelations of his anti-Semitic wartime journalism, see his *Memoires for Paul de Man*, trans. Cecile Lindsay, Jonathan Culler, Eduardo Cadava, and Peggy Kamuf (New York, 1989).

18. Adorno's phrase was: "After Auschwitz, it is no longer possible to write poems." *Negative Dialectics*, trans. E. B. Ashton (New York, 1973), 362. Adorno thus raises the issue of the "aestheticization" which language necessary entails that has become a recent source of debate over the appropriate modes of narrating the Holocaust, taken up most powerfully in the collection edited by Saul Friedlander, *Probing the Limits of Representation: Nazism and the "Final Solution"* (Cambridge, Mass., 1992); in Berel Lang, ed., *Writing and the Holocaust* (Ithaca, N.Y., 1988); and, most recently, in idem, "Is It Possible to Misrepresent the Holocaust?" *History and Theory* 34 (1995): 84–89, a response to articles by Hans Kellner, Wulf Kansteiner, and Robert Brown for a forum "Representing the Holocaust," in *History and Theory* 33 (1994).

19. Derrida, "Structure, Sign and Play," 292.

20. Technically, of course, Derrida, having been born in 1930, is a bit old to be properly classified as a member of the "second generation," particularly since, as a child in Algeria, he had experienced the effects of the war and its anti-Semitic policies in school, where he was excluded, as a Jew, from the privilege, granted to the top pupil of the class, of raising the flag every morning. Furthermore, in 1942, Derrida was expelled from school as a result of the lowering to 7 percent of the *numerus clausus* of Jews allowed to attend. Between then and the end of the war he attended a school run by Jews in Algiers. In this sense, Derrida certainly experienced the war and the anti-Semitism of the Pétain regime. Indeed, Bennington asserts that it was doubtless during these years when "the singular character of J.D.'s 'belonging' to Judaism [was] imprinted on him: wound, certainly, painful and practiced sensitivity to antisemitism and any racism . . . but also impatience with gregarious identification, with the militancy of belonging in general, even if it is Jewish." *Jacques Derrida*, 327. Nonetheless, in relation to the Holocaust and the experiences of European Jews, Derrida's childhood in Algiers, I believe, maintains a comparable position of marginality and belatedness that informs the psychology of the so-called second generation. Such chronological precision is, in any case, in my opinion misplaced, since the Holocaust and the revelations of its horrors are not the exclusive property of those who entered or engineered the camps—however privileged their experience might be. In a very real sense the Holocaust was an event in the history of Western Europe to which every sentient person is called upon to respond.

21. Fresco, "Remembering the Unknown," *International Review of Psychoanalysis* 11 (1984): 419. First published in the *Nouvelle Revue de Psychoanalyse* 24. As Laub explains, paradoxically "it is thus that the place of the greatest density of silence—the place of concentration where death took place . . . becomes for those children of survivors the only place which can provide an access to the *life* that existed before their birth." Felman and Laub, *Testimony*, 64. Survivors themselves were notably loath or unable to recount their experiences and, as Laub indicates, often "claim that they experience the feeling of belonging to a 'secret order' that is sworn to silence. Because of their participation in the Holocaust they have become the 'bearers of a secret' (*Geheimnisstraeger*) never to be indulged" (82). The sense of being the bearers of a secret was eerily echoed in Himmler's Posen speech (October 4, 1943), before an assembly of high-ranking SS officers, in which he praised the corps of SS members

for their heroic efforts in the camps, a heroism destined never to be celebrated because it could not be told. In Himmler's words, the extermination of the Jews constitutes "the most glorious page in our history, one not written and which shall never be written" (quoted in LaCapra, *Representing the Holocaust*, 62 n. 17). Thus, from all sides, this was a silence generated from within the Holocaust itself, whose transgressive, hence "unspeakable," nature was *intended* to afflict victim and perpetrator alike.

22. Fresco, "Remembering the Unknown," 420–23.

23. Personal communication.

24. Quoted in Ellen S. Fine, "The Absent Memory: The Act of Writing in Post-Holocaust French Literature," in Lang, *Writing and the Holocaust*, 44.

25. Steiner, *Language and Silence: Essays on Language, Literature and the Inhuman* (New York, 1986), 123.

26. Alvin Rosenfeld, *A Double Dying: Reflections on Holocaust Literature* (Bloomington, Ind., 1982), 28.

27. Steiner, *Language and Silence*, 4.

28. Quoted in Fine, "The Absent Memory," 41. One might compare to this Paul Celan's remarks on the German language, in which he continued to write even after surviving the camps, for it constituted his sole enduring possession from his dispossessed past, however damaged by the process through which it had passed: "Within reach, close and not lost, there remained, in the midst of the losses, this one thing: language. . . . This, the language, was not lost, was not lost but remained, yes, in spite of everything. But it had to pass through its own answerlessness, pass through a frightful falling mute, pass through the thousand darknesses of death-bringing speech." From Celan's Bremen speech, on receiving the Literature Prize of the Free Hanseatic City of Bremen (cited in Felman and Laub, *Testimony*, 28). Thus, like Steiner, Celan believes that language itself, and in particular German, did not pass unscathed through the crucible of the Holocaust. For Steiner's extended discussion of the fate of the German language in a post-Holocaust environment, see especially the essays "The Hollow Miracle" and "A Note on Günter Grass" in *Language and Silence*, 95–117.

29. The "unrepresentable" nature of the Holocaust is now the subject of a considerable literature. See, especially, the essays collected in Friedlander, *Probing the Limits of Representation*; idem, *Memory, History and the Extermination of the Jews of Europe* (Bloomington, Ind., 1993); Lang,

Writing and the Holocaust, passim; and LaCapra, *Representing the Holocaust*, passim.

30. Rosenfeld, *A Double Dying*, 33.

31. Primo Levi has taken this de-legitimation of speech to its extreme in claiming that even "we, the survivors, are not the true witnesses . . . we are those who by their prevarications, or abilities, or good luck did not touch bottom. Those who did so, those who saw the Gorgon, have not returned to tell about it, or have returned mute, but they are the 'Muslims,' the submerged, the complete witnesses, the ones whose deposition would have a general significance." *The Drowned and the Saved*, trans. Raymond Rosenthal (New York, 1988), 83–84. Only the dead, therefore, can truly speak, or speak truly; only they have experienced in full the real nature of the Holocaust.

32. Jean-François Lyotard, "Discussions or Phrasing 'after Auschwitz,'" in *The Lyotard Reader*, ed. Andrew Benjamin (Oxford, 1989), 364.

33. Steiner, "The Long Life of Metaphor," in Lang, *Writing and the Holocaust*, 157.

34. Quoted in Rosenfeld, *A Double Dying*, 87.

35. Edmund Jabès, "The Key," in Hartman and Budick, *Midrash and Literature*, 352. On these passages in Jabès, see Berel Lang, "Writing-the-Holocaust: Jabès and the Measure of History," in Lang, *Writing and the Holocaust*, 252.

36. Derrida, "Edmund Jabès and the Question of the Book," in *Dissemination*, 66, 71.

37. Derrida, "Plato's Pharmacy," 91.

38. Derrida, "Shibboleth," 340. It is not irrelevant that in his "gloss" to Bennington, Derrida harps constantly on questions of circumcision, insisting, for example, that "circumcision, that's all I've ever talked about, consider the discourse on the limit, margins, marks, marches, etc., the close, the ring (alliance and gift), the sacrifice, the writing of the body, the *pharmakos* excluded or cut off, the cutting/sewing of *Glas*, the blow and the sewing back up, whence the hypothesis according to it's that, circumcision, without knowing it, never talking about it, or talking about it in passing . . . that I was always speaking or having spoken." *Jacques Derrida*, 70. It was the fact of being circumcised that made it so difficult for Jewish males, and especially the "hidden children," to survive the war undetected, since it constituted the mark, the writing on the body, that betrayed identity. That Derrida assimilates the corpus of his

writing to this trace of inescapable identity powerfully suggests the un-acknowledged psychic roots of his intellectual turn.

39. There has been a great deal of discussion lately concerning the probable link between post-Holocaust and postmodern consciousness, beginning with Habermas's articulation of the general sense that "there [in Auschwitz] something happened, that up to now nobody considered even possible. There one touched on something that represents the deep layer of solidarity among all that wears a human face. . . . Auschwitz has changed the basis for the continuity of the condition of life within history." Cited in Friedlander, *Probing the Limits of Representation*, 2. Such a link is implicit in Lyotard's metonymic use of "the jews" in *Heidegger and "the jews"* (trans. Andreas Michel and Mark Roberts, introduction by David Carroll [Minneapolis, 1990]), as the very figure of postmodernity, that is, of precisely what can no longer be "phrased" "after Auschwitz"— the "excess" that disrupts and puts into question all former categories of being and knowledge. Among those most insistent on the connection between the "trauma" to Western European historical consciousness effected by the Holocaust and the thematics of postmodernism have been Dominick LaCapra and Eric L. Santner. For LaCapra, "much recent debate in critical theory and historiography is recast if the Holocaust is perceived as at least one more or less repressed divider or traumatic point of rupture between modernism and postmodernism. Postmodernism and the post-Holocaust become mutually entwined issues that are best addressed in relation to each other." *Representing the Holocaust*, 188. Santner argues even more forcefully that "the postmodern destabilization of certain fundamental cultural norms and notions, above all those dealing with self-identity and community, cannot be understood without reference to the ethical and intellectual imperatives of life after Auschwitz. For if the postmodern is, in a crucial sense, about the attempt to 'think difference,' we take on this task in the knowledge of what can happen if a society turns away from such labors." *Stranded Objects: Mourning, Memory, and Film in Postwar Germany* (Ithaca, N.Y., 1990), xiv. Both point to the prominence of themes of loss, death, impoverishment, and mourning that pervade much of postmodern criticism and writing. The significance of this insistence for the present inquiry is that it points clearly to the nonrestrictive impact of the Holocaust, beyond the circle of Jews and Germans to which it is often relegated. In this light, the Holocaust is now understood metonymically as the rupture in historical consciousness occasioned by the war and its catastrophes, an event in

Western European philosophy and thought as well as a psychological trauma affecting participants and their successors.

40. It might also be said, in this context, that the testimony of survivors indicates that the Holocaust reduced its victims to a state of pure corporeality, of a personhood shrunk to its barest minimum of bodily attributes and functions. The "local violence of desire" suffusing these bodies was, of course, not for sex but for food, and it is interesting to see the ways in which postmodern thought has dematerialized sexuality and the body, whereby the Flesh is made Word, in a kind of subconscious denial of both carnality and sexuality that discloses yet another level of anxiety, against which the pervasive preoccupation with sex in current academic discourse appears as a linguistic defense.

41. Derrida, *Positions*, 14.

42. Paul Zumthor, *Speaking of the Middle Ages*, trans. Sarah White (Lincoln, Neb., 1986), 37.

Chapter Three: Towards a Theory of the Middle Ground

1. Milan Kundera, *The Unbearable Lightness of Being*, trans. Michael Henry Heim (New York, 1985), 63.

2. From this perspective, it is interesting to see the ways in which deconstruction has become demonized as a threat to the whole value structure of Western civilization, a phenomenon that Dominick LaCapra relates to the passing of Soviet communism: "In the recent past the widespread belief that communism has failed and is no longer a serious threat to the West has induced a tendency to seek a stereotypical enemy and scapegoat elsewhere. Preposterous as the gesture may seem, deconstruction has itself at times been cast in this role as the homogeneous, anxiety-producing, politically and socially dangerous 'other.' " "The Personal, the Political and the Textual: Paul de Man as the Object of Transference," *History and Memory: Studies in the Representation of the Past* 4 (1992): 30.

3. Roger Chartier, "L'Histoire aujourd'hui: Doutes, défis, propositions," in Carlos Barros, ed., *Historia A Debate*, 3 vols. (Santiago de Compostela, 1995), 1: 119 and 120 for the citation from Foucault.

4. David Harlan, "Intellectual History and the Return of Literature," *American Historical Review* 94 (1989): 582.

5. Toews, "Intellectual History after the Linguistic Turn: The Autonomy of Meaning and the Irreducibility of Experience," *American Historical Review* 92 (1987): 901–2.

6. Partner, "Making Up Lost Time: Writing on the Writing of History," *Speculum* 61 (1986): 95.

7. Michel Foucault, "Nietzsche, Genealogy, History," in *Language, Counter-Memory, Practice*, ed. and trans. Donald F. Bouchard (Ithaca N.Y., 1977), 147.

8. Fredric Jameson, *The Political Unconscious: Narrative as a Socially Symbolic Act* (Ithaca, N.Y., 1982), 225–26. Jameson further stipulates that "it is not necessary that these analyses be homologous, that is, that each of the objects in question be seen as doing the same thing, having the same structure or emitting the same message. What is crucial is that, by being able to use the same language about each of these quite distinct objects or levels of an object, we can restore at least methodologically the lost unity of social life and demonstrate that widely distant elements of the social totality are ultimately part of the same global process."

9. Williams, *Marxism and Literature* (Oxford, 1977), 98.

10. An example of how this works is afforded by Michael Baxandall's use of the "Bougier principle," which states that "in the event of difficulty in establishing a relation between two terms, modify one of the terms till it matches the other, but keeping note of what modification has been necessary." Thus Baxandall, acknowledging that "art and society are analytical concepts from two different kinds of categorization of human experience"—are, therefore, "unhomologous systematic constructions put upon interpenetrating subject matters"—shows how some strands of modern criticism have modified the term *society* into the term *culture* in order to establish an analyzable, homologous relationship between the two. See his "Art, Society and the Bougier Principle," *Representations* 10 (1985): 40–41. For a discussion of Baxandall, see also Stephen Greenblatt, "Towards a Poetics of Culture," in H. Aram Veeser, ed., *The New Historicism* (New York, 1989), 11–12.

11. Quoted in Lee Patterson, *Negotiating the Past: The Historical Understanding of Medieval Literature* (Madison, 1987), xi. See also Williams, *Marxism and Literature*, 98–99, and idem, *Keywords: A Vocabulary of Culture and Society*, rev. ed. (New York, 1985), 204–6. Mediation in its "classical" sense here corresponds to Williams's definition (ii), though Adorno's falls within his category (iii).

12. Hunt, "History, Culture and Text," introduction to *The New Cultural History*, ed. Lynn Hunt (Berkeley, 1989), 10.

13. To borrow the formulation of Hayden White, "The Problem of Change in Literary History," *New Literary History* 7 (1975): 109. I derive

the term *constative* for language that is instrumental or descriptive from LaCapra's use of it in *Soundings in Critical Theory* (Ithaca, N.Y., 1989).

14. See Martin Jay, "Should Intellectual History Take a Linguistic Turn? Reflections on the Habermas-Gadamer Debate," in Dominick La-Capra and Steven L. Kaplan, eds., *Modern European Intellectual History: Reappraisals and New Perspectives* (Ithaca, N.Y., 1982), 110.

15. I have set aside in this discussion the hermeneutic problem of our reading of both categories of texts and the myriad ways in which we construe and misconstrue them, primarily because it is so fundamental to historical "reading" that it goes virtually without saying. I am not arguing for a return to a positivist belief in our capacity to recover a "true" account of *wie es eigentlich gewesen* or making a commonsensical appeal to the authenticity of "experience." But I do wish to open up an epistemological space that allows a degree of positive perception of the past, however imperfect and distorted by present ideological lenses.

16. Thus Judith Newton insists, "Taking the 'material' seriously, a material always apprehended within representation, changes the way that representation itself is represented." "History as Usual? Feminism and the 'New Historicism,'" in Veeser, *The New Historicism*, 166.

17. Jay, "Intellectual History," 110.

18. Roger Chartier, "Popular Culture: A Concept Revisited," paper presented at a conference on Popular Culture, MIT, October 16–17, 1993. I would like to thank Professor Chartier for giving me a copy of this paper.

19. LaCapra, *Soundings in Critical Theory*, 6

20. Stock, "History, Literature and Medieval Textuality," *Yale French Studies* 70 (1986): 17. Similarly, Edward Said, in arguing for a "secular criticism," maintains that "even if we accept . . . that there is no way to get past texts in order to apprehend 'real' history directly, it is still possible to say that such a claim need not also eliminate interest in the events and circumstances entailed by and expressed in the texts themselves." *The World, the Text and the Critic* (Cambridge, Mass., 1983), 4.

Chapter Four: In the Mirror's Eye

1. Rand, "Editor's Preface," *Speculum* 1 (1926): 4.
2. Patterson, "Introduction: Critical Historicism and Medieval Studies," in Lee Patterson, ed., *Literary Practice and Social Change in Britain, 1380–1530* (Berkeley, 1990), 2. See also his *Negotiating the Past: The His-*

torical Understanding of Medieval Literature (Madison, 1987), and idem, "On the Margin: Postmodernism, Ironic History and Medieval Studies," *Speculum* 65 (1990): 87–108.

3. Patterson, "Critical Historicism and Medieval Studies," 2.

4. Biddick, "Bede's Blush: Postcards from Bali, Bombay, Palo Alto," in John Van Engen, ed., *The Past and Future of Medieval Studies*, Notre Dame Conferences in Medieval Studies, 4 (Notre Dame, Ind., 1994), 16.

5. Cited in Allen J. Frantzen, *Desire for Origins: New Language, Old English and Teaching the Tradition* (New Brunswick, N.J., 1990), 16.

6. Peter W. Williams, "The Varieties of American Medievalism," *Studies in Medievalism* 1, no. 11 (spring 1982): 8.

7. Bede, *A History of the English Church and People*, trans. Leo Sherley-Price, rev. R. E. Latham (New York, 1977), 55–56.

8. Frantzen, *Desire for Origins*, 16.

9. P. W. Williams, "The Varieties of American Medievalism," 10.

10. F. N. Robinson, "Anniversary Reflections" [Presidential Address delivered at the Twenty-fifth Annual Meeting of the Medieval Academy], *Speculum* 25 (1950): 494.

11. Philip Gleason, "American Catholics and the Mythic Middle Ages," in *Keeping the Faith: American Catholicism Past and Present* (Notre Dame, Ind., 1987), 20. Unfortunately, space does not allow me to pursue the development of Catholic medievalism in North America, which, at least in its initial stages (before the Neo-Thomist revival) was conducted largely outside the mainstream of the Academy. Gleason's article offers a sensitive and comprehensive discussion. See also John Van Engen, "The Christian Middle Ages as an Historiographical Problem," *American Historical Review* 91 (1986): 519–52.

12. William J. Courtney, "The Virgin and the Dynamo: The Growth of Medieval Studies in North America 1870–1930," in Francis G. Gentry and Christopher Kleinhenz, eds., *Medieval Studies in North America: Past, Present and Future* (Kalamazoo, Mich., 1982), 21 n. 8.

13. Cited in ibid., 10.

14. Ibid., 5.

15. The judgment of his teaching offered by Courtney, ibid., 6.

16. See Patrick Geary, "Visions of Medieval Studies in North America," in Van Engen, *The Past and Future of Medieval Studies*, 51–52. Alternatively, however, Susan Mosher Stuard has argued that Adams was the first to focus on the "social balance" between the sexes, particularly in the family, as an important element in Europe's dynamic pattern of

growth, a phenomenon disrupted by the processes of state building. In that sense, Adams was among the first medievalists to introduce a concern with the family, women, and gender as a counterpart to the history of the state, a view with a potentially subversive edge for American historiography. See her "New Dimension? North American Scholars Contribute Their Perspective," in Susan Mosher Stuard, ed., *Women in Medieval History and Historiography* (Philadelphia, 1987), 84. But Stuard acknowledges that Adams failed to incorporate these concerns into his teaching, which was restricted to precisely the history of political reigns, wars, and administrative milestones whose centrality his writings might have contested.

17. Certainly, the most important writer of medieval history before Haskins was Charles Henry Lea. Lea, however, was not a professor but a publisher. Indeed, the first generation of American medievalists tended to be gentlemen-scholars, whose private wealth funded their amateur historical scholarship. It is a tribute to Lea's industry and intelligence that he could produce such important work on such a massive scale and still function as a publisher in Philadelphia. Another important medieval scholar of the turn of the century, author of a widely circulated book, *Thirteenth, Greatest of Centuries* (New York, 1912), was James J. Walsh, a medical doctor who had trained under Rudolph Virchow in Germany. Although Walsh was an important contributor to the tradition of popular medievalism, the impact of his work lay largely outside academia. On Walsh, see Gleason, "American Catholics and the Mythic Middle Ages," 19ff.

18. For the details of Haskins's and Strayer's lives and early careers, see Norman Cantor, *Inventing the Middle Ages: The Lives, Works, and Ideas of the Great Medievalists of the Twentieth Century* (New York, 1991), chap. 7, "American Pie, Charles Homer Haskins and Joseph Reese Strayer," passim.

19. Ibid., 252.

20. On Haskins's role in the formation of the Academy and *Speculum*, a role rather more restricted than Cantor intimates, see George R. Coffman, "The Medieval Academy of America: Historical Background and Prospect," *Speculum* 1 (1926): 5–18.

21. Charles Homer Haskins, "European History and American Scholarship," *American Historical Review* 28 (1923): 215.

22. Ibid., 218. Behind the profound passion of this statement lies, to be sure, an equally profound anxiety over just how marginal and irrele-

vant medieval history must seem to most Americans. In 1971, Strayer openly articulated the threat underlying the American practice of medieval history, warning a new generation of students to whom he addressed his remarks that, without concerted effort, they were in danger of being "shoved into the back corner along with Sanskrit, Assyriology and other subjects" (i.e., all the *dead* languages, betraying the threat of nonbeing that always haunts the medievalist's imaginary). Strayer reminded his young audience, "We should never forget our greatest danger: we began as antiquarians and we could end as antiquarians." "The Future of Medieval History," *Medievalia et Humanistica*, n.s., 2 (1971): 179. The insistence on continuity and relevance marked the American appropriation of the medieval past for decades. In his presidential address, "Humanistic Studies and Science," on the occasion of the fifth annual meeting of the Academy, John Matthews Manly sounded the plea once again, imploring that "the infinitely various and fascinating period we roughly call the Middle Ages must not be neglected. It lies close to us. In it arose many of our most important institutions. Our social life, our customs—our ideals, our superstitions and fears and hopes—came to us directly from this period; and no present-day analysis can give a complete account of our civilization unless it is supplemented by a profound study of the forces and forms of life, good and evil, which we have inherited from it." *Speculum* 5 (1930): 250. As late as 1963, S. Harrison Thomson, surveying the field, echoed Haskins's sentiment by declaring that "the Middle Ages are early American history and they should be so presented." See "The Growth of a Discipline: Medieval Studies in America," in Katherine Fischer Drew and Floyd Seyward Lead, eds., *Perspectives in Medieval History* (Chicago, 1963), 17.

23. Coffman, "The Medieval Academy of America," 17.

24. Charles Homer Haskins, *The Renaissance of the Twelfth Century* (rpt. New York, 1964), vii–viii.

25. Haskins's appreciation of the importance of science to medievalism's modernist agenda was implemented in his important research on medieval science (see his *Studies in the History of Mediaeval Science* [Cambridge, Mass., 1924]); in his hiring of George Sarton as the first historian of science at Harvard; and in their joint founding of the journal *Isis*, which continues to be an important venue for the history of science in the United States today. This aspect of Haskins's influence was continued and amplified by Lynn White's investigations into the history of technology, beginning in the 1950s, the effects of which were, in John

Van Engen's helpful phrasing, "to rewrite medieval culture to approximate American dynamism." See his "An Afterword on Medieval Studies, Or the Future of Abelard and Heloise," in Van Engen, *The Past and Future of Medieval Studies*, 414.

26. The term was popularized by Wallace K. Ferguson, *The Renaissance in Historical Thought: Five Centuries of Interpretation* (Boston, 1948).

27. Haskins, "European History and American Scholarship," 224, 226.

28. Space does not allow a full discussion of the impact of German positivism and philology on medieval studies in America, but its perduring effects would be difficult to overestimate. For a discussion of this from various points of view see, among others, Frantzen, *Desire for Origins*, passim; Patterson, *Negotiating the Past*, passim, and idem, "Critical Historicism and Medieval Studies"; and especially the wide range of essays in the volume edited by R. Howard Bloch and Stephen G. Nichols, *Medievalism and the Modernist Temper* (Baltimore, 1995). I would like to thank the editors for allowing me to read the book in manuscript. Especially useful essays in that volume are David Hult, "Gaston Paris and the Invention of Courtly Love"; and Stephen G. Nichols, "Modernism and the Politics of Medieval Studies." On the alliance of philology with French and German national movements, see also R. Howard Bloch, "Naturalism, Nationalism, Medievalism," *Romanic Review* 76 (Nov. 1985): 341–60; and Hans Ulrich Gumbrecht, "Un Souffle d'Allemagne ayant passé: Friedrich Diez, Gaston Paris and the Genesis of National Philologies," *Romance Philology* 40 (1986): 1–37.

29. According to William J. Courtney, the war's most striking effect on Americans was to redirect both attention and training away from Germany to France, Belgium, and England ("The Virgin and the Dynamo," 14ff.). One consequence of this shift was to inaugurate a small but powerful following in America for the Belgian historian Henri Pirenne, whose two most famous students were James Bruce Ross and Bryce Lyon. Another was the virtual extinction of German history as a field in North America, a phenomenon that remains true down to the present day. On this, see Edward Peters, "More Trouble with Henry: The Historiography of Medieval Germany in the Angloliterate World, 1888–1995," *Central European History* 28 (1995): 47–72.

30. Cantor, *Inventing the Middle Ages*, 249.

31. As in the title of his book, *On the Medieval Origins of the Modern State* (Princeton, 1970).

32. On Strayer's service in the CIA, see Cantor, *Inventing the Middle Ages*, 260.

33. Ibid., 258.

34. This was also Strayer's argument in his famous article, "Philip the Fair—A 'Constitutional King,'" *American Historical Review* 62 (1956): 18–32.

35. See his *Studies in Early French Taxation* (Cambridge, Mass., 1939), passim.

36. The first is published in John Benton and Thomas Bisson, eds., *Medieval Statecraft and the Perspectives of History: Essays by Joseph Reese Strayer* (Princeton, 1971): 12–27; the latter in Theodore K. Rabb and Jerrold E. Siegel, eds., *Action and Conviction in Early Modern Europe: Essays in Memory of E. R. Harbison* (Princeton, 1969), 3–16, reprinted in Benton and Bisson, *Medieval Statecraft and the Perspectives of History*, 300–314.

37. Strayer, "The Fourth and the Fourteenth Centuries," *American Historical Review* 77 (1972): 1–14.

38. See Strayer, "The Laicization of French and English Society in the Thirteenth Century," *Speculum* 15 (1940): 76–86, reprinted in Benton and Bisson, *Medieval Statecraft and the Perspectives of History*, 251–65.

39. Cantor, *Inventing the Middle Ages*, 254.

40. The term *postmodernism* first gained renown with the publication of Lyotard's *La condition postmoderne* (1979) but probably was not widespread in American historiography until the translation of Lyotard's book in 1984. On this, see William D. Paden, "Scholars at a Perilous Ford," in William D. Paden, ed., *The Future of the Middle Ages: Medieval Literature in the 1990s* (Gainesville, Fla., 1994), 8.

41. Eric L. Santner, *Stranded Objects: Mourning, Memory, and Film in Postwar Germany* (Ithaca, N.Y., 1990), 51.

42. On the negative appeal of the Middle Ages, see Paden. "Scholars at a Perilous Ford," 21.

43. To some extent, this kind of work might be thought to derive from Marc Bloch's emphasis on *mentalité*, an initially neglected aspect of the "*Annales* paradigm," but there has been very little work in medieval history in America that takes its primary impetus from the Annales school. Not only does there not exist an identifiable American school dedicated to the study of medieval *mentalités* (or a French one, for that matter, unless one wishes to include LeGoff and Schmitt under that rubric), neither can the profound changes represented by the rise of dis-

cursively oriented work really be traced back to the Annales, however compatible the *annaliste* emphasis on *mentalité* might at first seem to be with it. In truth, they employ quite different views of language, hence of the nature of medieval textuality and the uses to which it can, and should, be put.

44. Vance, "Semiotics and Power: Relics, Icons and the *Voyage de Charlemagne à Jérusalem et à Constantinople*," in Marina S. Brownlee, Kevin Brownlee, and Stephen G. Nichols, eds., *The New Medievalism* (Baltimore, 1991), 227.

45. For an overview of these developments in the field of medieval history see Stuard, "A New Dimension?" 81–99. See also the recent special volume of *Speculum* 68 (1993) dedicated to women's history, now published as Nancy Partner, ed., *Studying Medieval Women: Sex, Gender, Feminism* (Cambridge, Mass., 1993). An example of this work is Penny Shine Gold, *The Lady and the Virgin: Image, Attitude and Experience in Twelfth-Century France* (Chicago, 1985).

46. Here the work of Caroline Bynum has been decisive, especially her *Holy Feast and Holy Fast: The Religious Significance of Food to Medieval Women* (Berkeley, 1987), and her *Resurrection of the Body in Western Christianity, 200–1336* (New York, 1995).

47. See, for example, the collective article by E. Jane Burns, Roberta Krueger, and Helen Solterer, "Feminism and the Discipline of Old French Studies," in Bloch and Nichols, *Medievalism and the Modernist Temper*, 225–66.

48. An extremely useful survey of these changes is Michael Kammen's "The Historian's Vocation and the State of the Discipline in the United States," in Michael Kammen, ed., *The Past Before Us: Contemporary Historical Writing in the United States* (Ithaca, N.Y., 1980), 19–46; somewhat less informative is the essay on medieval historiography by Karl Morrison, "Fragmentation and Unity in American Medievalism," in ibid., 49–77.

49. Paul Freedman, "The Return of the Grotesque in Medieval Historiography," unpublished paper. I would like to thank Professor Freedman for letting me read his paper.

50. Ibid., 16.

51. Foucault, *The Archeology of Knowledge* (New York, 1972), 5

52. On the significance of treating texts as "monuments" rather than "documents," see Frantzen, *Desire for Origins*, who seeks to apply these principles to the study of Anglo-Saxon literature.

53. Recent examples of work done in this vein are: Joan Cadden, *The Meaning of Sex Differences in the Middle Ages* (Cambridge, 1994); John W. Baldwin, *The Language of Sex: Five Voices from Northern France around 1200* (Chicago, 1994); E. Jane Burns, *Bodytalk: When Women Speak in Old French Literature* (Philadelphia, 1993). There is, needless to say, a huge literature on medieval sexuality, beginning with the work of Vern L. Bullough, *Sexual Practices and the Medieval Church* (Buffalo, 1982); and James Brundage, *Law, Sex, and Christian Society in Medieval Europe* (Chicago, 1987).

54. See Bynum, *Holy Feast and Holy Fast.*

55. R. I. Moore, *The Formation of a Persecuting Society: Power and Deviance in Western Europe, 950–1250* (Oxford, 1987); idem, *The Origins of European Dissent* (New York, 1985); and idem, *The Birth of Popular Heresy* (New York, 1976). See also the series of works by Jeffrey Russell, *Dissent and Order in the Middle Ages: The Search for Legitimate Order* (New York, 1992); idem, *Lucifer: The Devil in the Middle Ages* (Ithaca, N.Y., 1984); and idem, *Religious Dissent in the Middle Ages* (New York, 1971). For a general bibliography, see Carl Berkout, *Medieval Heresies: A Bibliography, 1960–1979* (Toronto, 1981). Also relevant is the work of Edward Peters, *Heresy and Authority in Medieval Europe* (Philadelphia, 1988); idem, *Inquisition* (New York, 1988); idem, *Torture* (New York, 1985); and idem, *The Magician, the Witch and the Law* (Philadelphia, 1978); and with Alan Kors, *Witchcraft in Europe* (Philadelphia, 1972).

56. Norman Cohn, *The Pursuit of the Millennium* (London, 1957); idem, *Europe's Inner Demons: An Enquiry Inspired by the Great Witch-Hunt* (New York, 1975).

57. See William Chester Jordan, *The French Monarchy and the Jews: From Philip Augustus to the Last Capetians* (Philadelphia, 1989), and his *Women and Credit in Pre-industrial and Developing Societies* (Philadelphia, 1993), which in part concerns financial transactions (loans) between women and Jews.

58. The work of the late John Boswell is critical here, especially his *Christianity, Social Tolerance and Homosexuality: Gay People in Western Europe from the Beginning of the Christian Era to the Fourteenth Century* (Chicago, 1980) and *Same-Sex Unions in Premodern Europe* (New York, 1994). It is perhaps not surprising that, before he turned his attention to homosexuality, Boswell's first book, based on his Harvard dissertation, concerned Islam: *The Royal Treasure: Muslim Communities Under the Crown of Aragon in the Fourteenth Century* (New Haven, 1977).

59. See the work of Robert Chazan, *European Jewry and the First Crusade* (Berkeley, 1987); idem, *Daggers of Faith: Thirteenth-Century Christian Missionizing and Jewish Response* (Berkeley, 1989); and idem, "The Representation of Events in the Middle Ages," *History and Theory* 27 (1988): 40–55; and of Ivan Marcus, "History, Story and Collective Memory: Narrativity in Early Ashkenazic Culture," *Prooftexts* 10 (1990): 365–88.

60. See Eleanor Searle, *Predatory Kinship and the Creation of Norman Power* (Berkeley, 1988); and Thomas N. Bisson, "The 'Feudal Revolution,'" *Past and Present*, no. 142 (1994): 6–42.

61. Freedman, "The Return of the Grotesque," 9. Thus Lee Patterson has specifically advocated the adoption of an ironic mode of history as that best adapted to a postmodernist treatment of the medieval past. See his "On the Margin," passim.

62. Van Engen, "An Afterword on Medieval Studies," 414.

63. Santner, *Stranded Objects*, 7.

Chapter Five: Political Utility in Medieval Historiography

1. For a discussion of all the texts in this tradition, see my *The Chronicle Tradition of Saint-Denis: A Survey*, Medieval Classics: Texts and Studies, no. 10 (Leiden, 1979).

2. Some recent writings that are useful from this perspective are: Philippe Ariès, *Le Temps de l'Histoire* (Monaco, 1954); Helmut Beumann, "Die Historiographie des Mittelalters als Quelle für die Ideengeschichte des Königstum," *Historische Zeitschrift* 180 (1955): 449–88; William J. Brandt, *The Shape of Medieval History: Studies in Modes of Perception* (New Haven, 1966); Bernard Guenée, "Histoire, Annales, Chroniques: Essai sur les genres historiques au moyen âge," *Annales: Economies, Sociétés, Civilisations* 4 (1973): 997–1016; Robert Hanning, *The Vision of History in Early Britain* (New York, 1966); Benoît Lacroix, *L'Historien au moyen âge* (Paris, 1971); H. A. Myers, "The Concept of Kingship in the 'Book of Emperors' ('Kaiserchronik')," *Traditio* 27 (1971): 205–30; Joel T. Rosenthal, "Edward the Confessor and Robert the Pious: Eleventh-Century Kingship and Biography," *Medieval Studies* 33 (1971): 7–20; R. W. Southern, "Aspects of the European Tradition of Historical Writing," *Transactions of the Royal Historical Society*, 5th ser., 20 (1970): 173–96, 21 (1971): 159–79, 22 (1972): 159–80, 23 (1973): 243–63; Robert Stepsis, "Pierre de Langtoft's Chronicle: An Essay in Medieval Historiography,"

Mediaevalia et Humanistica, n.s., 3 (1972): 51–73. See also the important review of Lacroix's book by Robert Hanning, in *History and Theory* 12 (1973): 419–34.

3. Marc Bloch has described this mechanism precisely: "The very authority that was ascribed to tradition favored the change. For every act, especially if it was repeated three or four times, was likely to be transformed into a precedent—even if in the first instance it had been exceptional or even frankly unlawful." *Feudal Society*, trans. L. A. Manyon (Chicago, 1964), 1: 114.

4. See Walter Ullmann, *The Carolingian Renaissance and the Idea of Kingship* (London, 1969).

5. *From Max Weber*, ed. Hans H. Gerth and C. Wright Mills (New York, 1958), 78.

6. Strayer, in Jacques Barzun et al., eds., *The Interpretation of History* (Princeton, 1943), 10.

7. See *Les Grandes Chroniques de France*, ed. J. Viard, Société de l'Histoire de France, 10 vols. (Paris, 1920–53), 3: 160ff.

8. Guillaume le Breton, *Philippide*, bk. 8, v. 632 sq., 234; bk. 1, v. 285 sq., 18–19; *Nuncupatio*, v. 28, 3; and bk. 10, v. 698 sq., 310, in *Oeuvres de Rigord et de Guillaume le Breton*, ed. H.-F. Delaborde, vol. 2, Société de l'Histoire de France (Paris, 1885).

9. Cf. Beumann, "Historiographie des Mittelalters," 452–53.

10. Arnaldo Momigliano, "Time in Ancient Historiography," *History and Theory* 6 (1966): 15. Hence Herodotus, whose well-known opening words establish this life-saving function of history: "These are the researches of Herodotus of Halicarnassus, which he publishes in the hope thereby of preserving from decay the remembrance of what men have done and of preventing the great and wonderful actions of the Greeks and Barbarians from losing their due meeds of glory."

11. Hannah Arendt, *Between Past and Future* (Cleveland, 1965), 43.

12. Cassiodorus, *An Introduction to Divine and Human Readings*, trans. and intro. Leslie Webber Jones (New York, 1969), 43.

13. Suger, *Vita Ludovici Grossi Regis Franciae*, ed. Henri Waquet, Les Classiques de l'Histoire de France au moyen âge (Paris, 1964), 3.

14. "Regum et principum gesta recordatione dignissima qui antiquis temporibus regnaverunt, ne ab humana memoria viderentur excidere, et edaci vetustate ea contingeret aboleri, labor et diligentia historiographorum studuit literarum traditionibus tradere ad exemplum." Guillaume de Nangis, *Vita Sancti Ludovici regis Franciae*, ed. M. Daunou, *Recueil*

des Historiens des Gaules et de la France [hereafter cited as *RHF*], 20: 310.

15. See Bernhard W. Scholz, "Principles of a Medieval Rhetoric of History," unpublished paper.

16. "Nec in narratiuncula mea Tullianam eloquentiam aut flores recthoricos expectetis, quia mecum bene agitur si ex veteri confusione tracta et succinte facta digeries morsus reprehensionis evaserit." Bibliothèque Municipale, Soissons, MS 129, fol. 130r.

17. Scholz, "Principles of a Medieval Rhetoric of History," 6. Cf. Lacroix, *L'Historien au moyen âge*, 10ff.

18. "Scripsi enim quedam que propriis oculis vidi, quedam que ab aliis diligenter inquisita forsan minus plene didici, quedam mihi incognita penitus pretermisi." Rigord, Prologue, *Gesta Philippi Augusti*, in *Oeuvres de Rigord et de Guillaume le Breton*, 1: 5.

19. *Grandes Chroniques*, 1: 2. Cf. Guillaume de Nangis, Prologue, *Vita Sancti Ludovici*: "Praeterea lectorem hujus operis expostulo, ut moveat ipsum tam rudis hominis scribentis auctoritas, nec quis dicat, sed quae dicuntur attendat. Utile vero non judicatur dubiis verborum sententiis historiae seriem tradere, sed plano simplici loquendi genere, ut simplicibus et peritis intellectus capacitas sit communis." *RHF*, 20: 311.

20. Jean Leclercq connects this with a specifically biblical and monastic notion of edification as well. See *The Love of Learning and the Desire for God*, trans. C. Misrahi (New York, 1961), 194.

21. See Hannah H. Gray, "History and Rhetoric in Quattrocento Humanism" (Ph.D. diss., Radcliffe College, 1956). See also George H. Nadel, "Philosophy of History before Historicism," *History and Theory*, 3 (1963–64): 291–315; and Lacroix, *L'Historien au moyen âge*, 167–75: "historia est narratio rei gesta ad instructionem posteritatis" (168).

22. One notes the class bias in Primat's Prologue to the *Grandes Chroniques*, despite the fact that it is one of the first works of vernacular history in medieval France and presumably aimed at a wide audience: "Si puet chascuns savior que ceste oeuvre est profitable à fere pour fere cognoistre aus vaillanz genz la geste des rois et por mostrer à touz dont vient la hautece dou monde: car ce est examples de bone vie mener, meismement aus rois et aus princes qui ont terres à governor." *Grandes Chroniques*, 1: 3.

23. "Tanti principis commendabiles actus quasi speculum pre oculis semper habeatis in exemplar virtutis." Rigord, *Gesta Philippi Augusti*, 2–3.

24. Brandt, *The Shape of Medieval History*, 160. For an analysis of medieval scientific perception, see his chap. 1.

25. Cf. Georges Lefebvre, "L'infériorité de la critique apparaît dans l'absence de toute idée de développement historique. Pour eux, le passé était demi fableux, conventionnal, fixé une fois pour toutes, ou au contraire, beaucoup plus fréquemment, quelque chose de semblable au présent. Jamais, peut-être, depuis le temps primitifs, l'anachronisme n'a été cultivé au même degré." *La Naissance de l'historiographie moderne* (Paris, 1971), 44. See also the fervent argument to this effect by Peter Burke, *The Renaissance Sense of the Past* (London, 1969), chap. 1, "Medieval Historical Thought."

26. Bloch, *Feudal Society*, 1: 83.

27. Struever, *The Language of History in the Renaissance: Rhetoric and Historical Consciousness in Florentine Humanism* (Princeton, 1970), 186.

28. Tom F. Driver, *The Sense of History in Greek and Shakespearean Drama* (New York, 1960), 59, 60 (quoting Richardson).

29. On the importance of the Bible for understanding medieval historical thought, see Lacroix, *L'Historien au moyen âge*, 58ff.

30. See Hanning, *The Vision of History in Early Britain*, 14.

31. See the excellent remarks of Hanning (in *History and Theory*, 425–26) about the potentially misleading effect of chroniclers invoking rhetorical principles of historiography in their Prologues. In Hanning's view, the conscious articulation of rhetorical tradition, which occurs in so much medieval historical writing, has a paradoxical role "in providing not a guide to perceiving and communicating the meaning of history, but rather a context within which the author and audience share a common intention—to address themselves to the needs of the past for instruction and edification." These rhetorical commonplaces were intended, he believes, to provide a "verbal context" in which the historian could locate himself and win acceptance from his audience, but they do not, therefore, necessarily describe the methods or purposes which govern and inspire his work. My study of the chronicles of Saint-Denis bears out Hanning's observations.

32. See Joseph R. Strayer, "France: The Holy Land, the Chosen People and the Most Christian King," in Theodore K. Rabb and Jerrold E. Siegel, eds., *Action and Conviction in Early Modern Europe: Essays in Memory of E. R. Harbison* (Princeton, 1969), 3–16.

33. Driver, *The Sense of History*, 53.

34. See, for example, the Prologue to the First Continuation to the *Chronicon* of Guillaume de Nangis by the anonymous monk of Saint-Denis: "Verum cum breves sint homines dies, eorum paucitas ita finiatur in brevi, et caduca, mortalis et misera vita nostra, multis repleta miseriis et respersa tanquam vapor parens ad modicum non subsistat, sed ut fumus ocius evanescens." *Chronique Latine de Guillaume de Nangis*, ed. Hercule Géraud, Société de l'Histoire de France (Paris, 1843), 1: 327. The belief that medieval thought contained a strong bias towards the universal, unchanging, and timeless can still be found in even such sophisticated writers as John Pocock. See his *Politics, Language and Time: Essays on Political Thought and History* (New York, 1971), 81.

35. Etienne Gilson, *The Spirit of Medieval Philosophy*, trans. A. H. C. Downes (New York, 1940), 386.

36. *Grandes Chroniques*, 1: 1, 3–4. This organization was later dropped, but it was Primat's intended one.

37. There are two traditions, apparently independent, which create the myth of Frankish Trojan origins. The first and best known is that of the so-called *Chronicle of Fredegar*. The other is a tradition established at Saint-Denis in the eighth-century *Liber Historiae Francorum* (ed. Bruno Krusch, *Monumenta Germaniae Historica, Scriptores rerum merovingicarum*, 2: 215–38). For an argument concerning the independence of these two traditions, see John M. Wallace-Hadrill, *The Fourth Book of the Chronicle of Fredegar* (London, 1960), xii.

38. For the importance of genealogy in the effort of the chroniclers of Saint-Denis to write a history of France, see also Ariès, *Le Temps de l'Histoire*, 146.

Chapter Six: Genealogy

1. Gerald of Wales, *The Journey through Wales*, trans. Lewis Thorpe (New York, 1978), 116–17.

2. Galbraith, *Historical Research in Medieval England* (London, 1951), 11.

3. See Northrop Frye, *The Anatomy of Criticism* (New York, 1969), 15; and William J. Sayers, "The Beginnings and Early Development of Old French Historiography" (Ph.D. diss., University of California, Berkeley, 1966), 390.

4. Cassiodorus, *An Introduction to Divine and Human Readings*, trans. and intro. Leslie Webber Jones (New York, 1946), 116. Cf. Bernard

Guenée, "Histoire, Annales, Chroniques: Essai sur les genres historiques au moyen âge," *Annales: Economies, Sociétés, Civilisations* 4 (1973): 997–1016. The same terminology appears again, for example, as the title to Diceto's history (*Ymagines Historiarum*), based on testimony and direct knowledge, as opposed to his *Abbreviationes Chronicorum*, epitomes of written sources.

5. For a description of this method of pictorial illustration, see Kurt Weitzmann, *Illustration in Roll and Codex: A Study of the Origin and Method of Text Illustration* (Princeton, 1970), passim and p. 36 for the reference to the work of Robert. The affinity between this method of pictorial illustration and historical narration which I am proposing is not as arbitrary as it might first appear. Weitzmann demonstrates that the "cyclic" (also called "continuous") method was introduced into representational arts in Hellenistic times under the influence of literary narration as an attempt to render the contents of literary sources (17). One might possibly view them as reciprocal techniques of narration derived from a common procedure.

6. The paratactic construction of medieval historical narrative and its avoidance of genuine causal analysis has been emphasized by Nancy Partner, *Serious Entertainments: The Writing of History in Twelfth-Century England* (Chicago, 1977), especially chap. 7 (on evidence) and chap. 8 (on literary form). For the latter, see also William W. Ryding, *Structure in Medieval Narrative* (The Hague, 1971).

7. Guenée, "L'Historien par les mots," in Bernard Guenée, ed., *Le Métier d'historien au moyen âge* (Paris, 1977), 9–10. The conception of the historian as a compiler and his text as a vehicle of transmission points to the highly conventional nature of much medieval historiography and its social function as verbal communication.

8. On this development, see the important studies by Georges Duby, "Structures de parenté et noblesse dans la France du Nord aux XIe et XIIe siècles" and "Remarques sur la littérature généalogique en France aux XIe et XIIe siècles," both in *Hommes et structures du moyen âge* (Paris, 1973). They have been translated into English and appear in Georges Duby, *Chivalrous Society* (Berkeley, 1977). For a different view of the relation of genealogical literature to social developments, see Léopold Genicot, *Les Généalogies*, Typologie des Sources du Moyen Age Occidental (Turnhout, 1975).

9. Duby, "Structures de parenté et noblesse," 268.

10. "Considerans hystorie regum Francorum prolixitatem . . . temp-

tavi seriem cunctarum hystoriarum de ipsis loquentium sub quidam arboris formula redigere, adjungere ipsorum actus et victorias, quod et fastidientibus prolixitatem, propter subjectam oculis formam, sit oblectatio, et studiosis facile possit prehabita pre oculis memorie commendari." B.N. Lat. 6184, fol. 1r. The French version repeats this formal principle: "Je G. de Nangis . . . ay translate de Latin en francois . . . ce que j'avoye autreffoiz fait en Latin selon la forme d'un arbre de la generacion." Walters Art Gallery, MS 306, fol. 1r.

11. Anonymous of Béthune, *Histoire des ducs de Normandie et des rois d'Angleterre*, ed. F. Michel, Société de l'Histoire de France (Paris, 1840); *Les Grandes Chroniques de France*, ed. J. Viard, Société de l'Histoire de France, 10 vols. (Paris, 1920–53).

12. This is a characteristic of almost all vernacular histories that follow a genealogical model. Sayers, "The Beginnings and Early Development of Old French Historiography," 174. This practice continues even into the seventeenth century, as discussed by Orest Ranum, *Artisans of Glory* (Chapel Hill, N.C., 1980), 16.

13. See, for example, the Anonymous's description of the accession of William the Conqueror to the ducal throne: "Ses fils Guillaume tint le tierre apries lui. Des primes ot grant travail et grant paine: ses lignages le guerrois, qui grant desdaing avoit de chou qui il estoit dus et bastars." *Histoire des ducs de Normandie*, 58.

14. "Li commencemenz de ceste hystoire sera pris a la haute lignie des Troiens, dont ele est descendue par longue succession." *Grandes Chroniques*, 1: 4.

15. Ibid., 1: 3.

16. Frye, *Anatomy of Criticism*, 341. Also his "History and Myth in the Bible," in Angus Fletcher, ed., *The Literature of Fact* (New York, 1976), 1–9. The Anonymous of Béthune's *Histoire* lacks a prologue and does not, therefore, exhibit the same degree of self-consciousness about narrative structure as the *Grandes Chroniques*. But his work, too, is cast as dynastic history, following the dynastic and generational changes of Norman and English rulers. That genealogy as a conceptual metaphor was capable of organizing histories as opposed in principle to genealogical considerations as episcopal histories has been proposed by Michel Sot, who argues that the lists of bishops in the ninth-century *Gesta Episcoporum* function like a genealogy in family histories, establishing a pseudo-lineage for bishops which acts, as do genealogies, to legitimize the episcopal succession by asserting its ancient origins and unbroken

continuity. See his "Historiographie épiscopale et modèle familial au IX siècle," *Annales: Economies, Sociétés, Civilisations* 33 (1978): 433–46. While Sot's argument is extremely interesting and supports the notion that genealogical models penetrated historical thought in profound ways, he is aware, of course, that strictly speaking the continuity in episcopal office is established by spiritual succession, not blood descent and that, therefore, once broken, can be quickly restored, while family continuity is much more fragile and dependent entirely on human durability. However, many medieval genealogies overcome this historical fragility of the family by simply inventing ancestors to fill the gaps left by death, and most locate the founding of the line in a mythical ancestor of primitive times, in a process not unlike the episcopal practice of inventing apostolic origins for the See.

17. A point well made by Ranum, *Artisans of Glory*, 5.

18. Robert A. Nisbet, *Social Change and History: Aspects of the Western Theory of Development* (New York, 1969), 30.

19. Ryding suggests that notions of procreation pass as naive forms of causal explanation, although his fundamental position is that medieval narratives lack logical construction and therefore obstruct genuine intelligibility from the point of view of cause and effect. *Structure in Medieval Narrative*, 98.

20. Erich Auerbach, *Mimesis: The Representation of Reality in Western Literature*, trans. Willard R. Trask (Princeton, 1958), 73ff. In Auerbach's terms, we might prefer to say that genealogy restores the "horizontality" of history, which typology had broken by its vertical orientation to God alone, through whom the spiritual connection between *figurae* was guaranteed. However, even typological interpretation contained within it a notion of historical fulfillment which, when joined to genealogy, functioned as a medieval analogue to the notion of historical development over time, as I have argued elsewhere. See Chapter Five.

21. There is a fascinating discussion of the use of metaphors of procreation and filiation in relation to Vico's concept of gentile history—the history of the *gens* and *gentes* generated in time, in Edward Said, "On Repetition," in Fletcher, *The Literature of Fact*, 135–58.

22. For a similar point made in relation to literary narrative, see Tony Hunt's review of Ryding's *Structure in Medieval Narrative*, in "The Structure of Medieval Narrative," *Journal of European Studies* 3 (1973): 322.

23. Geertz, "Deep Play: Notes on the Balinese Cockfight," in *The Interpretation of Cultures* (New York, 1973), 449.

Chapter Seven: The 'Reditus Regni ad Stirpem Karoli Magni'

1. *Les Grandes Chroniques de France,* ed. J. Viard, Société de l'Histoire de France, 10 vols. (Paris, 1920–53), 5: 1–2.

2. That is, Merovingians, Carolingians, and Capetians. The blood tie between Merovingians and Carolingians was established in earlier volumes.

3. K. F. Werner, "Die Legitimität der Kapetinger und die Entstehung der reditus regni Francorum ad stirpem Karoli,'" *Die Welt als Geschichte* 12 (1952): 203 (hereafter referred to as Werner). Since the publication of this essay, additional work on the *reditus* fiction has appeared, notably by Andrew W. Lewis, "Dynastic Structures and Capetian Throne Right: The Views of Giles of Paris," *Traditio* 33 (1977): 225–52; Elizabeth Brown, "La Notion de la légitimité et la prophétie à la cour de Philippe-Auguste," in R.-H. Bautier, ed., *La France de Philippe-Auguste: Le temps des mutations* (Paris, 1982), 77–110; and Joachim Ehler, "Die *Historia Francorum Senonensis* und der Aufstieg des Hauses Capet," *Journal of Medieval History* 4 (1978): 1–26.

4. *Grandes Chroniques,* 1: 90; 6: 139.

5. There is some confusion about whether Hugh the Great or Hugh Capet is intended as the object of Valery's prophecy. The *Grandes Chroniques* actually specify Hugh the Great, but the earliest versions of the prophecy, those found in the *Historia Relationis Corporis S. Walarici* and the *Cronica Centulensi sive S. Richarii,* as well as Ordericus Vitalis, designate Hugh Capet. The wording of the passage in Vincent of Beauvais's *Speculum Historiale* is unclear, but a reading of the whole section in which the prophecy appears suggests Hugh Capet. Of the early versions I have consulted, only the *Gesta Ludovici Octavi* clearly states Hugh the Great, whence it enters the *Grandes Chroniques* in this form. There must, however, have been other early versions giving Hugh the Great, because a citation of the prophecy in the 1220 Register of Philip Augustus, which antedates the *Gesta Ludovici Octavi,* also reads Hugh the Great. I have deliberately referred to it as Valery's prophecy to Hugh Capet throughout, since this is its original and fundamental form in both medieval and modern historiography.

6. For an anonymous genealogy of the eleventh century establishing Ermengart as the daughter of Charles of Lorraine, see *Genealogia Caroli Magni qua Namurcensium comitum et Boloniens origo declaratur,* ed. D. Bouquet, *Recueil des Historiens des Gaules et de la France* [hereafter cited

as *RHF*], 13: 585. The so-called chronicle of Baldwin of Avesne later continued this genealogy up to Philip Augustus. Ibid., note c.

7. *Grandes Chroniques*, 7: 4–7.

8. Werner, 203.

9. *Gesta Ludovici Octavi*, ed. M. Brial, *RHF*, 17: 302–11. The chronicle dates from the last quarter of the thirteenth century.

10. Vincent of Beauvais, *Speculum Historiale* (Douai, 1624), 1275–76. This part of the *Grandes Chroniques* belongs to the second compilation, redacted circa 1286 or very shortly thereafter.

11. Werner, 205.

12. Ibid., 205. Andreas's text is partially published by G. Waitz in the *Monumenta Germaniae Historica* [hereafter cited as *MGH*], *Scriptores*, 26: 204–15. Several unpublished manuscripts are extant, including one at the Bibliothèque Nationale, MS. Lat. 8865, under the title *Historia Succincta de Regibus Francorum*.

13. B.N. lat. 8865, fol. 181r.

14. Werner, 220.

15. *Historia Relationis*, *RHF*, 9: 147–49.

16. *Cronica Centulensi*, *RHF*, 8: 273–75.

17. Ordericus Vitalis, *Historia*, *RHF*, 10: 234.

18. "Simul unus, bis quoque terni." *Historia Relationis*, 147, note c.

19. Vincent of Beauvais, *Speculum Historiale* (1624), 1276. Werner explains Vincent's remark by pointing to the existence of a manuscript of Andreas of Marchiennes's *Historia succincta* (ca. 1200) which reads *septimam sempiternam*, as well as later manuscripts which have only *sempiternam* (Werner, 276 n. 72). The confusion is easily understandable and could have appeared in many versions of the prophecy, much to the Capetians' benefit.

20. *Chronicon*, *RHF*, 10: 300.

21. F. Kern, *Kingship and Law in the Middle Ages*, trans. S. B. Chrimes (Oxford, 1956), 17.

22. Philip was himself descended from a Carolingian line through his mother, Adele of Champagne. See below.

23. "Simulque Francorum principes benedictione sancti Spiritus gratia confirmavit et tali omnes interdictu et excommunicationis lege constrinxit, ut nunquam de alterius lumbis regem in aevo presumant eligere, sed ex ipsorum." "*Clausula de Unctione Pippini*," *MGH*, *Scriptores rerum merovingicarum*, 1: 465.

24. R. Giesey, "The Juristic Basis of Dynastic Right to the French

Throne," *Transactions of the American Philosophical Society*, n.s., 51 (1961): 5.

25. There are some exceptions, of course. In 991, a scribe of Cahors dates a part of the reign of Charles by designating him king, *regnante Karolo Rege*, although Charles was never crowned. Similarly, scribes of the Midi used the telling formula: "Deo regnante regeque sperante"; regnante Domino nostro Jesu Christo Francis vero contra jus regnum usurpante Ugine rege." A last echo of these legitimist sentiments can be seen in 1009, when a scrupulous scribe juxtaposed might and right by bringing together the name of King Robert II and those of the two surviving Carolingian princes, Louis and Charles, to date his act: "Actum anno incarnationis Domini MVIIII regnante Roberto et Ludovico et Carolino." See P. Viollet, *Histoire des institutions politiques et administratives de la France* (Paris, 1898), 2: 28.

26. "Nam Franci Primates, eo [Charles] relicto, ad Hugonem, qui ducatum Franciae strenue tunc gubernabat . . . se conferentes, eum Noviocomo solio sublimant regio." *MGH, Scriptores*, 9: 375.

27. *Continuatio Chronici Odoranni Monachi Sancti Petri Vivi Senonensis, RHF*, 10: 165.

28. Ibid., note. "Donat [Ludovicus V] regnum uxori suae, sub praestiti sacramenti fide Hugonam obtestans, ut post datum legibus diem ducat in uxorem Blanchiam, regno suo potiturus et dominio."

29. "Qui [sc. Hugh] etiam cum sua venerabili conjuge, Adelaide nomina, filia Pictavorum comitis, de progenis Karoli Magni imperatoris." *Translatio Sancti Maglorii*, ed. R. Merlet, *Bibliothèque de l'Ecole des Chartes* 56 (1895): 247.

30. R. Fawtier, *The Capetian Kings of France*, trans. L. Butler and R. J. Adam (New York, 1966), 55–56.

31. Werner, 218. The Carolingians had managed to satisfy Germanic demands for blood kinship in much the same way by fabricating a marriage alliance between a son of the Carolingian saint Arnoul, bishop of Metz, and Saint Beggue, daughter of Pepin of Landen and mother of Pepin Heristal. The genealogy was included in the *Grandes Chroniques* (2: 198ff.) translating the *Liber Historiae Francorum*, and again in 6: 139ff., translating chapter 38 of Rigord, *Gesta Philippi Augusti*. A different version of the descent appeared in 7: 4, where Pepin, Charlemagne's father, is said to be descended from Blitide, a putative daughter of Clothair I. Through Blitide the Carolingians claimed to be, as Hincmar of Rheims testified at Metz in 869 before the consecration of Charles the

Bald, "of the race of Clovis." See J. de Pange, *Le Roi Très Chrétien* (Paris, 1949), 132. Pepin's Merovingian descent was an accepted fact throughout the Middle Ages and was iconographically authorized in the sculptural program of royal tombs at Saint-Denis in the thirteenth century, where Clovis II, son of Dagobert, was placed in the Carolingian line of tombs. See Georgia Sommers, "Royal Tombs at Saint-Denis in the Reign of St. Louis" (Ph.D. diss., Columbia University, 1966), 97.

32. *MGH, Scriptores*, 9: 364–69. Cf. Werner, 209ff.

33. *MGH, Scriptores*, 9: 367–68.

34. Werner, 203. I think Werner greatly exaggerates the impact of the *Historia Francorum Senonensis* on later writers. Typically, medieval chroniclers were able to maintain quite contradictory views of any given event at one time without it necessarily affecting their ultimate judgment. Thus Hugh of Fleury (writing ca. 1114) used both Aimoin of Fleury and the *Historia Francorum Senonensis* to construct his account of the *mutatio regni*. There is no evidence that the latter's prejudices unduly affected his opinion. In Hugh's version, Hugh Capet does not enter the narrative until after Charles of Lorraine's capture, which is seen primarily as the work of rebellious magnates and, especially, of Ascelinus. In sum, Hugh ascribes the *mutatio* to God's judgment: "Sicque deficiente secunda regum Francorum linea, translatum est regnum in terciam generacionem, Dei hoc optant iudicio qui quos vult elevat et quos vult humiliat." *Liber qui modernorum Regum Francorum continet actus*, ed. G. Waitz, *MGH, Scriptores*, 9: 384. On the other side of the coin, Andreas of Marchiennes, architect of the *reditus*, was no Capetian sympathizer and in the Prologue to Book 3 of his *Historia succincta* specifically underlines the illegal nature of Hugh's accession as an act not only against his rightful lord but in contravention of Stephen's consecration commandment: "Tunc Hugo Caputius comes Parisiensis et duc Francorum contra dominum suum et consobrinum Karolum ducem Lotharingiae regnum Francorum contra preceptum Romanae ecclesiae, qui omnes invasores regni anathematizaverat, iniuste invasit." B.N. lat. 8865, fol. 181v. The twelfth-century Latin chronicle compiled at Saint-Denis and published by Waitz under the title *Historia Regum Francorum* (also known as the *Abbreviatio*) did incorporate the Sens version (*MGH, Scriptores*, 9: 395–406), but important writers such as Rigord and Guillaume le Breton who used it as a source for their own histories simply dropped the Sens narration and substituted a more neutral account. See Rigord, *Gesta Philippi Augusti*, 61; Guillaume le Breton, *Gesta Philippi Augusti*, 176,

both published in *Oeuvres de Rigord et de Guillaume le Breton*, ed. H.-F. Delaborde, vol. 1 (Paris, 1885). Finally, the *Grandes Chroniques* themselves used the Sens history back to back with the *reditus*, apparently unconcerned with the possible slur on the Capetian name whose exaltation they had taken as their task. See *Grandes Chroniques*, 4: 365–67.

35. A. Luchaire, *Histoire des institutions monarchiques de la France sous les premiers Capétiens* (Paris, 1981), 1: 74.

36. Bloch, *Feudal Society*, trans. L. A. Manyon (Chicago, 1964), 2: 388. Bloch also believes that the thaumaturgical powers ascribed to the Capetians, starting with Robert II, signaled the beginnings of a new form of legitimacy for French rulers. See his *Les Rois thaumaturges: Etudes sur le caractère surnaturel attribué à la puissance royal particulièrement en France et en Angleterre*, Publications de la Faculté de l'Université de Strasburg, 19 (Strasbourg, 1924), passim.

37. Percy Schramm speaks of a "bound" election as early as Philip I (1059) and claims that between 987 and 1059 the "dynasty had secured the principle of blood-right." *Der König von Frankreich* (Weimar, 1960), 1: 102. Similarly, Viollet states that by the eleventh century, kingship "had become hereditary in France in fact." *Histoire des institutions*, 2: 52. All historians agree with Luchaire that heredity definitely "triumphed" in the second half of the twelfth century. Luchaire, *Histoire des institutions*, 1: 62. For a discussion of the literature, see Andrew W. Lewis, *Royal Succession in Capetian France: Studies on Familial Order and the State*, Harvard Historical Studies (Cambridge, Mass., 1981).

38. See Andrew W. Lewis, "Anticipatory Association of the Heir in Early Capetian France," *American Historical Review* 83 (1978): 906–27. Lewis proposes the model to test the advent of the constitutional principle of heredity, but it is also useful in dealing with questions of psychological legitimacy.

39. A. Molinier, ed., in *Vie de Louis le Gros par Suger suivie de l'Histoire du Roi Louis VII*, Collection de textes pour servir à l'étude et à l'enseignement de l'histoire (Paris, 1887), xxxiii.

40. These passages were incorporated into the *Grandes Chroniques*, 6: 6, which added a reference to God as guarantor of Capetian dynastic continuity: "por ce que Diex lor [the French] avoit doné lignie et tel remanant de lor bon segnor."

41. "A longo tempore fuit unicum et irremediabile totius regni desiderium, ut sua benignitate et misericordia largiretur Deus prolem de nobis que in sceptris post nos ageret et regnum moderari potest." Cited

in A. Cartellieri, *Philip II August, König von Frankreich*, 4 vols. (Leipzig, 1899–1921), 1: zehnte Beilage, 49. See A. Luchaire, *Etudes sur les Actes de Louis VII* (Paris, 1885), no. 522.

42. Rigord, *Gesta Philippi Augusti*, 7, 8.

43. Cartellieri, *Philip II August*, zehnte Beilage, no. 7; also nos. 8–10, 13, 18–19. This is true of Louis's early acts. According to Luchaire, dating by regnal years, including the king's, was dropped after 1175. *Etudes sur les Actes de Louis VII*, 20.

44. Fawtier gives a rather strange explanation for this delay: "On sait que Louis VII, seul roi depuis 1137, attendit longtemps un héritier mâle, que seule put lui donner sa troisième femme. C'est ce qui explique qu'il ait attendu presque la veille de sa mort pour s'associer son fils Philippe, le futur Philippe-Auguste." F. Lot and R. Fawtier, *Histoire des institutions françaises au moyen âge*, vol. 2, *Institutions royales* (Paris, 1958), 15. On the contrary, one would imagine that after waiting so long for a male heir, Louis would have been anxious to ensure his accession by immediate association, urged upon him by Alexander III. Louis's delay suggests that he believed Philip's succession was secure and did not require formal designation. That he changed his mind at the last moment is almost certainly due to his failing health.

45. See A. Luchaire: "Certains indices tendraient même à faire croire qu'il se substitua tout à fait à Louis VII et n'attendit pas sa mort pour expédier des diplômes où il s'intitulait *rex Francorum* sans aucune reserve du droit paternel." *Manuel des institutions françaises: Période des Capétiens directs* (Paris, 1892), 474–75. It is true that the formulae of Philip's charters do not differ from those redacted before and after Louis's death. Cartellieri, however, prefers to see Philip's inception into royal authority as taking place in two stages; while he exercised the plenitude of royal power to which he had been associated by his father throughout (Nov. 1, 1179–Sept. 19, 1180), even to the latter's detriment, he did so initially by virtue of his legal association, and only towards the end (after June 1180) can we speak of an actual "usurpation" of power. A. Cartellieri, "L'Avènement de Philippe-Auguste," *Revue Historique* 54 (1894): 28.

46. It is reported by Ralph de Diceto: "Ludovicus rex Francorum, quia ius suum et potestatem in Philippum regem transtulerat, ne quid in regno statuerat citra filii conscientiam, sigilli sui potestate privatus est." In Cartellieri, *Philip II August*, fünfte Beilage, 29–30. Cartellieri, here and in a series of three articles on Philip's accession in the *Revue Historique* (52 [1893]: 241–59, 261–79; 54 [1894]: 1–33), believes Philip did ap-

propriate the royal seal for his exclusive use, though he qualifies the action as forced upon Philip by absolute necessity, without attributing to Philip any desire to set aside his father's legitimate authority.

47. The evidence that relates to the birth of a royal heir according to the proposed model can be multiplied for Louis VIII. Thus even before Louis's birth, Philip seems to have been assured that any male heir would succeed. Rigord reports that Philip called a council in 1185 to allow legates from Jerusalem to preach the Crusade, but refused to take the cross himself because he had not yet secured the succession with the birth of an heir: "Ipse enim Philippus rex tunc regni Francorum gubernacula solus strenue regebat; nondum enim ex Elizabeth venerabili Regina, uxore sua sobolem desideratum susceperat, et ideo de consilio principam strenuos milites . . . de propriis reditibus sumptus sufficientes . . . Hierosolymam devote transmisit." *Gesta Philippi Augusti*, chap. 31, p. 48. See also Rigord's description of Louis's birth and the rejoicing it occasioned in Paris (chap. 54, pp. 80–81). Giles of Paris, in his poem *Carolinus*, addresses Louis as "puer, in regno regalis sanguinis haeres." Brial, ed., *RHF*, 17: 289. Philip's Testament of 1190 made no provision for the succession should both he and Louis die during the Crusade. This does not necessarily suggest, as Luchaire points out, that the realm would return to election by the magnates. According to Luchaire, the right of collateral heirs to succeed was no longer in question and Philip Augustus could not "a priori dismiss the idea that the crown might devolve to one of his paternal uncles." Luchaire, *Manuel des institutions françaises*, 467.

48. Migne, *Patrologia Latina*, 101: 1295.

49. The emperor ceased using the title after the reign of Henry IV (1056–1105). See G. Zeller, "Les Rois de France, candidats à l'Empire: Essai sur l'idéologie impériale en France," *Revue Historique* 173 (1954): 277. Ferdinand Lot has studied the progressive monopolization of the word *Carolingian* by the West Franks and attributes it, like Zeller, to the fact that the Carolingian dynasty ceased to reign in Germany three quarters of a century earlier than in western France. More important, Lot shows that the term was not restricted to the royal *race*, the descendants of Charlemagne, but came to stand for the subjects of a "Carolingian" king, ultimately for all the French. Thus, in the anonymous *Gesta Episcoporum Cameracensium*, "Carolingian" designates the French of the tenth and eleventh centuries as opposed to Germans and Lorrainers. In this work *partes Kerlensium* signifies France. In the chronicles studied by

Lot, Capetian kings are always considered as Carolingians. Hugh Capet is denoted *Rege etiam Karlingorum Hugone*; Robert is *rex Karlensium*; Henry I *rex Carolinorum* and *rex Caralingorum*. By extension, in the *Annales Magdeburgense*, for example, France is always *Karlingia*, even though at this time (end of the twelfth century) France had long ceased to be governed by a Carolingian. See F. Lot, "Origine et signification du mot 'Carolingien,'" *Revue Historique* 46 (1891): 68–73.

50. R. Folz, *Le Souvenir et la Légende de Charlemagne dans l'Empire germanique médiéval* (Paris, 1950), 138. North of the Alps eschatological speculation drew on the prophecy of Pseudo-Methodius, of Syriac origin, dating from the seventh century and known in France from the end of the eighth. Ibid., 139. Adso was in this transalpine tradition. The Sybille of Tibur originated in Lombardy and belonged to an Italo-Byzantine tradition which, because of its anti-Germanic tendency, was welcomed in France in the twelfth century.

51. Ibid., 144.

52. Otto of Freising, *The Deeds of Frederick Barbarossa*, trans. and annot. C. C. Mierow (New York, 1953), 26.

53. This is the famous *Descriptio qualiter Karolus Magnus Clavum et Coronam a Constantinopoli Aquisgrani detulerit qualiterque Karolus Calvus hoc ad sanctam Dyonisium retulerit*. See *Grandes Chroniques*, 3: 160 n. 1. It was written between 1080 and 1095 by the monks to authenticate their relics. C. Van de Kieft, "Deux Diplômes faux de Charlemagne pour Saint-Denis au XIIe siècle," *Le Moyen Age* 13 (1958): 401.

54. Charter no. 286, *MGH, Diplomata Karolinorum*, ed. E. Mühlbacher, 1: 428–30. R. Barroux argues for Suger as the author of the forgery and dates it to 1124 at the time of Louis VI's war against the threatened invasion of the German emperor. "Suger et la vassalité du Vexin," *Le Moyen Age* 13 (1958): 23–24. Van de Kieft insists that it cannot be dated before 1156, and prefers to attribute it to the hand of Odo of Deuil. "Deux Diplômes faux," 415, 432.

55. "Sanctissime domine Dionysi hiis regni Franciae insigniis et ornamentis libenter me spolio, ut deinceps eius regale habeas, teneas atque possideas dominium et in signum rei quattour modo aureos tibi offero bizancios, ut omnes tam presentes quam et futuri sciant et agnoscant, quod a deo solo et a te regnum Franciae teneo tuoque ac tuorum sociorum fretus auxilio et suffragantibus meritis illud ancipiti gladio defendo obsecrans atque obtestans omnes successores nostros reges." *MGH, Di-*

plomata Karolinorum, 1: 429. Louis IX was to reenact literally the conditions of the Charlemagne forgery by placing four pennies on the altar of Saint-Denis when he returned from the Crusade.

56. M. Sepet, "Le Drapeau de France," *Revue des Questions Historiques* 17 (1875): 516ff. See Schramm, *Der König von Frankreich*, 1: 139.

57. The first description of the king's going to Saint-Denis to receive the flag from the monks preparatory to battle is found in Suger, *Vita Ludovici Grossi* (in *Vie de Louis le Gros par Suger*, 101). Odo of Deuil, recounting Louis VII's departure for the East, already calls it a "customary procedure": "Dum igitur a beato Dionysio vexillum et abeundi licentiam petiit, qui mos semper victoriosis regibus fuit." *De Profectione Ludovici VII in Orientem*, ed. V. C. Berry, Records of Civilization, Sources and Studies, 42 (New York, 1948), 16. By the time of the *Grandes Chroniques* this flag is definitely identified as the Oriflamme. See *Grandes Chroniques*, 5: 237. On the Oriflamme, see the recent work of Anne Lombard-Jourdan, *Fleur-de-lis et Oriflamme: Signes célestes du royaume de France* (Paris, 1991). On the beginnings of nationalism in the time of Suger, see H. Koht, "The Dawn of Nationalism in Europe," *American Historical Review* 52 (1947): 265–80. Laetitia Boehm has proposed that the beginnings of French nationalism go back even further to the period of the First Crusade. See her "Gedanken zum Frankreich-Bewüsstsein im Frühen 12. Jahrhundert," *Historisches Jahrbuch* 74 (1955): 681–87.

58. Van de Kieft, "Deux Diplômes faux," 434.

59. Léon Gautier, "L'idée politique dans les Chansons de Geste," *Revue des Questions Historiques* 7 (1869): 84 n. 3.

60. Fawtier, *The Capetian Kings*, 85.

61. Folz, *Le Souvenir et la Légende de Charlemagne*, 207.

62. "Duxit uxorem, praecipue nobilitatis et spectandae pulchritudinis puellam nomine Adelam, filiam Comitis Theobaldi, quae de genere Karoli Magni Regis Francorum comprobatur esse hoc modo." *Historia, RHF*, 12: 290.

63. Guillaume le Breton, *Philippide, Nuncupatio*, both in *Oeuvres de Rigord*, 2: 3 (see also 58, 115); Giles of Paris, *Carolinus*, 297. Bertrand calls Philip "Charles, que fo dels mielhs de sos parents." Folz, *Le Souvenir et la Légende de Charlemagne*, 279.

64. Innocent III, *Novit Ille*, ed. Brial, *RHF*, 19: 458.

65. Werner (224) admits this and claims that Adele's descent was simply forgotten after the appearance of the *reditus*.

66. It is particularly noteworthy that this argument against the im-

portance of Elizabeth's descent was advanced as early as 1317 by Ivo, author of the *Vita et Passio Sancti Dionysii*, presented by Saint-Denis's abbot, Gilles of Pontoise, to Philip V. The Latin version of the *Vita* included a long section on the history of the kings of France in which Ivo disputed the legitimizing function of the *reditus* doctrine, claiming, as I have, that the Capetian dynastic tie to the Carolingians dated from Hugh Capet himself and in no way depended on the house of Hainault. Thus, after discussing Philip Augustus's marriage to Elizabeth and the subsequent birth of Louis, Ivo demurred: "dicunt igitur progeniem Karoli recuperatam fuisse per istam Ysabellam et per descendentes ab ea quam quidem progeniem Karoli Magni dicunt in Hugone Capucio defecisse. Verum licet ista Ysabellis de genere Karoli Magni descendit, non oportet Magni progeniem supra diximus in Hugone Capet minime defecisse, nam eum ibidem de eadem stirpe sufficienter probavimus descendisse." B.N. lat. 5286, fol. 200v. Hugh's Carolingian connection is given on folio 195r, which also cites Innocent III's decretal (*Novit Ille*) reporting Philip Augustus's Carolingian descent as evidence of the priority of the dynastic tie to the marriage with Elizabeth. This argument, coming as it does from within the heart of the Dionysian tradition itself, and a mere generation after the incorporation of the *reditus* doctrine into it, should not be slighted. Given the fidelity with which the monks of Saint-Denis continued the earlier traditions and works, it is compelling evidence that Saint-Denis never viewed the *reditus* as necessary to Capetian legitimacy. By referring to Hugh's Carolingian descent, Ivo, of course, attempted to establish the fully legitimate status of the house from its very inception (and thus deny the intervening period of illegitimate rule), a theory equally fictional. Nevertheless, in view of the modern historiographical interpretation of the *reditus*, it forces us to reconsider the status normally accorded that doctrine in its function of dynastic legitimation.

67. See Giesey, "The Juristic Basis of Dynastic Right to the French Throne," 5. The effect of consecration, with its notion of "rebirth of the ruler," in negating dynastic and familial continuity has been studied by Walter Ullmann, *The Carolingian Renaissance and the Idea of Kingship* (London, 1969), esp. chap. 4.

68. Fawtier, *The Capetian Kings*, 57.

69. Ibid., 57 n. 2. Fawtier also speculates that some of the opposition of the greater nobility to the regency of Blanche of Castille was due to "a half-formed conviction that the day of the Capetians was over, that the

prediction of St. Valery was about to be fulfilled by a change in dynasty."

70. C. Petit-Dutaillis, *Feudal Monarchy in France and England* (New York, 1964), 215.

71. Gerard of Wales, *De Principis Instructione Liber*, ed. G. F. Warner, Rolls Series, 21⁸: 294.

72. *Historia Regum, RHF*, 17: 426; Rigord, *Gesta Philippe Augusti*, chap. 21, p. 34.

73. Guillaume le Breton, *Philippide*, in *Oeuvres de Rigord*, bk. 8, v. 632 sq., 234; bk. 1, v. 285 sq., 18–19; idem, *Nuncupatio*: Viva Karolide virtus, v. 28, 3; and bk. 10, v. 698, 310.

74. *Recueil des Actes de Philippe Auguste*, ed. H.-F. Delaborde (Paris, 1966), 1: xxvii.

75. Paris, Archives Nationales, JJ 26, fol. 309r–v.

76. An unexplained reference to the *reditus* can be found in the anonymous *Chronica Strozziana*, found in the library of Leo Strozzi and dating from circa 1200. The chronicle states: "De progenie Ermengardis processit Balduinis Baiucensis, cujus filiam Elizabeth Philippus II rex Francorum uxorem duxit, ex qua Ludovicum genuit. Si iste post patrem regnavit, constat Regnum reductum ad progeniem Caroli Magni." *RHF*, 10: 273. Otto of Freising gives a parallel expression to the *reditus* when saying of Henry III: "in ipsoque dignitas imperialis quae per longam iam tempus a semine Karoli exclaverat ad generosum et antiquum germen Karoli reducta est." Cited in Werner, 204 n. 8. The presence of the doctrine in these texts is not yet explained, and Werner, nevertheless, concluded that the credit for the political usefulness of the *reditus* goes to Vincent of Beauvais (224). Neither Cartellieri nor Petit-Dutaillis found any reference to the *reditus* in contemporary French documents before Vincent. See Petit-Dutaillis, *Bibliothèque de l'Ecole des Chartes* 60 (1899): 292.

77. Suger, *Vita Ludovici Grossi Regis*, 106. I am indebted to Professor Charles Wood for pointing out the passage's significance as the defeat of an emperor.

78. Innocent III, *Novit Ille*, 458–59.

79. John W. Baldwin, *Masters, Princes and Merchants: The Social Views of Peter the Chanter and His Circle* (Princeton, 1970), 1: 210, 2: 147 n. 33. On Philip Augustus's territorial acquisitions, see now idem, *The Government of Philip Augustus: Foundations of French Royal Power in the Middle Ages* (Berkeley, 1986).

80. Fragments of Rigord's *Short Chronicle of the Kings of France* have been published by Delaborde, following a manuscript in the Biblio-

thèque Municipale of Soissons. *Bibliothèque de l'Ecole des Chartes* 45 (1884): 600–604. The reference here is to p. 604.

81. Rigord, *Gesta Philippi Augusti*, 6.

82. Guillaume le Breton tells of *Hymnos triumphales* sung that day and describes "omnes autem cujusque generis, sexus et etatis homines ad tanti triumphi (sic triumphali) spectacula concursantes." *Gesta Philippi Augusti*, 296.

83. J. Strayer, in Jacques Barzun et al., eds., *The Interpretation of History* (Princeton, 1943), 10.

84. Thus, for example, the fourteenth-century French canonist Guillaume de Montlauzon (d. 1343) observed that the king of France recognized no superior because Charlemagne, in whose person the empire was transferred to the Germans, had not intended that his own special patrimony—i.e., the kingdom of France—should be subject to anyone: "de jure rex Francie et quidam alii imperatorem in suum superiorem minime recognoscant, maxime cum Karolus Magnus, in cuius personam fuit translatum in germanos imperium non videtur verisimiliter suum speciale patrimonium, quod erat regnum Francie, velle alicui subiecisse." Cited in G. Post, "Two Notes on Nationalism in the Middle Ages," *Traditio* 9 (1953): 310 n. 66.

85. Zeller has reviewed all the French campaigns for the emperorship up to and including the eighteenth century. See his "Les Rois de France, candidats à l'Empire."

86. See L. Boehm, "De Karlingis imperator Karolus, princeps et monarchia totius Europae! Zur Orientpolitik Karls I von Anjou," *Historisches Jahrbuch* 88 (1968): 1–35. Boehm shows how earnestly Charles pursued imperialistic ventures and the tight connection that existed in his mind between his political actions and the claim of blood descent from Charlemagne.

87. Zeller, "Les Rois de France, candidats à l'Empire."

Chapter Eight: The Cult of Saint Denis and Capetian Kingship

1. Bernard Guenée, *L'Occident au XIVe et XVe siècles: Les Etats* (Paris, 1971), 121, and idem, "Etat et nation en France au moyen âge," *Revue Historique* 237 (1967): 17–30.

2. "Huius tempore viri episcopi ordenati ad praedicandum in Galliis missi sunt, sicut historia passiones sancti martyres Saturnini denarrat. Ait enim: sub Decio et Grato consolibus, sicut fideli recordationem reteni-

tur, primum ac summum Tholosana civitas sanctum Saturninum habere coeperat sacerdotem. Hii ergo missi sunt . . . Parisiacis Dionysius episcopus. . . . De his vero beatus Dionisius Parisiorum episcopus, diversis pro Christi nomine adfectus poenis, praesentem vitam gladio inminente finivit." Gregory of Tours, *Historia Francorum*, ed. W. Arndt, *Monumenta Germaniae Historica* [hereafter cited as *MGH*], *Scriptores rerum merovingicarum*, 1: 48.

3. Sumner Crosby, *The Abbey of Saint-Denis 475–1122*, Yale Historical Publications (New Haven, 1942), 39.

4. "Igitur sanctus Dionysius, qui tradente sancto Clemente Petri Apostoli successore, verbi divini semina gentibus eroganda susceperat . . . . ac Parisius Domino ducente pervenit." M. Félibien, *Histoire de l'Abbaye royal de Saint-Denys en France* (Paris, 1706), clxiv, clxv.

5. *Vita Genovefae virginis Parisiensis*, ed. B. Krusch, *MGH, Scriptores rerum merovingicarum*, 3: 215–38.

6. Hilduin, *Areopagitica sive Sancti Dionysii vita*, in Migne, *Patrologia Latina*, 106: 14–50 (hereafter cited as *PL*).

7. The *Vie de Saint Denis*, written in the mid-thirteenth century, explicitly mentions that Rusticus and Eleutherius accompanied Denis to Paris. See B.N. n.a. fr. 1098, fol. 8v.

8. Crosby, *The Abbey of Saint-Denis*, 95.

9. "Quorum memoranda et gloriosissima passio e regione urbis Parisiorum in colle qui ante mons Mercurii, quoniam inibi idolum ipsius principaliter colebatur a Gallis, nunc vero mons martyrum vocatur . . . qui ibidem triumphale martyrium perpatrarunt, celebrata est VII idus Octobris." *PL*, 106: 50. See L. Levillain, "Etudes sur l'abbaye de Saint-Denis à l'époque Mérovingienne," *Bibliothèque de l'Ecole des Chartes* 82 (1921): 40.

10. "Et facta est comes multitudo coelestis exercitus exanimi ejus corpori, caput proprium ab ipso monte, ubi fuerat decollatus, per duo fere millia deportanti usque ad locum in quo nunc Dei dispositione et sua electione requiescit humatum, sine cessatione hymnis dulcisonis Deum laudans." *PL*, 106: 47.

11. L. Levillain, "Etudes sur l'abbaye de Saint-Denis," 49.

12. The *Passio* says only: "In hac ergo fidei constantia permanentes, reddentes terrae corpora, beatus coelo animas intulerunt; talique ad Dominum meruerent professione migrare, ut amputatis capitibus, adhuc putaretur lingua palpitans Dominum confiteri." Félibien, *Histoire de l'Abbaye royal de Saint-Denys*, clxiv.

13. Rigord, *Gesta Philippi Augusti*, in *Oeuvres de Rigord et de Guillaume le Breton*, ed. H.-F. Delaborde, Société de l'Histoire de France (Paris, 1882), 1: 114–15.

14. The theory that Denis had lost a portion of his cranium had a certain iconographic life in thirteenth-century France. L. Demaison, "Les statues du portail de gauche de la cathédrale de Reims," *Bulletin de la Société Nationale des Antiquaires* (1916): 185, discovered two seals of the Abbey of Saint-Denis de Montmartre that depict Saint Denis with his head cut above the eyebrows, carrying the remnant between his hands. The oldest extant exemplar seals a charter of the month of June 1216, which is the earliest date that can be established for these figures of Saint Denis amputated at the cranium. In a supporting discussion, H.-F. Delaborde, "Relique du crâne de Saint Denis à Notre-Dame de Paris," *Bulletin de la Société Nationale des Antiquaires* (1916): 190, pointed out that there existed at Notre-Dame de Paris a relic from Saint-Étienne-des-Grès which purported to be the top of Saint Denis's head, a fact that explains why the figure of Saint Denis on the portal of Notre-Dame carries only this part of his head.

15. Félibien, *Histoire de l'Abbaye royal de Saint-Denys*, clxv–clxxii.

16. Haimo actually makes no specific mention of the head, being more concerned to authenticate the identity of the saint. Rigord, in his review of this incident, however, explicitly adds: "et aperto vase Beati martyris Dionysii, totum corpus ipsius cum capite inventum est, exceptis duobus ossibus de collo." *Gesta Philippi Augusti*, 62. The *Grandes Chroniques* use the original text of Haimo but follow Rigord in this interpolation. See *Les Grandes Chroniques de France*, ed. J. Viard, Société de l'Histoire de France (Paris, 1930), 6: 145.

17. H.-F. Delaborde, "Le procès du chef de Saint Denis en 1410," *Mémoires de la Société de Paris et de l'Ile-de-France* 11 (1884): 297–409.

18. R. Bossuat, "Traditions populaires relatives au martyre et à la sépulture de Saint Denis," *Le Moyen Age* 11 (1956): 479–509. See the fifteenth-century text of the Religieux de Saint-Denis, B.N. lat. 5949A, fol. 319r.

19. *Epistola XII Ludovici ad Hilduinum Abbatem S. Dionysii anno 835,* in *PL*, 104: 1328.

20. *The Story of Abelard's Adversities*, ed. J. Muckle (Toronto, 1964), 53, 55.

21. "Abbati et conventui monasterii Sancti Dionysii in Francia scribitur, et, quia ab aliquibus dubitabatur an corpus beati Dionysii, quod in eodem monasterio requiescit, fuerit corpus beati Dionysii

Areopagitae, qui mortuus fuit in Graecia, vel alterius, dominus Papa mittit eis de veris reliquiis, sive corpus illius beati Dionysii Areopagitae, et concedit omnibus visitantibus quadraginta dies." Innocent, *Registrum*, in *PL*, 216: 993. While the Register seems to conclude that the relics sent by Innocent were those of Dionysius the Areopagite, who, having "died in Greece," could not have been the apostle to Gaul, the account of this transaction in the *Vita et actus Beati Dionysii*, written shortly afterwards in 1223, states explicitly that the gift made by Innocent was the body of Saint Denis, bishop of Corinth, not that of the Areopagite. See C. Liebman, *Etude sur la Vie en prose de Saint Denis* (New York, 1942), 209. Moreover, the *authenticum* of Innocent, copied into the *Vita*, retains a great deal more ambiguity over which body Innocent thought he was sending than the Register's version implies. The Religieux of Saint-Denis, in the fifteenth century, describes this affair under the rubric *De corpore sancti Dionysii Corynthiorum episcopi ad ecclesiam Sancti Dionysii translato*, reaffirming the Dionysian position that Saint Denis of Corinth was not the Areopagite. See B.N. lat. 5949A, fol. 375r. A feast of Saint Denis of Corinth was celebrated at the monastery on April 18. Félibien, *Histoire de l'Abbaye royal de Saint-Denys*, ccxix.

22. Félibien, *Histoire de l'Abbaye royal de Saint-Denys*, clxv. It seems logical that had the *Passio* intended to refer to the church built by Sainte Geneviève, it would have mentioned her role in the foundation. The passage must therefore refer to an earlier shrine, possibly even a small church, which later became dilapidated, since the *Vita Genovefae* gives as the reason for Geneviève's foundation the terrible condition of the saint's shrine. See *Vita Genovefae*, 222.

23. *Vita Genovefae*, 224.

24. Gregory of Tours, *Liber in gloria martyrum*, ed. W. Arndt, *MGH*, *Scriptores rerum merovingicarum*, 1: 535–36.

25. Crosby, *The Abbey of Saint-Denis*, 44.

26. It was Levillain who established Hincmar as the probable author of the *Miracula*. "Etudes sur l'abbaye de Saint-Denis," 58–114. See also A. Luchaire, "Etudes sur quelques manuscrits de Rome et de Paris, Les *Miracula Sancti Dionysii*," *Bibliothèque de la Faculté des Lettres* 8 (1899): 20–29.

27. Hincmar, *Gesta Dagoberti I regis Francorum*, ed. B. Krusch, *MGH*, *Scriptores rerum merovingicarum*, 2: 401.

28. Ibid., 402–3.

29. The story of Dagobert's vision was incorporated into all subse-

quent legedaries of the saint. Compare the accounts in the *Vita et Actus* (Liebman, *Etude sur la Vie en prose de Saint Denis*, 187 ff.), *Vie de Saint Denis* (B.N. n.a. fr. 1098, fol. 20v–21r), and *Grandes Chroniques*, 2: 103ff.

30. Hincmar, *Gesta Dagoberti*, 411.

31. Crosby, *The Abbey of Saint-Denis*, 44.

32. Ibid., 38.

33. Liebman, *Etude sur la Vie en prose de Saint Denis*, 10.

34. See, for example, the translation of Saint Hilary of Poitiers by Dagobert (Liebman, *Etude sur la Vie en prose de Saint Denis*, 202); the translation of Saints Patroclus, Romanus, and Hilary of Toulouse (ibid., 202–3); and the translation of Saints Cucphatus and Hypolitus by Charlemagne (ibid., 204–5).

35. Such, Léopold Delisle believed, was the origin of the piece. See "Notice sur un livre de peinture exécuté en 1250 dans l'Abbaye de Saint-Denis," *Bibliothèque de l'Ecole des Chartes* 38 (1877): 444.

36. On Ivo, see ibid., 455ff., and Delisle, "Notice sur un recueil historique présenté à Philippe le Long par Gilles de Pontoise, abbé de Saint-Denis," *Notices et Extraits des manuscrits de la Bibliothèque Impériale* 21, pt. 2 (1865): 249–65. See also H. Martin, *Légende de Saint Denis: Reproduction des miniatures du manuscrit original présenté en 1317 au roi Philippe le Long* (Paris, 1908); and B. Haureau, "Ives, moine de Saint-Denys," *Histoire Littéraire de la France* 31 (1893): 143–51.

37. See Ivo's *Vita et passio sancti Dionysii*, B.N. lat. 5286, fol. 3v.

38. "In rebus que bellicis pugnatores victoriossimi eiusdem patronum sui dyonisii protegente eos in omnibus ea qua apud Deum praecellit potencia dum nec ad bella quicumque solliti sunt praefati reges procedere quin primus ad eiusdem peculiaris patronum sui Dyonisii venerabile monasterium humiliter accedentes extractis de locis suis . . . commune totius francorum exercitus vexillum . . . sperantes per sanctorum suffragia praedicorum et hostium superbiam deprimere ac de ipsis victoriam obtinere." B.N. lat. 5286, fol. 117r.

39. Delisle, "Notice sur un livre de peinture," 454.

40. Rigord, *Gesta Philippi Augusti*, 11.

41. Benedict of Peterborough, *Gesta regis Henrici Secundi Benedicti Abbatis*, ed. W. Stubbs, Rolls Series, 49: 240–42.

42. Rigord, *Gesta Philippi Augusti*, 12 n. 1.

43. The *Grandes Chroniques* qualify Rigord's phrase by adding a reference to the kingdom: "patrons et defense des rois et dou roiaume de France" (6: 93). Thomas himself recognized the greatness of Saint Denis

and in his dying words, reported by Herbert of Bosham, commended the cause of his church to the French martyr: "et beato Dionysium Francorum apostolo commendans, ut illi inter martyres potissimum Deo inspirante sic commendaretur ecclesiae causa, cui ipse in ecclesia per martyrium simile jam assimilabitur in poena, isto sicut et illo decalvato. Se itaque exposito mox causam ecclesie quam egerat patronis commendavit, et pro suis oravit." *Vita Sancti Thomae archiepiscopi et martyris auctore Herberto de Boseham*, in *Materials for the History of Thomas Becket, Archbishop of Canterbury*, ed. J. C. Robertson, 7 vols., Rolls Series, 67³: 499.

44. *Grandes Chroniques*, 6: 203.

45. Guillaume de Nangis, *Vita Sancti Ludovici regis Franciae*, ed. M. Daunou, *Recueil des Historiens des Gaules et de la France* [hereafter cited as *RHF*], 20: 344.

46. *Grandes Chroniques*, 7: 106ff.

47. *Chronique Latine de Guillaume de Nangis de 1113 à 1300 avec les continuations de cette chronique*, ed. H. Géraud, 2 vols. (Paris, 1843), 2: 38.

48. "Quadem autem die, dum, pro negotiis regni agendis, rex per villam Beati Dionysi transitum faceret, in abbatiam Beati Dionysii, sicut in propriam cameram suam descendit." Rigord, *Gesta Philippi Augusti*, 65. Compare the *Grandes Chroniques* on the death of Philip Augustus: "Il garda et defendi l'eglise de Saint Denis en France sor totes autres, come sa propres chambre" (6: 370). The passage in Guillaume le Breton on which this text is based omits the reference to the chamber (*Gesta Philippi Augusti*, 324). Suger projects a similar picture of Louis VI's native affection for Saint Denis and his hope and confidence in the martyr's concern: "Altus puerulus, antiqua regum Karoli Magni et aliorum excellentiorum, hoc ipsum testamentis imperialibus testificantium, consuetudine, apud Santum Dionysium tanta et quasi nativa dulcedine ipsis sanctis martyribus suisque adhesit, usque adeo ut innatam a puero eorum ecclesie amiciciam toto tempore vite sue multa liberalite et honorificentia continuaret et, in fine, summe post Deum sperans ab eis, seipsum et corpore et anima, ut, si fieri posset, ibidem monachus efficeretur, devotissime deliberando contraderet." *Vita Ludovici Grossi regis Franciae*, ed. Henri Waquet, Les Classiques de l'Histoire de France au moyen âge (Paris, 1964), 6.

49. The *Couronnement*, while concerned with the coronation of Louis the Pious, was probably directed towards the coronation of the infant Louis VII in 1131, at the age of ten. The poem makes Louis the Pious an infant, although in fact by 813, the date of his coronation, he was

already thirty-five or thirty-six years old. For this and other arguments, see A. Lanly, ed., *Le Couronnement de Louis: Chanson de Geste du XIIe siècle*, ed. A. Lanly (Paris, 1969), 8ff.

50. *Le Couronnement de Louis*, ed. E. Langlois, Les classiques français du moyen âge (Paris, 1920), 46, 112.

51. Jordan of Fantosme, *Chronique de la guerre entre les Anglois et les Ecossois en 1173 et 1174*, ed. R. Howlett, Rolls Series, 82³: 206.

52. "Antiquitus solebant fieri, sicut et nunc quoque fiunt, processiones ab ecclesiis ad ecclesias a religiosis pastoribus sancte matris ecclesiae, subsequente eos humillima devotione populi. Et hoc fieri consueverat quotiens aliqua urgens necessitas compulisset, videlicet si mortalitas hominum, si late vagans pestilentia, si aeris inequalitas, aut si inter reges aut principes bellorum immanitas deseviret." In Liebman, *Etude sur la Vie en prose de Saint Denis*, 205.

53. The principal source of this legend is the *Chanson de Roland*, which explains that "Saint Pierre fut, si aveit num Romaine / Mais de Munjoie iloec out pris eschange." M. Sepet, "Le Drapeau de France," *Revue des Questions Historiques* 17 (1875): 516. The *Nova Gesta Francorum*, written at the Abbey of Saint-Denis in the early twelfth century, reiterates this legend: "Mox ut Leo in eius loco successit missis legatis ad pium regem Karolum clavis confessionis Sancti Petri simul et vexillum romane urbis direxit." B.N. lat. 11793, fol. 27v.

54. Sepet, "Le Drapeau de France," 516.

55. Suger, *Vita Ludovici Grossi*, 220.

56. "Dum igitur a beato Dionysio vexillum et abeundi licentiam petiit, qui mos semper victoriosis regibus fuit." Odo of Deuil, *De Profectione Ludovici VII in Orientem*, ed. V. C. Berry, Records of Civilization, Sources and Studies, 42 (New York, 1948), 16.

57. See A. Cartellieri, *Philip II August, König von Frankreich*, 4 vols. (Leipzig, 1899–1921), 1: 145 n. 3.

58. Historians such as Sepet have claimed that the confusion of the two standards dates as early as the reign of Louis VII ("Le Drapeau de France," 518). But no clear-cut evidence exists before the historians of Philip Augustus. See H.-F. Delaborde, in *Oeuvres de Rigord*, 98–99. By the time of the *Grandes Chroniques*, the original banner of the Vexin is described as the Oriflamme at the moment of Philip's acquisition of the county and the obligation to carry in it battle as part of the service of the fief of the Vexin. For additional references to the Oriflamme, see Philippe Contamine, *L'Oriflamme de Saint-Denis aux XIVe et XVe siècles*

(Nancy, 1975); and Anne Lombard-Jourdan, *Fleur-de-lis et Oriflamme: Signes célestes du royaume de France* (Paris, 1991).

59. For the political uses of the dynastic tie between Carolingians and Capetians, see Chapter Seven. For the flag's connection with the cult of Charlemagne during the reign of Philip Augustus, see Schramm, *Der König von Frankreich* (Weimar, 1960), 1: 139–40. The *Traité du Sacre* by Jean Golein later emphasizes its imperial connotation for Charlemagne and, through him, for all French kings: "Si veulent aucuns dire que celle banniere baillée par la vision de l'empereur de Constantinople à Charlemaine pronostiquoit qu'il devoit estre empereur du peuple romain, si comme il fu apres, et appelé patrician et empereur; et celle enseigne imperial voult lassier en France en signe de Empire perpetuel par succession de hoir masle." Cited in Marc Bloch, *Les Rois thaumaturges: Etudes sur le caractère surnaturel attribué à la puissance royal particulièrement en France et en Angleterre*, Publications de la Faculté de l'Université de Strasburg, 19 (Strasbourg, 1924), 486.

60. Guillaume de Nangis, *Vita Sancti Ludovici*, 370.

61. Primat, *Chronique Latine*, ed. N. de Wailly, *RHF*, 23: 40.

62. Guillaume de Nangis, *Gesta Philippi regis Francorum, filii Sanctae memoriae regis Ludovici*, *RHF*, 20: 474, 502–5.

63. Guillaume de Nangis, *Chronique Latine*, 345.

64. Félibien, *Histoire de l'Abbaye royal de Saint-Denys*, cclxii.

65. Guillaume de Nangis, *Vita Sancti Ludovici*, 468.

66. The dating of this charter is uncertain, and it bears an ambiguous relation to a passage in the *Pseudo-Turpin* which it closely resembles. Schramm (*Der König von Frankreich*, 1: 135) dates it later than the *Pseudo-Turpin*, which he believes was written circa 1140. C. Van de Kieft ("Deux Diplômes faux de Charlemagne pour Saint-Denis au XIIe siècle," *Le Moyen Age* 13 [1958]: 432) believes it could not have been written before 1156 and awards Odo of Deuil a principal part in its fabrication. R. Barroux ("Suger et la vassalité du Vexin," *Le Moyen Age* 13 [1958]: 15), on the contrary, attributes it to Suger and dates it shortly after 1124. He believes it results from the same impulse that underlay Suger's account of Louis VI's assumption of the Oriflamme—namely, a desire to depict France as a vassal of the abbey. Least likely is the opinion of Buchner ("Das gefälschte Karlsprivileg für St. Denis BM2 nr. 482 und seine Entstehung, zugleich ein Beitrag zur Geschichte Frankreichs im 12 Jahrhundert," *Historisches Jahrbuch* 42 [1922]: 12–28, 250–65), who dates it to 1149 and considers it a response of Suger to the rebellion of Robert

of Dreux after the failure of Louis VII's crusade. Since the charter's notion that the king of France is the vassal of Saint Denis underlies the iconography of the abbey's *Porte des Valois*, dating shortly after 1175, this seems to constitute a *terminus ad quem* for the fabrication of the charter. The passage in the *Pseudo-Turpin Chronicle* to which it should be compared can be found in Symser's edition, *The Pseudo-Turpin* (Cambridge, Mass., 1937), 106.

67. Charter no. 286, *MGH, Diplomata Karolinorum*, ed. E. Mühlbacher, 1: 429.

68. Georgia Sommers, "Royal Tombs at Saint-Denis in the Reign of St. Louis" (Ph.D. diss., Columbia University, 1966), 70–71. Other iconographic features of the thirteenth century emphasize the bond between the king and the abbey. According to Robert Branner (*Saint Louis and the Court Style* [London, 1965], 46), the presence of royal coats of arms among the ornaments of the Gothic work reflects a desire to express the abbey's relationship to the crown. On the tomb program of Saint-Denis, see also Alain Erlande-Brandenburg, *Le Roi est Mort: Etude sur les funérailles, les sépultures et les tombeaux des rois de France jusqu'à la fin du XIIIe siècle*, Bibliothèque de la Société Française d'Archéologie, 7 (Paris, 1975).

69. Suger, *Vita Ludoici Grossi*, 220.

70. H.-F. Delaborde, "Pourquoi Saint Louis faisait acte de servage à Saint Denis," *Bulletin de la Société Nationale des Antiquaires* (1897): 256.

71. "Partant, si ne doit-on pas cuider ce soit servages, ainz est droiz establissemenz de franchise; car ensi fist Alixandres le Granz, quant il ot conquis tout Orient, que tuit cil qui le rendoient IIII deniers fussent quites de toutes autres costumes. Dont li rois de France paient chascun an IIII besanz d'or et les offrent desus lor chiés aus martyrs en recognoissance que il tienent de Dieu et de li le roiaume de France: qui il ne feissent en nule maniere, se ce fust en nom de servage." *Grandes Chroniques*, 3: 289.

72. *Gesta Sancti Ludovici Noni Francorum regis auctore monacho Sancti Dionysii anonymo*, ed. M. Daunou, *RHF*, 20: 51–52.

73. This story is repeated by Ivo: "Omni etiam anno in prefato festo aut intererat vel si tunc occupatus interesse non poterat, quam citius postea accedens ad altare sancti Dyonisii cum maxima devotione, nudo capite, flexis genibus, oratione praemissa vocato ad hoc presente filio suo domino Philippo, ponens quatuor bisantios primo super caput suum tenens cum manu postmodum cum multa reverencia eosdem bisantios,

osculans altare, super illud devotissime offerebat." B.N. lat. 5286, fol. 207r. On the questions of the hereditary implications of the act, see Paul R. Hyams, "The form of manumission charters and ideas about freedom," unpublished paper. I would like to thank Professor Hyams for sending me a copy.

74. *Vie de Saint Louis par le Confesseur de la reine Marguerite*, ed. M. Daunou, *RHF*, 20: 76.

75. Delaborde, "Pourquoi Saint Louis faisait acte de servage à Saint Denis," 255.

76. Vatican, MS Ottoboni Lat. 2796; Register A, fol. 12v. I would like to thank Professor Baldwin for sharing this discovery with me and for his advice concerning its dating.

77. R. Bossuat, "Traditions populaires relatives au martyre et à la sepulture de Saint Denis," 483.

78. Gorski, "La naissance des Etats et le Roi-Saint: Problème de l'idéologie féodale," in *L'Europe aux IXe–XIe siècles*, Colloque International sur les origines des Etats Eupropéens aux IXe–XIe siècles (Warsaw, 1968), 425–32. Gorski points out that one of the benefits of this ideal model of the holy king was its freedom from influences of the Roman Empire. It could, thus, serve as an instrument of national claims against imperial hegemony.

79. Joseph Strayer, "France: The Holy Land, the Chosen People and the Most Christian King," in Theodore K. Rabb and Jerrold E. Siegel, eds., *Action and Conviction in Early Modern Europe: Essays in Honor of E. R. Harbison* (Princeton, 1969), 5.

80. Schramm, *Der König von Frankreich*, 1: 177.

81. Strayer, "France," 5.

82. Bernard Guenée, "L'Histoire de l'état en France à la fin du moyen âge vue par les historiens français depuis cent ans," *Revue Historique* 237 (1967): 346.

83. E. Kantorowicz, "Kingship under the Impact of Scientific Jurisprudence," in M. Clagett et al., eds., *Twelfth-Century Europe and the Foundations of Modern Society* (Madison, 1966), 101; and idem, *The King's Two Bodies: A Study in Medieval Political Theology* (Princeton, 1966).

84. G. Langmuir, "Community and Legal Change in Capetian France," *French Historical Studies* 6 (1970): 286.

85. Strayer speaks of a cult of the kingdom of France as early as 1300, in *On the Medieval Origins of the Modern State* (Princeton, 1970), 54.

86. P. Viollet, *Histoire des institutions politiques et administratives de la France* (Paris, 1898), 2: 20.

Chapter Nine: History as Enlightenment

1. For Suger's role in the inception of royal historiography at Saint-Denis, see my *The Chronicle Tradition of Saint-Denis: A Survey*, Medieval Classics: Texts and Studies, no. 10 (Leiden, 1979), 39–40.

2. Apart from the introductions to his published works, no genuine study of Suger's historical writings has ever been undertaken. Even the better biographies of Suger, such as those by Otto Cartellieri, *Abt Suger von Saint-Denis*, Historische Studien, 11 (Berlin, 1898; rpr. Millbrook, N.Y., 1965), and Marcel Aubert, *Suger* (Paris, 1950), discuss his historiography only briefly.

3. See A. Molinier, ed., *Vie de Louis le Gros par Suger suivie de l'Histoire du Roi Louis VII*, Collection de textes pour servir à l'étude et à l'enseignement de l'histoire (Paris, 1887), xvii–xviii; and Spiegel, *The Chronicle Tradition of Saint-Denis*, 41.

4. See Simon Luce, "La Continuation d'Aimoin et le manuscrit Latin 12711 de la Bibliothèque Nationale," *Notices et Documents publiés par la Société de l'Histoire de France à l'occasion du cinquantième anniversaire de sa fondation* (Paris, 1884), 57–70; and Jean-François Lemarignier, "Autour de la royauté française du IXe au XIIe siècle. Appendice: La continuation d'Aimoin et le manuscrit Latin 12711 de la Bibliothèque Nationale," *Bibliothèque de l'Ecole des Chartes* 113 (1955): 25–36.

5. Jules Lair, "Mémoire sur deux chroniques latines composées au XIIe siècle à l'abbaye de Saint-Denis," *Bibliothèque de l'Ecole des Chartes* 33 (1874): 543–80.

6. Spiegel, *The Chronicle Tradition of Saint-Denis*, 78.

7. For a review of the manuscript tradition and printed editions, see Henri Waquet, *Vie de Louis le Gros*, Les Classiques de l'histoire de France au moyen âge, 11 (Paris, 1929), xvii–xxvi. Three additional manuscripts which possess copies of the *Vita Ludovici*, unknown to Waquet, are: Rome, Biblioteca Apostolica Vaticana, Reg. Lat. 550, a copy of the *Continuation of Aimoin* written, according to Marc Du Pouget, around 1202–5 ("Recherches sur les chroniques latines de Saint-Denis: Commentaire et édition critique de la *Descriptio clavi et corone domini*" [thesis, Ecole des Chartes, 1977], 16) and housed in the library of Saint-

Denis, where it later served as the basis for the initial portion of B.N. lat. 5925, itself largely a copy of the *Continuation of Aimoin*. The second and third manuscripts consist of two versions of a newly discovered early vernacular prose history entitled *Chronique des Rois de France*, written in Francien between 1210 and 1229–30, in all probability in Paris or its environs. Both manuscripts—Rome, Biblioteca Apostolica Vaticana, Reg. Lat. 624, and Chantilly, Musée Condé, MS 869—include the first translation of Suger's *Vita Ludovici* into French, and Pierre Botineau has established that Primat, when he came to translate the *Vita Ludovici* in the first installment of the *Grandes Chroniques*, used this vernacular text as a source. See Pierre Botineau, "Une Source des *Grandes Chroniques de France*: L'Histoire de France en prose française de Charlemagne à Philippe-Auguste," unpublished typescript. On the Vatican manuscript, see Elie Berger, "Notices sur divers manuscrits de la Bibliothèque Vaticane," *Bibliothèque des Ecoles françaises d'Athènes et de Rome* 6 (1879): 10; Ronald N. Walpole, "La Traduction du *Pseudo-Turpin* du Manuscrit Vatican Regina 624: A Propos d'un livre récent," *Romania* 99 (1978): 484–514; Pierre Botineau, "L'Histoire de France en français de Charlemagne à Philippe-Auguste: La Compilation du Ms. 624 du Fonds de la Reine à la Bibliothèque Vaticane," *Romania*, 90 (1969): 79–99; and on both the Vatican and Chantilly manuscripts, see Ronald N. Walpole, "Prolégomènes à une édition du Turpin français dit le *Turpin I*," *Revue d'Histoire des Textes* 10 (1980): 199–230, and 11 (1981): 325–70. Gillette Labory of the Institut de Recherche d'Histoire et des Textes in Paris has studied the first 165 folios that make up the translation of the *Continuation of Aimoin*. See her "Essai d'une histoire nationale au XIIIe siècle: La Chronique de l'Anonyme de Chantilly-Vatican," *Bibliothèque de l'Ecole des Chartes* 148 (1990): 301–54. A new translation of the *Vita Ludovici* into French has just been published by Michel Bur, *Suger: La Geste de Louis VI*, Acteurs de l'Histoire (Paris, 1994). On the text as a whole, see my *Romancing the Past: The Rise of Vernacular Prose Historiography in Thirteenth-Century France*, The New Historicism (Berkeley, 1993), chap. 6.

8. For Guillaume's biography of Suger, see Guillaume, *Vita Sugerii*, in *Oeuvres Complètes de Suger*, ed. A. Lecoy de la Marche, Société de l'Histoire de France, 139 (Paris, 1867), 382, 389.

9. Jean Baudouin, *Le Ministre Fidèle représenté sous Louis VI en la personne de Suger, Abbé de S. Denys en France et Régent du Royaume sous Louis VII* (Paris, 1640).

10. See Waquet, *Vie de Louis le Gros*, xii; *Oeuvres Complètes de Suger*, ed. Lecoy de la Marche, iii; Aubert, *Suger*, 116; and Erwin Panofsky, *Abbot Suger on the Abbey Church of Saint-Denis and Its Art Treasures* (Princeton, 1946; 2d ed., 1979), xi.

11. As in the recent books of Colin Morris, *The Discovery of the Individual 1050–1200* (New York, 1972); and Karl Weintraub, *The Value of the Individual Self and Circumstance in Autobiography* (Chicago, 1978). Georg Misch, in his *Geschichte der Autobiographie*, 4 vols. (Frankfurt-am-Main, 1949–69), vol. 3, similarly includes Suger's personal testimonies as evidence for the growing consciousness of personality in the twelfth century.

12. I confess to having said as much myself; see my *The Chronicle Tradition of Saint-Denis*, 46–47.

13. Brandt, *The Shape of Medieval History: Studies in Modes of Perception* (New Haven, 1966), chap. 7.

14. *Vita Ludovici*, 10, in Waquet, *Vie de Louis le Gros* (hereafter cited as *Vita Ludovici*).

15. Ibid. Suger's Latin here has caused some confusion. He states: "quia nec fas nec naturale est Francos Anglis, immo Anglos Franci subici." Waquet (11) translates this as: "parce ce qu'il n'est ni permis ni naturel que les Français soient soumis aux Anglais, ni même les Anglais aux Français." However, *Les Grandes Chroniques de France* (ed. J. Viard, Société de l'Histoire de France, 10 vols. [Paris, 1920–53], 5: 85) understood the text in the way I have translated it and gives a reading of: "mes por ce que ce n'est pas droiz ne chose naturel que François soient en la subjection d'Anglois: ainz est droiz que Anglois soient sugiet à François." It seems fairly clear that *immo* is best taken to mean "but rather" or "on the contrary," instead of "nor" as Waquet translates it. For the complex relations between the Capetians and the Anglo-Norman kings over the question of homage owed the kings of France, see C. Warren Hollister, "Normandy, France and the Anglo-Norman *Regnum*," *Speculum* 51 (1976): 202–47. Also useful are Jean-François Lemarignier, *Recherches sur l'hommage en marche et les frontières féodales* (Lille, 1945), and idem, *La France médiévale: Institutions et sociétés* (Paris, 1970); and John Le Patourel, *The Norman Empire* (Oxford, 1976), 218–21.

16. *Vita Ludovici*, 12.

17. Ordericus Vitalis, *Ecclesiastical History*, ed. and trans. Marjorie Chibnall (Oxford, 1978), 6: 240. Suger does, of course, acknowledge

Louis's defeat but says only that he "withdrew, not without great damage to his host" (non tamen sine magno erratici exercitus detrimento). *Vita Ludovici*, 198.

18. *Vita Ludovici*, 200.

19. Georges Duby, *The Three Orders: Feudal Society Imagined*, trans. Arthur Goldhammer (Chicago, 1980), 113, 228.

20. For a summary of this development, see Chapter Eight. See also Sumner Crosby, *The Abbey of Saint-Denis 475–1122*, Yale Historical Publications (New Haven, 1942]), 14ff.; Gabriel Théry, O.P., "Contribution à l'histoire de l'Aréopagitisme au IXe siècle," *Le Moyen Age* 25 (1923): 111–53; and Panofsky, *Abbot Suger on the Abbey Church*, 18.

21. Pseudo-Dionysius, *Letter 8*, in Ronald E. Hathaway, *Hierarchy and Definition of Order in the Letters of Pseudo-Dionysius* (The Hague, 1969), 146.

22. Marie-Dominique Chenu, "The Platonisms of the Twelfth Century," in Jerome Taylor and Lester Little, eds. and trans., *Nature, Man and Society in the Twelfth Century* (Chicago, 1968), 82.

23. Marie-Dominique Chenu, "The Symbolist Mentality," in Taylor and Little, *Nature, Man and Society in the Twelfth Century*, 115, n. 40. John is elaborating the principle, stated at the beginning of the "Celestial Hierarchy" by Pseudo-Dionysius, that "it is not possible for our mind to be raised to that immaterial representation and contemplation of the heavenly hierarchies without using the material guidance suitable to itself, accounting the visible beauties as reflections of the invisible comeliness . . . and the ranks of the orders here, of the harmonious and regulated habit with regard to Divine things." All English quotations from Pseudo-Dionysius are taken from the English translation by John Parker, *The Works of Dionysius the Areopagite* (rpr., London, 1976). The quoted passage is from "On the Celestial Hierarchy," 3.

24. Chenu, "Symbolist Mentality," 123.

25. Panofsky, *Abbot Suger on the Abbey Church*, 19.

26. Chenu, "Symbolist Mentality," 132, 126.

27. Pseudo-Dionysius, *Ecclesiastical Hierarchy*, 84–85.

28. Hathaway, *Hierarchy and Definition of Order*, 142.

29. Ibid., 52.

30. *Vita Ludovici*, 134, 86.

31. It is in this context that Suger's famous dictum that the king of France cannot do homage—or would, *si non rex esset*—should be understood. Not because it violates feudal custom (which before Louis VI's

time is silent on this point), but out of an absolute ontological incapacity
to break rank, to submit to a lower order of being. As with so much else
in Suger's thought, the roots of his originality lie in his application of
Pseudo-Dionysian theology, in this case to feudo-vassalic relations. Suger's
statement occurs in the context of Louis's assumption of the Oriflamme,
the banner of the Vexin, which the king held in fief from Saint-Denis, at
the time of Henry V's threatened invasion of France in 1124: "Rex Francorum Ludovicus filius Philippi, accelerans contra imperatorem ro-
manum insurgentem in regnum Francorum, in pleno capitulo beati
Dionysii professus est se ab eo habere, et jure signiferi, si non rex esset,
hominium ei debere." Suger, *Liber de rebus in Administratione sua gestis*,
in *Oeuvres Complètes de Suger*, ed. Lecoy de la Marche, 162.

32. *Vita Ludovici*, 130.

33. Pseudo-Dionysius, *Ecclesiastical Hierarchy*, 86, 142.

34. *Vita Ludovici*, 286.

35. See the similar conclusion of Barbara Nolan, with respect to
Suger's rebuilding of the abbey church, in her interesting book, *The
Gothic Visionary Perspective* (Princeton, 1977), xv, 46–50.

36. Suger, *Liber de administratione*, 191.

37. *Vita Ludovici*, 4.

38. Chenu, "Platonisms," 86.

Chapter Ten: Social Change and Literary Language

1. Anonymous of Béthune, *Chronique des Rois de France*, ed. Léopold
Delisle, *Recueil des Historiens des Gaules et de la France* [hereafter cited as
RHF], 24: 770.

2. See Georges Duby, "Situation de la noblesse de France au début
du XIIIe siècle," in *Hommes et Structures du Moyen Age* (Paris, 1973),
343–52. An English translation is reprinted as "The Transformation of
the Aristocracy: France at the Beginning of the Thirteenth Century," in
Chivalrous Society, trans. Cynthia Postan (Berkeley, 1977), 179–85. Also
useful for the social and political history of the period is the collection of
articles based on a colloquium organized in Paris in 1980 on the occasion
of the 800th anniversary of Philip Augustus's accession to the throne,
now published as R.-H. Bautier, ed., *La France de Philippe-Auguste: Le
temps des mutations* (Paris, 1982).

3. On the beginnings of vernacular prose historiography, see Paul
Meyer, "Discours de M. Paul Meyer, membre de l'Institut, Président

pendant l'exercice de 1889–1890: Quelques vues sur l'origine et les premiers développements de l'historiographie française,'" *Annuaire-Bulletin de la Société de l'Histoire de France* 27 (1890): 82–106; William J. Sayers, "The Beginnings and Early Development of Old French Historiography" (Ph.D. diss., University of California, Berkeley, 1966); Brian Woledge and H. Clive, *Répertoire des plus anciens textes en prose française depuis 842 jusqu'aux premières années du XIIIe siècle*, Publications Romanes et Françaises, 79 (Geneva, 1964); Omer Jodogne, "La naissance de la prose française," *Bulletin de la Classe des Lettres et des Sciences Morales et Politiques, Académie Royale de Belgique* 49 (1963): 296–308; Henry Chaytor, *From Script to Print: An Introduction to Medieval Literature* (Cambridge, 1945); Diana B. Tyson, "Patronage of French Vernacular History Writers in the Twelfth and Thirteenth Centuries," *Romania* 100 (1979): 180–222; Ronald N. Walpole, "Philip Mouskés and the Pseudo-Turpin Chronicle," *University of California Publications in Modern Philology* 26 (1947): 327–440; and Brian Woledge, "La Légende de Troie et les débuts de la prose française," *Mélanges de linguistique et de la littérature romanes offerts à Mario Roques*, 2 vols. (Paris, 1953), 2: 313–24.

4. Nicolas's original version no longer survives, but a later recension, associated with a corpus of local history known as the *Chronique Saintongeaise*, is preserved in three extant manuscripts: B.N. fr. 124, B.N. fr. 5714, and the so-called Lee manuscript, now published by André de Mandach, *Chronique dite Saintongeaise: Texte Franco-Occitan inédit "Lee": A la découverte d'une chronique gasconne du XIIIe siècle et de sa poitevinisation* (Tübingen, 1979). Auracher published an edition based on the Paris manuscripts in *Die sogenannte Poitevinische Übersetzung des Pseudo-Turpin* (Halle, 1877). See also C. Meredith-Jones, "The Chronicle of Turpin in the Saintonge," *Speculum* 13 (1938): 160–79; and Ian Short, "A Note on the Pseudo-Turpin Translations of Nicolas of Senlis and William of Briane," *Zeitschrift für Romanische Philologie* 86 (1970): 525–32. For a general discussion of both the Latin and Old French manuscript traditions, see André de Mandach, *Naissance et développement de la Chanson de Geste en Europe I: La Geste de Charlemagne et de Roland*, Publications Romanes et Françaises, 69 (Geneva, 1961).

5. The "Johannes" version is published by Ronald N. Walpole, *The Old French "Johannes" Translation of the Pseudo-Turpin Chronicle: A Critical Edition*, 2 vols. (Berkeley, 1976), while that of Michel of Harnes was edited by A. Demarquette in *Mémoires de la Société Centrale d'Agriculture et du Département du Nord*, 2d ser., 3 (1860). On Michel himself, see

idem, *Précis historique sur la maison de Harnes* (Douai, 1856); and H. E. Warlop, *The Flemish Nobility before 1300*, 4 vols. (Kortrijk, 1975), 1: pt. 1. On Renaud of Dammartin, see Henri Malo, *Un grand feudataire Renaud de Dammartin et la coalition de Bouvines: Contribution à l'étude du règne de Philippe-Auguste* (Paris, 1898).

6. The Francien version was incorporated into some manuscripts of the *Chronique des Rois de France* by the Anonymous of Béthune (see below, note 15) and is also found in a Francien text dating from 1210–30, similarly called *Chronique des Rois de France*, which survives in two manuscripts, Vatican Reg. Lat. 624 and the newly discovered Chantilly, Musée Condé, MS 869. In this text, as in the Anonymous of Béthune, the *Turpin* figures as part of royal history and is inserted into the section on Charlemagne. The Francien version has been given the name of *Turpin I* by Ronald Walpole, who has published a new critical edition of it in *Le Turpin français dit le Turpin I* (Toronto, 1985). For a full discussion of the manuscripts, see idem, "Prolégomènes à une édition du Turpin français dit le Turpin I," *Revue d'Histoire des Textes* 10 (1980): 199–230, and 11 (1981): 325–70. The *Turpin* portion of Vat. Reg. Lat. 624 has been published separately by Claude Buridant, *La Traduction du Pseudo-Turpin du Manuscrit Vatican Regina 624*, Publications Romanes et Françaises, 142 (Geneva, 1976). The Hainaut-Flanders-Artois affiliated version is found in Ronald N. Walpole, *An Anonymous Old French Translation of the Pseudo-Turpin Chronicle: A Critical Edition of the Text Contained in B.N. MSS. fr. 2137 and 17203 and Incorporated by Philip Mouskés in His Chronique Rimée*, Medieval Academy of America (Cambridge, Mass., 1979). Ian Short has edited the Anglo-Norman version in *The Anglo-Norman Pseudo-Turpin of William of Briane*, Anglo-Norman Text Society, 25 (Oxford, 1973). For a different view of Briane's sources, see André de Mandach, "Réponse à M. Ian Short," *Zeitschrift für Romanische Philologie* 86 (1970): 533–37. The text of the Burgundian version is found in Ronald N. Walpole, "The Burgundian Translation of Pseudo-Turpin," *Romance Philology* 2 (1948–49): 77–255, and 3 (1949–50): 83–116.

7. Villehardouin, *La Conquête de Constantinople*, ed. Edmond Faral, Les Classiques de l'Histoire de France au moyen âge, 2 vols. (Paris, 1973); Henri de Valenciennes, *Histoire de l'Empereur Henri de Constantinople*, ed. J. Longnon, Documents relatif à l'Histoire des Croisades, 2 (Paris, 1948); Robert de Clari, *La Conquête de Constantinople*, ed. Philippe Lauer, Classiques Français du Moyen Age (Paris, 1924). On Robert, see Peter F. Dembowski, *La Chronique de Robert de Clari: Etude de la langue*

et du style (Toronto, 1964), and A. Pauphilet, "Sur Robert de Clari," *Romania* 57 (1931): 280–3ll.

8. William of Tyre, *Roman d'Eracles*, ed. Paulin Paris, 2 vols. (Paris, 1879–80); *Chronique d'Ernoul et de Bernard le Trésorier*, ed. L. de Mas-Latrie, Société de l'Histoire de France (Paris, 1871). On these texts, see M. R. Morgan, *The Chronicle of Ernoul and the Continuations of William of Tyre*, Oxford Historical Monographs (Oxford, 1973).

9. This text remains unedited. The base manuscript of the first recension is B.N. fr. 20125. The *Histoire Ancienne* was among the most popular medieval historical works and is preserved in some fifty-nine manuscripts, forty-seven of which belong to the first recension. On the manuscript tradition, see Brian Woledge, *Bibliographie des romans et nouvelles antérieurs à 1500: Supplément 1954–1973*, Publications Romanes et Françaises, 130 (Geneva, 1975). Although unpublished, it has been the object of considerable study, beginning with Paul Meyer, "Les premières compilations françaises d'histoire ancienne," *Romania* 14 (1885): 1–81. Especially useful are the studies by Guy Raynaud de Lage, " 'L'Histoire Ancienne jusqu'à César' et les 'Faits des Romains,' " *Moyen Age* 55 (1949): 5–16; idem, "Les romans antiques dans *l'Histoire Ancienne jusqu'à César*," *Moyen Age* 63 (1957): 267–309; idem, "Les romans antiques et la représentation de la réalité," *Moyen Age* 68 (1961): 247–91; idem, "L'Histoire Ancienne," *Dictionnaire des lettres françaises I: Le Moyen Age* (Paris, 1964). A detailed study of the Macedonian section and its sources is provided by D. J. A. Ross, "The History of Macedon in the *Histoire Ancienne jusqu'à César*," *Classica et Mediaevalia* 24 (1963): 181–231. Meyer sought to identify the clerical author of the *Histoire Ancienne* with Wauchier de Denain ("Wauchier de Denain," *Romania* 32 [1903]: 583–86), in which opinion he was joined by Ferdinand Lot ("*Compte rendu* de J. Frappier, *Etude sur la Mort Le Roi Artu*," *Romania* 64 [1938]: 120–22), but the reasoning behind this hypothesis remains unconvincing to most students of the text.

10. Jean de Thuin, *Li Hystore de Jules César*, ed. F. Settegast (Halle, 1881). For an interesting discussion of Jean de Thuin, see J. Frappier, "Remarques sur la peinture de la vie et des héros antiques dans la littérature française du XIIe et du XIIIe siècle," in A. Fourrier, ed., *L'Humanisme médiéval dans les littératures romanes du XIIe au XIIIe siècle* (Paris, 1964), 13–54.

11. *Les Empereurs de Rome par Calendre*, ed. G. Millard, Contributions in Modern Philology (Ann Arbor, 1957). See also M. Roques, "Le

manuscrit Fr. 794 de la Bibliothèque Nationale et le scribe Guiot," *Romania* 73 (1952): 177–99; Mireille Schmidt-Chazan, "Un lorrain de coeur: Le champenois Calendre," *Cahiers Lorraine* 3 (1979): 65–75; and Michel Bur, "Les comtes de Champagne et la 'Normanitas': Sémiologie d'un tombeau," *Proceedings of the Battle Conference* (1980): 22–32.

12. *Li Fet des Romains*, ed. L.-F. Flutre and K. Sneyders de Vogel, 2 vols. (Paris, 1938). On the manuscript and textual tradition, see L.-F. Flutre, *Les manuscrits des Faits des Romains* (Paris, 1932), and idem, *Li Fet des Romains dans les littératures françaises et italiennes du XIIIe au XVIe siècle* (Paris, 1933) . The dating of the work to 1211–14 is discussed by K. Sneyders de Vogel, "La date de la composition des 'Faits des Romains,'" *Neophilologus* 17 (1932): 213–14, 277. Among the many studies of this history, the most comprehensive is that by Jeanette M. A. Beer, *A Medieval Caesar*, Etudes de Philologie et d'Histoire, 30 (Geneva, 1976). See also Mireille Schmidt-Chazan, "Les traductions de la 'Guerre des Gaules' et le sentiment national au Moyen Age," *Annales de Bretagne* (1981): 387–407; and Meyer, "Les premières compilations d'histoire ancienne," 1–32. On the public for ancient history and on the later use of the *Faits des Romains*, see Jacques Monfrin, "Les traducteurs et leur public au Moyen Age," in Fourrier, *L'Humanisme médiéval*, 247–64; Bernard Guenée, "La culture historique des nobles: Le succès des Faits des Romains," in Philippe Contamine, ed., *La Noblesse au Moyen Age* (Paris, 1976), 263–88; and Robert Bossuat, "Traductions françaises des *Commentaires de César* à la fin du XVe siècle," *Bibliothèque d'Humanisme et Renaissance* 3 (1943): 253–411.

13. See Jacques Monfrin, "Humanisme et traductions au Moyen Age," in Fourrier, *L'Humanisme médiéval*, 221ff.

14. The first mention of the Chantilly manuscript appeared in a review article by Ronald N. Walpole, "La Traduction du *Pseudo-Turpin* du Manuscrit Vatican Regina 624: A Propos d'un livre récent," *Romania* 99 (1978): 484–514. While engaged in a search for manuscripts of the vernacular *Turpin*, Professor Walpole noticed that the version of *Turpin* contained in Chantilly, MS 869, closely resembled one published in 1976 by Claude Buridant (see above, note 6) from a thirteenth-century manuscript preserved at the Vatican, and he suggested that perhaps the Chantilly exemplar was a second copy of the text as a whole, although his own observations were confined to the section on *Pseudo-Turpin*. The existence of the Vatican manuscript was first noted by Elie Berger in 1879 ("Notices sur divers manuscrits de la Bibliothèque Vaticane," *Biblio-*

thèque des Ecoles françaises d'Athènes et de Rome 6 [1879]: 10), but it was not until Pierre Botineau undertook a complete study of it that its importance as one of the earliest histories of France in Old French was appreciated. See his "L'Histoire de France en français de Charlemagne à Philippe-Auguste: La Compilation du Ms. 624 du Fonds de la Reine à la Bibliothèque Vaticane," *Romania* 90 (1969): 79–99. Unfortunately, both Buridant and Botineau were unaware of the existence of the second and more complete version of the text at Chantilly. Walpole's suggestion that MS 869 might be a second copy of the chronicle is confirmed by an examination of the work as a whole. For a full description of both manuscripts, see Walpole, "Prolégomènes," passim. For a detailed analysis of the sources utilized in the first 165 folios of the Chantilly manuscript (containing the *Continuation of Aimoin*), see Gillette Labory, "Essai d'une histoire nationale au XIIIe siecle: La Chronique de l'Anonyme de Chantilly-Vatican," *Bibliothèque de l'Ecole des Chartes* 148 (1990): 301–54. On the chronicle itself, see my "Moral Imagination and the Rise of the Bureaucratic State: Images of Government in the *Chronique des Rois de France*, Chantilly, Ms. 869," *Journal of Medieval and Renaissance Studies* 18 (1988): 157–73, and my *Romancing the Past: The Rise of Vernacular Prose Historiography in Thirteenth-Century France*, The New Historicism (Berkeley, 1993), chap. 6.

15. The only complete manuscript of the Anonymous of Béthune's *Chronique des Rois de France* is B.N. n.a. fr. 6295. On the Anonymous, see Léopold Delisle, "Notice sur la Chronique d'un Anonyme de Béthune du temps de Philippe-Auguste," *Notices et Extraits des Manuscrits* 34, pt. 1 (1891): 365–80; Charles Petit-Dutaillis, "Une nouvelle Chronique du règne de Philippe-Auguste, l'Anonyme de Béthune," *Revue Historique* 50 (1892): 63–71; and idem, *Etudes sur la vie et le règne de Louis VIII* (Paris, 1964). The final, contemporary, section of the Anonymous's *Chronique* is published by Léopold Delisle, "Chronique de l'Anonyme de Béthune," *RHF*, 24: 750–75.

16. Giles's prologue is published by Paul Meyer in *Romania* 6 (1877): 494–98.

17. C. R Borland and R. G. L. Ritchie, "Fragment d'une traduction en vers de la Chronique en prose de Guillaume le Breton," *Romania* 42 (1913): 1–22.

18. Charles Petit-Dutaillis, "Fragment de l'Histoire de Philippe-Auguste: Chronique en français des années 1214–1216," *Bibliothèque de l'Ecole des Chartes* 87 (1926): 98–141; and Léopold Delisle, "Fragment de

l'histoire de Philippe-Auguste," *Histoire Littéraire de France* 32 (1898): 232–42.

19. Only a small portion of the Ménestrel's chronicle has been published (*RHF*, 10: 278–80, 11: 319, 12: 22–27, 17: 429–33). Kathleen James has prepared a new edition based on all eleven surviving manuscripts, "Critical Edition of *La Chronique d'un Ménestrel d'Alphonse de Poitiers* as contained in B.N. fr. 5700" (Ph.D. diss., University of Maryland, College Park, 1984). On the Ménestrel, see Mandach, *Chronique dite Saintongeaise*; and Ian Short, "The *Pseudo-Turpin Chronicle*: Some Unnoticed Versions and Their Sources," *Medium Aevum* 38 (1969): 1–22.

20. On the *Grandes Chroniques*, see my *The Chronicle Tradition of Saint-Denis: A Survey*, Medieval Classics: Texts and Studies, no. 10 (Leiden, 1979), 72–88.

21. Eugene Vance, "'Aucassin et Nicolette' as a Medieval Comedy of Signification and Exchange," in Minnette Grunmann-Gaudet and Robin F. Jones, eds., *The Nature of Medieval Narrative*, French Forum Monographs, 22, (Lexington, Ky., 1980), 61; and Nancy S. Struever, "The Study of Language and the Study of History," *Journal of Interdisciplinary History* 4 (1974): 401–15.

22. R. Howard Bloch, *Medieval French Literature and Law* (Berkeley, 1977), 10.

23. Eugene Vance, "Roland et la poétique de la mémoire," *Cahiers d'Etudes Médiévales* 1 (1975): 103. See also the expanded version of this article in *Mervelous Signals: Poetics and Sign Theory in the Middle Ages* (Lincoln, Neb., 1986).

24. Vance, "Roland et la poétique de la mémoire," 104. The ritualistic nature of this attitude to history in traditional societies has been explained by Mircea Eliade, *The Myth of the Eternal Return or Cosmos and History* (Princeton, 1965). For its implications for the understanding of medieval historiography in particular, see Chapter Five.

25. R. Howard Bloch, *Etymologies and Genealogies: A Literary Anthropology of the French Middle Ages* (Chicago, 1983), 15. On the rise of silent reading, see the important article by Paul Saenger, "Silent Reading: Its Impact on Late Medieval Script and Society," *Viator* 13 (1980): 367–414; and on literacy, Brian Stock, *The Implications of Literacy: Written Language and Models of Interpretation in the Eleventh and Twelfth Centuries* (Princeton, 1983).

26. Robert Hanning, *The Individual in Twelfth-Century Romance* (New Haven, 1977), 143.

27. Vance, "Roland et la poétique de la mémoire," 106.

28. As discussed in Northrop Frye, *The Great Code: The Bible and Literature* (New York, 1982), 22, 227.

29. On the nature of oral performance, see Ruth Crosby, "Oral Delivery in the Middle Ages," *Speculum* 11 (1936): 88–110; and on its relation to written texts, Franz Bäuml, "Transformations of the Heroine: From Epic Heard to Epic Read," in Rosemarie Morewedge, ed., *The Role of Women in the Middle Ages* (Albany, 1975): 23–40; and idem, "Varieties and Consequences of Medieval Literacy and Illiteracy," *Speculum* 55 (1980): 237–65.

30. On emplotment as a crucial element in historical narrative, see Hayden White, "The Question of Narrative in Contemporary Historical Theory," *History and Theory*, 23 (1984): 1–33; and idem, "Historicism, History and the Figurative Imagination," *History and Theory* 14, *Beiheft* 14 (1975): 48–67. Frank Kermode, in *The Genesis of Secrecy: On the Interpretation of Narrative* (Cambridge, Mass., 1979), like White, sees historical narrative as intrinsically no different from fictional narrative except in its pretense to objectivity and referentiality.

31. These techniques are discussed in Joseph J. Duggan, *The Song of Roland: Formulaic Style and Poetic Craft* (Berkeley, 1973). For medieval narrative generally, see William W. Ryding, *Structure in Medieval Narrative* (The Hague, 1971).

32. Roland Barthes has argued that historical discourse seeks reversion towards the level of pure referent, becoming in the process "the utterance for which no one is responsible." "Historical Discourse," in Michael Lane, ed., *Introduction to Structuralism* (New York, 1970), 151.

33. Variant readings of the Latin sources common to the *Chronique des Rois de France* and the *Grandes Chroniques* have been studied by Pierre Botineau, "Une Source des *Grandes Chroniques de France*: L'Histoire de France en prose française de Charlemagne à Philippe-Auguste," unpublished typescript. I would like to thank Gillette Labory, of the Institut de Recherche d'Histoire et des Textes in Paris, for bringing this paper to my attention.

34. "Apres sera dit en commun / Coment le Wandele, Got, et Hun / France pelfirer et guasterent / et les iglises desrouberent / E des Normans vos iert retrait / E lor conqueste et lor fait / Coment destruirent Germanie / Couloigne et France la guarnie / Anjou, Poitou, Borgoigne tote / De ce ne rest il nule doute / Que Flandres Wandes n'envaïssent / E

Mout de maus ne lor feïssent / Des quels gens Flandres fu puplée / Vos iert bien l'estoire contée." B.N. fr. 20125, fol. 2–2v.

35. Raynaud de Lage, " 'L'Histoire Ancienne jusqu'à César' et les 'Faits des Romains,' " 5.

36. The sections are those designated by Meyer, "Les premières compilations d'histoire ancienne," 38–49.

37. B.N. fr. 20125, fol. 2v. On the complex relationship of the *Histoire Ancienne* to its romance sources, see Raynaud de Lage, "Les romans antiques dans *l'Histoire Ancienne jusqu'à César*," passim.

38. Woledge, *Bibliographie des romans et nouvelles*, 42ff.

39. B.N. fr. 20125, fols. 10v, 41v, 43, 62, 180v, 273v–74. The moralizations are discussed in Guy Raynaud de Lage, "La morale de l'histoire," *Moyen Age* 69 (1963): 365–69; and Renate Blumenfeld-Kosinski, "Moralization and History: Verse and Prose in the 'Histoire Ancienne jusqu'à César,' " *Zeitschrift für Romanische Philologie* 97 (1982): 41–46.

40. Conversely, ten, or nearly half, of the moralizations fall within the first section devoted to biblical history, where no such contamination might be feared.

41. B.N. fr. 20125, fols. 10v, 14.

42. Blumenfeld-Kosinski, "Moralization and History," 44; and Meyer, "Les premières compilations d'histoire ancienne," 58.

43. Frye, *The Great Code*, 8.

44. For a new explanation of the chronicler's attack on poetic discourse, see my "Forging the Past: The Language of Historical Truth in the Middle Ages," *History Teacher* 17 (1984): 267–88. For a fuller discussion, see my *Romancing the Past*, chap. 2.

45. "Maintes gens si en ont oi conter e chanter mes n'est si menconge non co qu'il en dient e en chantent cil chanteor ne cil ioglcor. Nus contes rimies n'est verais, tot es menconge co qu'il en dient car il n'en sievent rienz fors quant par oir dire." B.N. fr. 124, fol. 1.

46. B.N. fr. 573, fol. 147.

47. B.N. fr. 1621, fol. 208.

48. "Mes que que li autre aient osté et mis, ci poez oir la verité d'Espaigne selonc le latin de l'estoire que li cuens Renauz de Boloigne fist par grant estuide cerchier e querre es livres a monseignor Saint Denise." Walpole, *The Old French "Johannes" Translation*, 130.

49. Sayers, "The Beginnings and Early Development of Old French Historiography," 110.

50. See above, note 25.

51. For a more extensive discussion of this argument, see my *"Pseudo-Turpin, the Crisis of the Aristocracy, and the Beginnings of Vernacular Historiography in Thirteenth-Century France," Journal of Medieval History* 12 (1986): 207–23; and my *Romancing the Past,* chap. 2.

52. Patterson, "The Historiography of Romance and the Alliterative *Morte Arthure," Journal of Medieval and Renaissance Studies* 13 (1983): 1–32.

Chapter Eleven: Medieval Canon Formation and the Rise of Royal Historiography in Old French Prose

1. See Nora, "Between Memory and History: Les Lieux de Mémoire," *Representations* 26 (1989): 21. The other two, in Nora's view, occur first, with the destruction of the legend of the French monarchy's Trojan origins and the restoration of France's Gallic heritage, in Etienne Pasquier's *Recherches de la France* (1599), which also effected a significant shift away from the kind of dynastic history represented by the *Grandes Chroniques* to a more "modern" understanding of the history of a people as a nation; and finally, with the historiography of the late Restoration, which ushered in the modern conception of France as a nation-state. On the *Grandes Chroniques de France,* see my *The Chronicle Tradition of Saint-Denis: A Survey,* Medieval Classics: Texts and Studies, no. 10 (Leiden, 1979), 72–89.

2. Michel Tyvaert, "L'Image du Roi: Légitimité et moralité royales dans les histoires de France au XVIIe siècle," *Revue d'Histoire Moderne et Contemporaine* 21 (1974): 521–46.

3. The existence of an Old French *Chronique des Rois de France* at the Musée Condé in Chantilly was first reported by Ronald N. Walpole in 1978. See his "La Traduction du *Pseudo-Turpin* du Manuscrit Vatican Regina 624: A Propos d'un livre récent," *Romania* 99 (1978): 484–514. On the Vatican manuscript, see Pierre Botineau, "L'Histoire de France en français de Charlemagne à Philippe-Auguste: La Compilation du Ms. 624 du Fonds de la Reine à la Bibliothèque Vaticane," *Romania* 90 (1969): 79–99; and idem, "Une Source des *Grandes Chroniques de France*: L'Histoire de France en prose française de Charlemagne à Philippe-Auguste," unpublished typescript. I would like to thank Gillette Labory, of the Institut de Recherche d'Histoire et des Textes in Paris, for letting me read a copy of Botineau's article at the Institut. Claude Buridant has

published an edition of the version of *Pseudo-Turpin* found in Vatican Reg. Lat. 624. Both manuscripts have now been submitted to a detailed analysis by Gillette Labory, especially with respect to their common reliance upon a group of Latin sources that also served Primat in the compilation of the *Grandes Chroniques* at Saint-Denis. See her "Essai d'une histoire nationale au XIII siècle: La Chronique de l'Anonyme de Chantilly-Vatican," *Bibliothèque de l'Ecole des Chartes* 148 (1990): 301–54.

4. The fullest text of the *Chronique des Rois de France* is preserved in Paris, B.N. n.a. fr. 6295. The final, contemporary section was edited and published by Léopold Delisle in the *Recueil des Historiens des Gaules et de la France*, 24: 750–75. On the manuscript tradition of the Anonymous's histories, see Ronald N. Walpole, *An Anonymous Old French Translation of the Pseudo-Turpin Chronicle: A Critical Edition of the Text Contained in B.N. MSS. fr. 2137 and 17203 and Incorporated by Philip Mouskés in his Chronique Rimée*, Medieval Academy of America, 89 (Cambridge, Mass, 1979); idem, *Le Turpin français dit le Turpin I* (Toronto, 1985); idem, "Philip Mouskés and the Pseudo-Turpin Chronicle," *University of California Publications in Modern Philology* 26 (1947): 327–440; idem, "Prolégomènes à une édition du Turpin français dit le *Turpin I*," *Revue d'Histoire des Textes* 10 (1980): 199–230, 11 (1981): 325–70; Léopold Delisle, "Chronique française des Rois de France par un Anonyme de Béthune," *Histoire Littéraire de la France* 32 (1898): 219–34; idem, "Chronique des Ducs de Normandie," *Histoire Littéraire de la France* 32 (1898): 182–94; idem, "Notice sur la Chronique d'un Anonyme de Béthune du Temps de Philippe Auguste," *Notices et Extraits des Manuscrits* 34, pt. 1 (1891): 365–80; idem, "Annales [B.N. fr. 10130]," *Histoire Littéraire de la France* 32 (1898): 207–8; Marc Du Pouget, "Recherches sur les Chroniques Latines de Saint-Denis: Commentaire et édition critique de la *Descriptio clavi et corone domini*" (thesis, Ecole des Chartes, 1977); Philippe Lauer, "Louis d'Outremer et le Fragment d'Isembart et Gormont," *Romania* 26 (1897): 161–74; Victor Le Clerc, "Notices Supplémentaires Chroniques [Anonyme de Béthune]," *Histoire Littéraire de la France* 21 (1895): 669–71; Paul Meyer, "Notice du Manuscrit fr. 17177 de la Bibliothèque Nationale," *Bulletin de la Société des Anciens Textes Français* (1895): 80–118; idem, "Notice sur le Ms. II.6.24 de la Bibliothèque de Cambridge," *Notices et Extraits des Manuscrits de la Bibliothèque Impériale* 32, pt. 2 (1888): 37–81; idem, "Compte-rendu de L. Delisle, Notice sur la Chronique d'un Anonyme de Béthune du Temps de Philippe-Auguste," *Romania* 21 (1892): 302–3; Alain Marechaux, *Chronique d'un Anonyme de*

Béthune (thèse du troisième cycle, Université de Lille, 1976); Charles Pe-tit-Dutaillis, "Une nouvelle Chronique du Règne de Philippe-Auguste, l'Anonyme de Béthune," *Revue Historique* 50 (1892): 63–71; idem, *Etude sur la vie et le règne de Louis VIII* (Paris, 1964); Brian Woledge and H. P. Clive, *Répertoire des plus anciens textes en prose française depuis 842 jusqu'aux premières années du XIIIe siècle*, Publication Romanes et Françaises, 79 (Geneva, 1964).

5. The house of Béthune traced its ancestry back to Robert I Fasci-culus, advocate of Arras around the year 1000, possibly a descendant of the counts of Arras, given that he and his heirs continued to hold the of-fice of advocate of Arras, although there is no documentary evidence to support this hypothesis. It is likely, in any case, that Robert I Fasciculus descended from Carolingian nobility, since the sources consider him a *princeps* and his son and successor Robert II is called *nobilis* in 1066. Gal-bert of Bruges specifically names Robert IV of Béthune (1090–1128) as belonging to the *primi terrae Flandriarum* and counts him among the peers (*pares*) of Flanders. *The Murder of Charles the Good, Count of Flan-ders*, ed. and trans. James Bruce Ross (New York, 1967), 29, 196. Although Robert IV was not expressly designated *nobilis*, all his descendants were considered to be noble in the twelfth and thirteenth centuries.

During the lifetime of his parents and elder brother Daniel, Robert VII was a relatively poor knight without lands of his own, which perhaps explains his readiness to enlist on the side of King John, whose largesse to potential vassals in his bid for Flemish support against Philip Augus-tus was renowned. Indeed, among the Flemish barons singled out for fa-vors from King John, Robert VII figures most frequently in the Rolls as the recipient of royal attention and gifts. Relations between the house of Béthune and the kings of England went back at least to the time of Henry II. The name Béthune appears as one of three peers on the list of Flemish nobles confirming the "recognitio servitii quod barones et castel-lani et ceteri homines comitis Flandriae debent Henrico regi Angliae si-cut domino pro feudis quae de ipso habent," dated 1163, indicating that members of the family were already receiving money-fiefs, if not actual land, from the English king. See H. E. Warlop, *The Flemish Nobility be-fore 1300*, 4 vols. (Kortrijk, 1975–76), 1: 261). Territorial grants to the Béthunes may have begun as early as 1175, when Count Philip of Flan-ders had occasion to send Robert VII's grandfather, Robert V "Le Roux," on a mission to England, where, perhaps in return for services rendered, he obtained important holdings in fief. Robert's father, Guillaume II, also received lands in England from Henry II, grants rapidly augmented under Richard I and John. Privileges were added to possessions when Guillaume's brother, Jean de Béthune, prévôt of Douai and future bishop of Cambrai, was given formal support by the king of England to obtain the deanship of York. See Gaston G. Dept, "Les Influences Anglaises et Françaises dans le Comté de Flandre au début du XIIe siècle," *Université de Gand Recueil de Travaux publiés par la Faculté de Philosophie et Lettres* 39 (Gand/Ghent, 1928): 55. By the turn of the twelfth century, then, the whole Béthune family was to some extent already under English influence.

This pattern of service and reward continued well into the next generation. Both Robert and his elder brother Daniel are found on the receiving end of royal favors in the Close and Patent Rolls for John's reign. When Guillaume II died in 1214, John confirmed to Robert the full seisin of all the lands and revenues that his father had enjoyed in England, which now devolved to Robert by hereditary right (*Rotuli Litterarum Clausarum*, ed. Thomas Duffy Hardy [London, 1833], 1: anno 1214, 208b). On April 11 of the same year, the king offered Robert an additional £100 (ibid., 184b), followed shortly thereafter by a gift of £200 (*Rotuli Litterarum Patentium*, ed. Thomas Duffy Hardy [London, 1835], anno 1214, 138). Given this extraordinary pattern of royal generosity to Robert VII of Béthune, it is not surprising that when Count Ferrand of Flanders sent Baldwin of Nieuwpoort to England to request John's aid against Philip Augustus, the count's messenger immediately identified Robert as a particular royal favorite among the group of Flemish nobles gathered at the English court. According to the Anonymous, who had accompanied his master across the Channel, Baldwin met with "vi haus homes de Flanders . . . et plusiors autres bacelors" (six high men of Flanders . . . and several other bachelors), who elected Robert VII to plead the Flemish cause before the English king. *Histoire des ducs de Normandie et des rois d'Angleterre*, ed. Francisque Michel, Société de l'Histoire de France (Paris, 1840), 128. Robert did so successfully, helped to lead the expedition that surprised the French fleet at Damme, and continued to play an important role in the war against Philip Augustus throughout 1213 and 1214.

6. For example, Walpole, "Philip Mouskés and the Pseudo-Turpin Chronicle," 327–440; William J. Sayers, "The Beginnings and Early Development of Old French Historiography" (Ph.D. diss., University of California, Berkeley, 1966); Charles Petit-Dutaillis, "Une nouvelle

Chronique du règne de Philippe-Auguste," 63–71; and idem, *Etude sur la vie et le règne de Louis VIII.*

7. On the manuscript at Chantilly, see Walpole, "Prolégomènes," 199–230, 325–70. See Claude Buridant, *La Traduction du Pseudo-Turpin du Manuscrit Vatican Regina 624*, Publications Romanes et Françaises, 142 (Geneva, 1976). He has also embarked on an edition of the last section of the *Chronique*, which consists of a prose translation of Guillaume le Breton's *Philippide*. See his "La Traduction du *Philippide* de Guillaume le Breton dans la *Chronique des Rois de France*" (thèse du troisième cycle, Université de Lille, n.d.).

8. "Ce que vous me demandez me donna voustre pere et vous mesmes m'avez ja confermé le don par voz lettres royaulx. Pour cette raison ay je desclairé mon droit en ce que vous requerez.
Ne troublez pas la paix du royaume, et que ceulx qui vous doivent obeïr ne vous soient ennemys. Il ne appartient pas que don de roy soit ainsi quassé. Ne n'est pas chose honneste que le roy se desdie. . . . Je suis saisi de par vostre pere et de par vous, et ma tenue me deffand ma droicture. . . . Ce me aye esté donné loyaument de mes seigneurs liges, et ainsi excuse droicte loyaulté et droit tiltre la letre que j'ay du fons de ceste querelle que je tiens sans faire tort a nully. Et bien sachez droictement que nulle chose qui aye esté donnee loyaument a ung homme ne la doit perdre sans forfait." Chantilly, MS 869, fols. 334r–34v.

9. "Ce que mon pere vous octroya a Rains a avoir et tenir par aucun temps ne vous puet pas garantir si brief temps que l'avez tenue." Ibid., fol. 334v.

10. "Gentilz Roy, tel temps ne telle heure ne requiert pas bataille. Ne si puissant roy ne se doit point combatre de nuyt, aincoys convient avant ordonner et deviser ses batailles et bailler a chacune son connestable et que chacun sache quel lieu il doit tenir et qui il doit suivre. . . . Bon roy, ne te mesprise mie tant que toy qui es sire de si grant empire de gens, que tu te vueilles et ton peuple mectre en tel peril." Ibid., fol. 337r.

11. Georges Duby, *Le Dimanche de Bouvines* (Paris, 1973), 127.

12. Chantilly, MS 869, fol. 337r.

13. The small group of royal counselors is described in the *Chronique* as: "Ceulx qui tousiours est [*sic*] avec le roy en guerres, et en batailles, et en ostelz et en palais, et ne souloit guieres aler nulle part sans eulx. Car ceulx pour voir souloient estre et aler avec lui plus continuellement que nul autre et lui aidoient et de conseil et de chevalerie et de quant que chacun d'eulx povoit. . . . Car à ces troys en qui il croyoit moult il souloit

prendre son conseil et descouvrir son cueur de ce qu'il vouloit faire." Ibid., fols. 385r, 378v.

14. "Rengez et ordonnez chacun en sa bataille, chevaliers de grant prouesce et inspirez de grant hardiesce qui tenoient leurs eschielles serrees et se tenoient prests tous de vistement combatre et courir sur eulx de quelque heure que les trompectes sonneroient l'assemblée de bataille." Ibid., fol. 387r.

15. On this development, see C. Warren Hollister and John W. Baldwin, "The Rise of Administrative Kingship: Henry I and Philip Augustus," *American Historical Review* 83 (1978): 867–905.

16. See my *The Chronicle Tradition of Saint-Denis*, 72–89; and, for a more recent insistence upon this point, Bernard Guenée, "Les Grandes Chroniques de France: Le Roman aux Roys (1274–1518)," in Pierre Nora, ed., *La Nation* (Paris, 1986), 189–213; and Raymonde Foreville, "L'Image de Philippe Auguste dans les sources contemporaines," in R.-H. Bautier, ed., *La France de Philippe Auguste: Le temps des mutations* (Paris, 1982), 122ff.

17. "Li François, qui vourent avoir roi aussi comme les autres nations." *Les Grandes Chroniques de France*, ed J. Viard, Société de l'Histoire de France, 10 vols. (Paris 1920–53), 1: 19.

18. Bernard Guenée, *Histoire et Culture Historique dans l'Occident Médiéval* (Paris, 1980), 340.

19. A point well made by Guenée, "Les Grandes Chroniques de France," 195.

20. Ibid.

21. Raymond Williams, *Culture* (Glasgow, 1981), 201.

Index

Index

Index

Index

Library of Congress Cataloging-in-Publication Data

Spiegel, Gabrielle M.
    The past as text : the theory and practice of medieval historiography /
Gabrielle M. Spiegel.
        p.   cm. — (Parallax)
    Includes bibliographical references and index.
    ISBN 0-8018-5555-1 (alk. paper)
    1. Middle Ages—Historiography.   2. Civilization, Medieval—
Historiography.   I. Title.   II. Series: Parallax (Baltimore, Md.)
D116.S685   1997
909.07—dc21   96-36987
                                                                    CIP

The problem of miracles (xii) (xiii)
History as propaganda (xii)
What do you think of her "middleground"? ,54
Is any of this useful to your thinking
  about chronicles?
Her summones of Saussure + Derrida (chap. 1 + 2
  are very good.
very hopeful + positive on p9
see p 23, 27, 45   } do 27 + 54 outline
24 is important   the same kind of
                                    project?

less certainty about cultural/historical context
  than about what is there on the page
  before him